Sociology of Waiting

Sociology of Waiting

How Americans Wait

Paul Christopher Price

LEXINGTON BOOKS
Lanham • Boulder • New York • London

Published by Lexington Books
An imprint of The Rowman & Littlefield Publishing Group, Inc.
4501 Forbes Boulevard, Suite 200, Lanham, Maryland 20706
www.rowman.com

6 Tinworth Street, London SE11 5AL, United Kingdom

British Library Cataloguing in Publication Information Available

Library of Congress Cataloging-in-Publication Data

Names: Price, Paul-Jahi Christopher, author.
Title: Sociology of waiting : how Americans wait / Paul Christopher Price.
Description: Lanham : Lexington Books, [2021] | Includes bibliographical references and index.
Identifiers: LCCN 2021008021 (print) | LCCN 2021008022 (ebook) |
   ISBN 9781793640697 (cloth) | ISBN 9781793640703 (ebook) |
   ISBN 9781793640710 (pbk)
Subjects: LCSH: Waiting (Philosophy) | Socialization. | Social structure. |
   Decision making. | Expectation (Psychology)
Classification: LCC B105.W24 P75 2021 (print) | LCC B105.W24 (ebook) |
   DDC 302.5—dc23
LC record available at https://lccn.loc.gov/2021008021
LC ebook record available at https://lccn.loc.gov/2021008022

Dedication

Willie Nora Price

This book is dedicated to my mother, Willie Nora Price. She died in April 2017, and rarely a day goes by that I do not think about her life, her journey. I miss her. Parents shape children in different ways; and in some cases, children don't realize that they are being molded. This was my mother. She had ways of influencing her social circle. Through her instruction and examples, she taught me consistency. She was a dedicated Sunday school teacher, attending the same church for over fifty-five years. As director of Christian Education, she produced annual plays and programs for the church. Such programs included Christmas plays, Easter plays, Thanksgiving, Children's day, Mother's Day celebrations, Pastor Appreciations, Black history month programs, missionary society, and so on. This environment affected me in ways that continue to influence my life. And as a young man, I participated in most of her programs. Her final church production was "The Church Garden." This drama connected gardens to churches. It was about garden diversity and how such diversity might enhance or spoil the atmosphere, and therefore, how church diversity and church membership must be ministered to. "The Church Garden" used vegetable metaphors to characterize the pros and cons of church life. This performance targeted squash, berries, lettuce, and turnips. For example, squash *church gossip,* turnip *(turn-up) for meetings,* berry *(bury) church division, and* lettuce *(let us) pray. Planting seeds that reap significant harvest. My sister, Diana, contends that gardens do not simply exist, they "require patient-labor and attention." Thus, at the end of the day, you reap what you sow.*

Working in her personal garden brought joy and peace. She loved the fruits of her labor. Similarly, she loved the fruits of her church labor; the children she taught and influenced; the pastors and members she affected, and the conferences she attended. Working in the church was her life. Spending lots of time at the church, she acquired entrance keys, opening the sanctuary for others, for rehearsals, and often preparing the church before service (before the start of church). When not at church, she frequently completed church projects at home. Church work and the small church atmosphere define my mother; that's who she was. She was a lover of church and therefore a lover of God and humanity. I love you Momma, and miss you much.

Contents

Preface

How long have you waited for your package to arrive? How long have you waited for your fiancé to pop the question? How long have you waited for escrow to close? How long have you waited for the train? How long have you waited for that dress to go on sale? And how long have you waited for your numbers to hit? Waiting is a fascinating topic. It is an *activity* that we all do. Given that we all do it, waiting is universal. Such activity and its universality are my reasons for writing this book. I wanted to understand *how* individuals wait. I contend that waiting is an activity, and such activity involves doing. For example, what are persons *doing* while waiting? Are they knitting, reading, conversing, planning, working, computing, listening, watching, etc.? Such *doing* represents activity.

During my research, I was driven by the details of waiting and how certain entrepreneurs capitalized on waiting by developing creative ventures. For example, selling flowers to motorists while they wait at traffic signals; or selling snacks (popcorn, chips, gum, candy, etc.) to visitors standing in line at Men's Central Jail. Each level of waiting led to another exciting observation and analysis. Clearly, waiting as a research topic is rich and intriguing.

One of the most stimulating discoveries was *wait explanations*. If I am told that my car will be ready in thirty minutes, and I return—yet it is not. If I am promised that my food is coming out next, though it does not. If I am told that the doctor will see me next, but he/she does not. What am I to do? Write a negative review? What are my expectations of the institution? And what are the institution's expectations of me. Am I owed a reason? If so, how is such explanation delivered?

Wait observations were fascinating. I found myself going deeper and deeper into waiting. It kept my interest; it maintained my attention. Within this book, I want readers to experience a variety of wait-situations. That is not to say that readers do not experience waiting. My intent is to expose *you* to waiting situations that you have not or rarely go through, and develop those wait-experiences that *you* have tolerated and continue to occur.

Acknowledgments

GOD AND FAMILY

God and Family are important to me. Often, when writing, I went inside myself and pulled out amazing thoughts that I did not know existed. Creativity and analysis were fresh! For this, I praise God. Additionally, I thank my wife (Sherrie) and children (Briana and Kyra) for their constant support. Deciding where to observe was at times influenced by my wife. Sherrie participated in Black Friday annually. When I finally decided to attend with her, I was amazed by this fruitful source of *wait data*!

PROFESSOR/EDITOR BEVERLY TATE

Professor Beverly Tate is a most encouraging faculty, editor, and friend. Frequently, we discussed waiting and her unexpected suggestions pointed me in new directions. I appreciate Professor Tate for her patience, challenges, interview suggestions, and overall concern for this project. Your soft criticisms were acknowledged and addressed. Your encouragement was and is appreciated. Thank you for editing this manuscript.

PROFESSOR BAKHTAWAR (BUCKY) BHADHA

My chapter drafts are complete and I need someone to review and provide feedback. I asked several faculty members to review and critique my chapters. All declined except Professor Bakhtawar Bhadha, affectionately known as

Bucky. Bucky seemed interested, and when I asked her, she shrugged her shoulders and nonchalantly said, "yes, no problem." She read through my chapters quickly, editing and suggesting. Professor Bhadha's chapter reviews were complete before I could consider and revise her previous chapter editions. Thank you, Bucky. I appreciate you and your spirit.

Introduction

SOCIOLOGY OF WAITING

Collectively watching from the north sideline, Coach Johnson's players roared in disapproval as the referee signaled touchdown. Many players believed that opposing wide receiver, Quickness, stepped out of bounds before entering the end zone. Responding to the apparent error and sideline emotion, head coach, Mike Johnson tossed out the red flag, a challenge to the official's ruling, shortly after the official signaled touchdown. For challengers, there is little time to waste when objecting to the referee's judgment. Failing to contest before the next play nullifies any further objection to that play. So, throwing a flag onto the field begins the process of "waiting for a decision," a decision to overturn official ruling or maintain ruling. The questionable play is now under formal review, and while waiting, *everyone* examines and assesses the same play, enabling each person to form an opinion. *Everyone* includes all those watching the game, for example, stadium fans, TV viewers, commentators, coaches, players, camerapersons, etc. While waiting, each group reconsiders and evaluates "the play" as they see it, skewing their interpretation to benefit their positions. In short, many view the same play differently. There is discussion among viewers about why officials should rule one way or the other. But clearly the referee's decision has consequences for the following play or plays, coaches' strategies, and even the outcome of the game. Given the possible consequences, some groups wait with more anxiety than others. Prolonged reviews by officials produce additional speculation and concern by viewers. "Waiting for a decision" then puts the game (or any situation) on hold until rulings are rendered. Given their "neutrality," officials are sensitive to this process; that is, they recognize that viewers have opinions, that there are consequences to official decisions, that one cannot proceed until

1

decisions are made, and that decisions must be made in a timely but efficient manner. Finally, most officials desire to make the right decisions thus justify their findings.

Waiting for decisions is a major part of our lives and our society. On a macro level, the Supreme Court renders decisions that impact societal norms, operations, and organizations. For example, the Brown decision, the rulings on quotas, affirmative action, abortion, and gay marriage have all affected societal interactions and institutions. Yet, the common denominator in each decision was *waiting*. Waiting for officials to make decisions. For in waiting, there is usually an audience, and like the Quickness catch, which was ruled a catch and therefore a touchdown, spectators typically have their own views of events. Groups must wait in order to proceed, and strategies cannot be implemented until final decisions. Thus, persons recognize that they must adapt and adjust to new decisions, for these decisions organize our behaviors, that is, the outcome of the decision influences how we proceed. On a micro level, individuals are required to wait on decisions regarding jobs, promotions, college admissions, travel arrangements, medical procedures, etc. Waiting for a decision is rarely arbitrary. When waiting on college admissions, a student knows that he/she has applied and decisions are forthcoming. It is the specific situation (jobs, promotions, education, etc.) that guides one's waiting and may therefore frame one's anxiety. So much of what we *do* involves waiting, and *how we wait* is the subject of this book.

It goes without saying that "waiting on decisions" is one of several wait-types. For instance, cooks wait for cakes to brown; customers wait for deliveries; patients wait for appointments and results; passengers wait for trains; students wait for grades; and diners wait for meals. There are different types of waiting and different types of wait-environments. Waiting is complex; it is not linear; there are twists and turns that complicate waiting. There is no single answer; there are many, and in some cases, there is confusion about waiting which could lead to conflict, and/or new and creative ways of waiting. All in all, we are all a part of this experience called waiting.

What Is the *Sociology of Waiting?*

The sociology of waiting investigates *how people wait*. It examines and analyzes what people *do* while waiting. Waiting suggests that we are waiting on *something* or waiting for something to happen; thus, we are likely to remain or stay until persons (or objects) arrive, tasks are complete, decisions rendered, and turns taken. The driving *force* of this research is *how* people wait. Consequently, I am interested in what people *do* while waiting and how such *doing* assists them in passing time. Certain questions naturally emerge when investigating waiting, for example, how do norms develop while waiting? What norms are followed while waiting? What norms are broken while waiting? Are sanctions applied to wait-violators? To what extent are structure, order, and organization connected to waiting? And, how do we *learn* to wait? These and other questions are addressed throughout the chapters, but for the sake of clarity, I will offer one example regarding *wait-socialization* or learning to wait. If a baby cries because he/she is hungry, yet milk or food is not ready, parents typically caress baby-Beth or rock her and/or sing to her until the food is ready. While babies do desire immediate gratification, gradually through experience and encounter, they *learn* to wait. Such methods (rock, caress, or sing) calm and distract babies until their needs are met. Similarly, while in day care, toddlers learn to wait their turn in playing with certain popular toys—failure to wait may result in "time-out." Kindergartners, first and second graders learn to wait by forming lines and taking turns for the restroom, water fountain, computer games, and even recess. Teaching children how to wait often leads to order and stability in society. Moreover, such experiences have implications for waiting throughout the life course.

Waiting further suggests a certain maturity and consideration for others. We recognize that there is a process to waiting, and thus, decisions, repairs, appointments, and flight departures do not occur instantly. Part of waiting involves planning, for example, how do we plan to wait? By reading? By listening to music? By social media? By scheduling advanced appointments? Planning and patience leads to maturity in waiting. When delays are unplanned, children may have more difficulty waiting than adults, and this is partly due to age and inexperience. Additionally, consideration of others, while waiting, reflects a general concern and acknowledgment of others. For example, if a child is noticeably sick or a senior has difficulty standing, some individuals will permit the infirmed or disabled to go ahead. Or if one is late to an appointment and explains his/her tragic situation to those in front, he/she may likely bypass waiting. Considerations suggests that one is sensitive to the ill-fated circumstance thus allows individuals faster access; one then sacrifices his/her place in line to assist someone else, which in turn increases his/her wait time. Less sensitive individuals may refuse consideration arguing, "If I have to wait, so should he," or "she should get-up earlier so she won't be late."

Waiting is universal and at some point, everybody waits or has waited. We wait in drive-through lines, wishing those ahead would speed their order. We wait in airports, in train, and bus stations; we wait in virtual lines; we wait for stores to open; we wait for vaccines; we wait for friends; we wait for class to start (sometimes wishing professors will not show); we hope that weddings and funerals will start on time. In fact, there is no way to avoid waiting; waiting is as much a part of our life as life itself; waiting is natural;

it is normal. Waiting is spontaneous and planned—but either way, we are waiting. Waiting has produced an industry that focuses on minimizing our wait and/or making our wait more comfortable. Waiting areas are constructed to assist our wait, and waiting regions have socialized and influenced our methods of waiting, that is, waiting areas guide our wait behavior. Our wait then is habitually structured and controlled. Often, if there is no waiting area, persons develop one, for many have internalized waiting.

Some persons are better *waiters* than others; put another way, some individuals are more patient and more prepared. Does patience imply rewards in that "good things come to those who wait?" Or is patience linked to culture; whereby, certain countries, regions, and groups are more accustomed to slower lifestyles and frown on haste? Does one's ability to wait signal past experiences, creating more patience or anxiety while waiting? Whether patient or impatient, these questions help us to critically reflect on waiting and how it is experienced. Taken together, *the sociology of waiting is the study of how individuals wait. There is no single waiting method, and in most cases, there are established norms and physical structures that guide our waiting.*

Significance of Waiting

Why is waiting sociologically significant? We live in a society that requires waiting. Waiting has always been a major part of the United States and other cultures; it is a universal phenomenon. Mothers wait nine months to give birth; embryos take time to develop; seeds are planted, and they require time to grow. Waiting is a natural and ever-evolving process. Sociologically, waiting gets at order and our ability or inability to pause. Crowds cannot rush into concert venues; supermarkets cannot check out customers simultaneously and L.A. freeways require patience during rush hours. So, we must wait! Get in line, and wait! In all our waiting, *we've developed strategies and structures for "delays"*—and such methods and structures provide order as well as understanding, for example, we recognize why we wait. In some cases, our waiting is comforted by certain structures like waiting rooms, permitting the possible emergence of patience, social interaction, and even rest.

Further, waiting has potential social effects. For example, conversations might develop while parents wait for their children during ballet and swim practice; similarly, dialogue may arise while customers wait in line at the post office. Complaints about delays and/or talk about child's abilities make waiting social. The line formation at supermarkets, Department of Motor Vehicles (DMVs), dental offices, and airports enhances the sociability of waiting. The rails, ropes, arrows, and signs within supermarkets, airports, and hospitals guide our wait. Status is less significant and often unknown while individuals wait. We recognize that waiting is a process and that all participants are socialized to wait. Such socialization gets at our ability to internalize our wait-culture; thus, we come to expect others to wait as we do, for example, to obey wait rules and etiquette. Failure to adhere to waiting norms could lead to conflict; this is why wait signs, rails, lines, and sometimes security are necessary, that is, to instruct our waiting thus avoid quarrel. On one level, quarrels reflect wait breakdowns or some perceived confusion about waiting.

Waiting therefore becomes important not only for order and sociability, but also it gets at acceptance and adherence to norms of waiting. Internalizing wait-norms, thus accepting them as part of a stable society, raises questions and considerations about respect. Adhering to wait-norms implies a certain respect for others and one's society. Respect now drives our willingness to wait, our desire for order. Respect suggests that we not only understand our culture, but it is activated by consideration of others. For example, though I am in a hurry, I still must wait to process my appointment.

As waiting is an important part of our everyday lives, investigations regarding the sociology of waiting are sparse, ethnographically, and otherwise. It is therefore significant to explain and understand how people wait; and while waiting is necessary, how is it done? How is it accomplished? What strategies are used? How is waiting avoided or postponed? How is waiting compromised or even rationalized? These questions are crucial to our investigation; they permit us to focus on everyday-routine waiting; they allow us to explore why some prefer to wait and others don't. In a fast-paced society that is programmed for short-term gratification and quick fixes, "going nowhere fast" is a phrase often used to describe haste without thought, while the wise observe and wonder why individuals refuse to slow down.

We live in a society that is designed to accomplish tasks rapidly and efficiently. We want what we want, and we want it now! Often our socialization includes learning and completing assignments quickly and correctly, that is, a brief on-the-job training and a shorter potty training. Technology and human impatience have driven our fast-pace society, sometimes referred to as the *McDonaldization of Society* (George Ritzer, 1993). Our attention span has decreased so gimmicks are used to maintain our conscious. Computer technology promotes ever-increasing speeds. Frequently, microwaves are used instead of conventional ovens and fast food restaurants fill orders faster than traditional restaurants—as they (McDonalds, In-N-Out Burger, Burger King, and others) promise customers "in-n-out" service. Fast-track courses, online courses, and abbreviated academic (and vocational) programs are touted as the wave of the future. Supermarket customers are rewarded for "10 items or less," "self-service," and "cash only," but while online banking, shopping, and airline ticket purchases are convenient, mistakes in cyberspace are often disastrous, invasive, and time consuming. Further, certain municipal districts include night court, and believers desire that God answer their prayer(s) now! During the 1960s movement, a popular slogan among civil right activists was "freedom now!" In short, we live in a society that emphasizes speed and efficiency; yet in many cases, demand and conditions exceed supply. Consequently, we must wait. How does one wait in an impatient society? How does one resolve this societal strain and push toward immediate gratification versus long-term planning?

The sociology of waiting is a classic piece of *everyday sociology*, a timeless piece of routine behavior and activity. Waiting is as natural as breathing, eating, and drinking; indeed, mothers wait nine months before infants are brought to term, and summer will always follow spring—yet cyclically, we must wait for the natural course of events. At times, waiting is something we do, and do not fully realize that we're doing it. Waiting is part of our nature in that it is a natural and normal element of our daily experiences. Waiting provides its own *lessons*. That is, by watching cars weave through traffic and receive citations from police, we learn that waiting may have saved time and money. We also learn that rushing through traffic could cause fatal accidents; and, cutting a long post office line could lead to conflict. Additionally, we learn patience and opportunities for self-reflection. Thus, not only does waiting provide significant life lessons, it offers *benefits* as well. For instance, Tasha expressed that she had the most pleasant conversation while waiting to ride the rollercoaster. Waiting for over an hour, she met and talked with strangers about a variety of topics, including how to develop and manage business accounts. Talk seemed to shorten or distract her wait thus making her ride more enjoyable. Brittney shared that her waiting was rewarded with free food from Jack-N-the-Box. Whether waiting is imposed by others, required by the situation or self-applied, there is a certain value to waiting.

Further, the sociology of waiting is significant because there is far more to waiting than imagined, but often overlooked and taken for granted. It is an area of research that has received little attention, yet the discovery of wait-explanations, waiting places, social waiting, unexpected waiting, and alternatives to waiting permits knowledge and understanding that better explains wait patterns and wait behavior. Moreover, shining the light on waiting permits a far superior understanding of order and how our society organizes itself around taking turns, leisure, and "killing time." Waiting then is no small matter; it is a *matter* that takes up much of our valuable time and resources— consequently, reducing wait time has become big business. Finally, though waiting is a taken for granted activity, many have learned to utilize their down time. For example, customers and patients who wait for service are frequently seen making business calls, childcare arrangements, doing home and/or office work, and counseling loved ones. The significance of such activity gets at one's knowledge, preparation, and anticipation of waiting. Those who fail to prepare often regret this oversight and simply end up killing time.

Critical Writings

Some of the earliest work on waiting includes Mann (1969), Man and Taylor (1969), Schwartz (1974), Schwartz (1975), and Lipsky (1980). This body of literature is consistent in that thematically, order and rules are addressed, and yet each author recognizes the social dimensions of waiting. Mann (1969), in particular, focuses on social systems and how they are developed while people wait in line. That is, during lengthy waits, tents emerge, rules are respected, shift systems develop, and queue jumping is monitored. Eventually, strangers begin interacting and the adventure of queuing is well on its way. While Mann (1969) is interested in culture and social systems, Mann and Taylor (1969:95) depart from this analysis and are more concerned with the "relationship between apparent (estimated) position and actual position in line in situations where (a) there is a limited supply of the commodity and (b) priority for the commodity is determined by position in line." For Mann and Taylor, whether one overestimates or underestimates the numbers ahead depends on one's position in line. In these studies, "the line" is crucial to their analysis of waiting (Grushin, 2010).

To what extent is waiting a waste of time? In a postindustrial society, Barry Schwartz (1974) is concerned with the efficiency of waiting in productive societies. In part, Schwartz argues that time is a valuable commodity that is wasted while waiting. He further recognizes the power relationship between client and server is often stratified, arguing that servers have power to impose waits on others; abuse of this power may lead to the client reneging or refusing to wait. At the same time, Schwartz maintains that supply and demand influence time spent waiting. That is, we are more likely to spend more time waiting when product demand is high and supply is low, for example, the number of *servers* is low. Yet, in the end, clients are typically dependent on servers for goods and services, and *urgency* is another variable that determines their likelihood of waiting. So, while waiting is a necessary situation in all social systems, power is an important feature in the distribution of time and how persons wait.

Schwartz's (1975) second offering is far more ambitious, for example, *Queuing and Waiting: Studies in the Social Organization of Access and Delay*. While the second offering is an extension of his first article, "Waiting, Exchange and Power" (1974), Schwartz is primarily concerned with three issues: waiting time; the internal organization and order of queues; and the manner in which delay is interpreted by clients and servers. Interestingly, Schwartz examines medical emergency departments as a way to arrive at various factors that diminish waiting time. Additionally, his book examines the *American Journal of Sociology* and their inability to keep up with the growing number of papers submitted to them, for example, manuscript delay. While several other issues are discussed, Schwartz makes clear the cost of delay and offers useful solutions.

Innovative Techniques

While a study of waiting is not new, contemporary discussion of waiting as a research project makes for interesting and intriguing conversation. Each time I shared my research topic, persons habitually appeared stunned and baffled; some even frowned, as to communicate, "What do you mean?" Others simply repeated the term ("Waiting?") as for clarity. Whether verbally or nonverbally puzzled, each case required more explanation. I described that my study of waiting focuses on *how* individuals wait. For example, *how* people wait in line, or *how* they wait in traffic, or at the doctor's office. After grasping the idea, I could see the light come on—with a smile, a raised eyebrow, and/or a comment, "interesting." "Interesting" was the most frequently used term to describe the *sociology of waiting*. One respondent said, "What an interesting topic!" Another commented, "Hmm, that's interesting," and many simply said, "That's interesting." Other terms used to describe my project include "deep" ("that's deep man"), "clever," and "intriguing." One colleague expressed:

> I'm also intrigued by your study of waiting. At first, I thought it might be about waiting in line. But then I realized how the concept of waiting can also apply to so many other aspects of life—waiting for a baby to be born, waiting the return of a loved-one at war, waiting for an illness to run its course, waiting for a depression to end, waiting to be released from prison, waiting for Santa to come, etc. I realize how much our lives are spent waiting, especially in the Western world where we tend to be so future-oriented. Sounds like an exciting project.

The initial comments and gestures were followed by a need to say more in that respondents were frequently compelled to convey their wait experiences, stories, or "wait-issues" that I should consider. Needless to say, as respondents communicated "wait experiences and stories," such information became part of my data collection—which makes for an interesting methodological technique (Emerson et al., 1995). Still, the sharing, conveyance of stories, experiences, and encounters are valid in that they spotlight some aspect of *waiting*. The uniqueness lies in its natural and conversational revelations of wait experiences (see Hennink et al., 2011; Hammersley and Atkinson, 1983).

Others conveyed their stories with more conviction as if it should be included in my research. When I told Hannah, gymnastics coach, about my research project, she said, "You should talk to me! I can tell you a lot about waiting." Instantly and voluntarily, she began sharing her experiences and wait-emotions. Naturally, I did not dissuade anyone from sharing; I listened intently, probed and questioned when necessary; my ears and brain were open to every story, every emotion, and every situation (Emerson et al., 1995). Hannah confessed, "I will not go to the doctor unless I have the first appointment or unless it's an emergency. I cannot sit there and wait because I feel I'm wasting my time . . . In everything I do, I try to figure out how I can avoid waiting. Because I can't wait, it drives me crazy!" Hannah admitted that her inability to wait stems from her cultural socialization in Germany. Similarly, when Judge Sanders, retired judge, learned of my research, he shared how a waiting room was developed due to several court interruptions by babies. That is, the conflict among parents during custody proceedings led children to act out, cry, and side with one of the parents. All such interruptions led to delays. Consequently, a wait-room was constructed where children could go during custody hearings. And Ralph (ballet instructor) not only joked, but also complained about his wait-encounters; seemingly, he used this opportunity to vent: "The worst waiting situation is to wait for delivery. They'll give you a time, say 10am to 1pm, and you have to be there. Why can't they tell you from 10 to 11 or 11 to 12pm? They don't care! And if you're not there, you're screwed. Another is when you wait in line and you finally make it to the front; then, you find out there are no more tickets. They are sold out. Now that really makes me mad!" These stories imply that waiting is a common and unique experience. And while most persons express their views and opinions, their reactions were an essential source of data. Methodologically, I simply let it happen. I let them talk until they were finished. In part, this is the uniqueness of data collection. Each researcher is equipped with a certain demeanor. How does his/her demeanor and personality influence and encourage others (respondents) to talk or share, rather than conceal?

At times, obtaining information was almost effortless in that most people wished to discuss waiting, because *waiting* situations regularly exist. For example, while waiting in the bank or post office, I habitually recorded field notes. Yet, given the aforementioned wait-stories, the challenging question is—why did individuals so freely disclose their wait experiences? In part, it is because everyone waits, it is not personal, and most have something to say. Talking about waiting is not like discussing religion, politics, and/or race— where conversations are guarded. Waiting is not as sensitive, and people's stories provide evidence that they have in fact waited. Seemingly, individuals wanted to communicate their wait-stories and tales (see Bonilla-Silva, 2006 for distinction) to me, a researcher. Why? It is likely they wanted to vent, share, contribute to my research and have someone (researcher) remedy their wait-issues. Thus, in some cases, I became a substitute for the "grievance department"—and I soon learned that many complainants have better ways of reducing and handling wait situations.

The above instances and others are crucial in that they emerged naturally (Prus, 1995). How we manage waiting is significant to our current concerns. Methodologically, sharing voluntarily makes for an interesting and unique research technique, for in the course of respondent sharing, questions are voluntarily answered that I typically ask during structured interviews. Consequently, there is less questioning and more probing—while the possibility of discovering something new is readily apparent (see Prus, 1995; Corbin and Strauss, 2008). It follows then that my interviews were structured ($N = 83$) and unstructured ($N = 108$); that is, researchers must flow and adapt to research situations (Price, 2005). Additionally, this investigation included 311 open-ended surveys in which respondents wrote of their wait-experiences, such as self-imposed waits, wait-explanations, wait-decisions, wait-conflict, waiting with strangers, and refusing to wait. Respondents included high school students, undergraduate and graduate students, adults in general wait situations (airport, bank, concert line, hospital waiting room, etc.), homeless persons, and adults with specific statuses (judge, bank teller, court clerk, sheriffs, teachers, professors, ministers, etc.). Furthermore, African Americans, Asian Americans, Armenian Americans, Arab Americans, Latinos, whites, females, males, and seniors are included in this study.

One significant ethnographic principle is "let the issue choose you," not vice versa, for example, "you choose the issue." "Letting the issue choose you" is more natural and presents less bias. Choosing the issue could result in bias and preconceived notions of what one intends to find. *Letting the issue choose you* emerges naturally as one participates in the setting. How does it work? Ethnographers are trained to take notes on everything, and later, focus on issues that emerged. Within the setting, interactions, conversations, gestures, and so forth are taking place. While I investigated waiting, what issue(s) emerged? Well, standing in line at the donut shop, I noticed instances of customers cutting line. One does not know what to anticipate, and yet, I was not expecting someone to cut-the-line, but he did. In such instances, this becomes a fruitful source of data, and I honed in, observing how customers and employee handled the line-cutter. It became an *issue* to observe and record. I cite this example to show that cutting naturally emerged as I was present. And so, such an occurrence gives me an issue to study and focus on. In short, I did not choose the issue, cutting; the issue chose me. It follows then that within this book, topic selection is guided by this technique.

Participant observation was/is the most fruitful form of data collection. I spent over two years collecting and analyzing data. The importance of being in the field, for example, being present, is that investigators may hear, see, feel, and question individual responses to wait situations. Here, waiting scenarios and talk emerged naturally; it was critical that I placed myself in situations of wait—I needed to hear and feel what others were experiencing.[1] Positionality was crucial (Hennink et al., 2011). Watching someone cut in line and how it was handled proved invaluable. Watching clerks and how they managed crowds was crucial; listening to wait-explanations by managers and whether customers believed their excuses was another significant angle. Some customers don't believe explanations; other customers accept them and still others express anger. Therefore, whether customers accept explanations or not, an explanation is given. Finally, observing those who refused to wait gets at mental health and priorities, and yet an important source of data. The observer recognizes that different wait-environments exist and such situations conjure up different emotions and wait patterns—all of which are important to the *sociology of waiting*. For example, is there any *difference* between airport explanations and restaurant explanations? And of course, is there *similarity* among airport and restaurant explanations? Comparing and contrasting allowed me to make sense of wait-explanation, how it was delivered, and the specific context and environment in which it was issued. Here, one clearly learns that certain patterns and norms emerge in similar wait situations; but one also rediscovers that waiting is a natural and universal element in our social world.

Admittedly, my "research cap" was *on* frequently. That is, a scheduled Black Friday research observation habitually went beyond this event. I often went for a cup of coffee after observations. While sitting, sipping, and reflecting, it was not unusual for me to observe those waiting to order; and, it was not unusual to jot down notes of the wait-situation. Why? The wait-situation is "in the moment," and may prove a valuable piece of data. My research behavior then gets at my attachment to this project.

The excitement and challenge of ethnographic research is that one never knows what she/he will discover and/or encounter. Following up on a tip to wait at Men's Central Jail, I had no idea what to expect. I arrived and was met by a line of 40 persons that would soon swell to over 100 individuals. All were there to visit loved ones in jail. In length, the line was over 90 yards, which stretched beyond the facility and onto the sidewalk. The wait was informative in that watching and conversing with others proved fruitful. One conversation suggested that visiting on weekends was "the worst." When I showed up on Saturday, the line was twice as long. Observing and talking to sheriffs was also fascinating in that they control how many visitors enter the waiting room and how visitors wait in line; moreover, their interaction with visitors resembles an "us versus them" relationship. Part of what I discovered was *how* to wait at Men's Central Jail (MCJ) and *how* the wait itself was part of the experience for visitors.

I often timed how long it took to complete various waits. Some waits, like Black Friday waits, were longer than others; but interestingly, some waits were shorter than anticipated. While the DMV wait is typically long (over forty minutes), customers appeared pleasantly surprised when completing their license renewal in less than forty minutes. In contrast, waits that should have been short aroused annoyance among certain individuals whose wait was longer than anticipated. It soon became clear that persons have different internal time clocks regarding appropriate wait duration (see Flaherty, 1999). Wait time varied from place to place, yet, in most wait-environments persons expect to wait. We live in a *society of waiters*; that is, we are socialized to wait, and wait patterns get at order and organization within our communities.

For high school seniors, how do they wait to hear of their acceptance or rejection from college? I attempted to gain access to a private upper-middle-class high school. I wanted to distribute open-ended surveys to get a sense of their wait-experiences. The principal appeared uncomfortable with my project and rejected my request. This was problematic because the same request at a public high school was granted. Not only was it granted but after the survey, an informal discussion emerged with one senior class and their teacher. Certainly, this was useful, but I had nothing to compare. Through friends and high school teachers, eventually, I located private high school seniors who talked and wrote about their college admission experiences. Why is this important? Methodologically, this was clearly a *research challenge* and yet it was crucial to find another way. For example, when one research door closes (private high school), how does one find a similar group to survey?

Finally, all names used in this book are fictitious. While names and identities are important in certain scenarios, they are not in others. Waiting is general; everybody waits, so identity is equally as important as *the situation of wait*. Depending on the encounter, the *wait-situation* gives waiting its general appeal and point of analysis. In short, the starting point is always the wait-situation.

BOOK OVERVIEW

Structure of Waiting examines wait-patterns and how wait arrangements develop. The structure of waiting gets at social order, organization, material objects, formation, and cultural norms attached to waiting. Signs, rails, and arrows are clear examples of how waiting is organized and experienced. Waiting has become normative in that there is order and rules to waiting.

While conflict may occur, clashes are rare given our conventional understanding and acceptance of formal and informal wait rules and values. "First come, first serve" along with appointments are often acknowledged and honored protocols to waiting. Generally, persons adhere to established wait-patterns. Once individuals understand wait-structures, for example, how boarding passes are used to board planes or waiting in the doctor's office, we are likely to conform to perceived wait arrangements. Structurally, our waiting is assisted by *wait-props*, such as rails, ropes connected to poles, floor markings, number counters, symbols, and signs instruct people how, where, and what to expect while waiting. Waiting then is institutionalized, as wait structures, emerging structures, and cultural values exist to maintain wait order and wait boundaries.

Waiting Places investigates various venues where waiting occurs. A waiting place refers to a certain seat or area where persons spend time waiting. Sometimes, we prefer to wait at a certain table (Duneier, 1992) or chair or area, but if such spaces are taken, we adjust and wait elsewhere. Additionally, *waiting places* involve a variety of settings where waiting occurs, such as barbershops, beauty salons, dance studios, auto repair shops, break rooms, police stations, hallways, juror assembly rooms, and several other locations. Active or passive, waiting is an activity that we *do* and the places where we wait could have profane and/or sacred meaning. This chapter then examines three types of wait regions that describe the sort of waiting one will experience. For example, distinctions are made among *wait rooms, enclosed wait sections,* and *open wait areas*—all of which influence our wait behavior. Waiting is rarely exciting, so how are distractions employed to prevent boredom and keep customers from leaving?

Wait Utilization examines *how* people wait, that is, what people *do* while waiting. Given one's need to meet deadlines, what persons *do* with wait-time is significant. *Doing* or *not doing* gets at one's preparedness to wait. One high school teacher exclaimed, "When I wait, I take along my crossword puzzle to keep me occupied." A college professor remarked, "When I wait, I prepare myself. I take books, papers, magazines and crochet." For the above teachers and certain others, it is important to have something to *do*, to utilize their time, either by pleasure or work activities. *Wait Utilization* then focuses on *doing* and *how* one manages his or her time while waiting.

Waiting for Service investigates the process and condition of waiting in line or elsewhere for an organization's assistance and/or service. The typical picture illustrates standing in line at airports, grocery stores, or coffee shops. The primary focus is on the *experience of the wait*; that is, as customers wait, I hone in on what they see, how they feel, what they encounter, what they learn, and how they define and interpret their observations and experiences. Further, *waiting for service* gets at a condition; for instance, under what conditions do customers wait? Do customers wait in rain, snow, humidity, or noonday heat? Do customers wait in waiting rooms or the privacy and comfort of their vehicles and homes? Do customers wait in early morning, overnight, or even in shifts? The process and condition of waiting varies by organization and desired product. One is not likely to wait for playoff tickets in a hospital waiting room; just, as one will not wait for surgery in financial institutions. Thus, while *waiting for service* is a common situation, our wait often reflects a desired product and specific venues.

Wait Explanations give reasons for delays; they generally explain why one is waiting. There are times when individuals are stalled and long to know why. "What could be taking so long?" "Why am I held-up?" "Why did he get his food before me?" Wait explanations provide a basis for standstills. They offer cause and understanding for delay or stoppage. Such inquiries suggest that persons are attentive while waiting; they are attentive to time and order, thus when there is discrepancy, customers may confront those in charge. Wait explanations are sometimes accompanied with apologies, attempting to patronize, and appease customers, for example, "I'm sorry, the cook misread my handwriting, but your order should be out next." While explanations give reasons for delays, they frequently contain promise and hope; promise that service will soon materialize, and hope that service or product is worth the wait. There is nothing more disappointing than to wait for unsatisfactory service or disgusting outcomes. Conversely, the promise is something individuals anticipate, and carrying out the promise determines whether original explanation was true, for example, "I'm sorry, the cook misread my handwriting, but your order should be out next." After lengthy delays, customers count on their order being next. Inconsistencies could lead to distrust and credibility concerns. Hence, explanations not only remind individuals why they are waiting, but such explanations suggest that institutions are considerate of their time. Finally, this chapter examines explanation strategies, social status, no explanation, lies as explanations, and functions of wait explanations.

Minimizing customer delays to maintain business is one way of examining the *Business of Waiting*. It is a conventional strategy that focuses on satisfying and keeping one's client base. This chapter is not interested in the conventional model; I am more interested in expanding the business of waiting by examining waiting through different angles. For example, *waiting* is at the *center* of the *business of waiting*; here, one is not concerned with wait-reduction, one is more concerned with waiting as an enterprise ("How might I make money by people waiting?"). The "business of waiting" focuses on *how* organizations or individual entrepreneurs profit from those waiting. It is a unique market niche. As noted earlier, waiting is a necessary condition; we all must wait. And given this condition, organized establishments have set up vending machines, slot machines, snack bars, coffee shops, and newsstands near waiting areas. Such innovations are designed to take one's mind off of waiting, that is, distraction, and simultaneously make money.

Waiting in line presents opportunities for individuals to entertain themselves by watching and evaluating strangers. In fact, persons become linked to strangers in various wait-situations. For instance, waiting at bus stops, waiting for trains, and waiting in financial institutions are situations where persons are surrounded by strangers; several of our experiences exist around people we do not know. The bus stop, the train station, and the financial institution are familiar situations where strangers abound. Given our many trips to the bank or ATM, individuals are not uncomfortable—for this situation is familiar, and yet strange (see Peter Berger, 1963). Order and organization are present in that strangers adhere to conventional norms for specific settings. Such situations only become uncomfortable when "unusual" and "scary" strangers are present and inconsiderate. It is clear then that one's linkage to strangers occurs in everyday situations. *Waiting with Strangers* focuses on how strangers wait among each other, that is, how space is used and whether communication is likely.

Technology has spilled over into wait-structures providing flexibility and *Alternatives to Waiting*. Our fast pace, quick-fix-society has ushered in wait-options that are utilized by many. *Alternatives to Waiting* examines *how* societal institutions and individuals reduce waiting and thus attempt to obtain services sooner. For instance, instead of standing in line at the bank, ATMs and online banking have evolved as worthy alternatives; similarly, microwaves have tweaked our dining routines. Options then provide alternatives to those who are rushed, prefer technological advancements, or simply don't want to wait.

Waiting for a loved-one to die triggers several emotions. Needless to say, death involves a range of emotions that assist persons in getting through a difficult circumstance. It is precisely *this wait* that permits emotions to emerge and manifest themselves. What type of emotions is experienced during "dying and death"? How are emotions managed when loved ones are near death? How is waiting used to comfort loved ones and significant others? Here, *I am interested in emotions of individuals who lose loved-ones and how they manage their emotions? How they wait for loved-ones to die?* Simply put, my focus is on the *Emotions and Waiting* of survivors.

The concluding chapter explores and introduces a *Theory of Waiting*. Initially, distinctions are made between *waiting games* and *wait-and-see situations*. Such distinctions are required to clear up confusion; these distinctions guide our usage of commonly used phrases. A theory of waiting captures the remainder of final chapter. Without question, a theory of waiting is designed to explain our wait-behavior and experiences.

NOTE

1. During my fieldwork, I waited in the following situations and environments: grocery stores, auto repair shops, body shops, laundry mats, bank lines, ATMs, post offices, immigration agencies, hospitals, DMVs, Black Friday, restaurants (fast food & reservation), courtrooms, jury rooms, car traffic, subways, buses, lines at men's central jail, barbershops, coffee shops, iPad and iPhone lines, X-box lines, waiting on the phone, airports, tarmacs, churches, movie lines, theater lines, concert lines, waiting for children, for furniture, for appointments, hotel lobbies, medical results, for decisions, waiting in crowds, at rallies, and so forth.

Chapter 1

Structure of Waiting

While waiting in amusement parks, one is often confronted with long lines and frequent stoppage. It is not uncommon to wait two or three hours for one's favorite ride. Some rides post appropriate height, weight, and wait length, allowing customers to make informed decisions about waiting. Deciding not to wait may slightly reduce wait-time for other ride-waiters, but the line, in fact remains. The end of the line curves around snack bars and restrooms; a rope is used to direct waiting, but as customers draw closer to the front, they enter a maze type area that collapses the long line into a confined arrangement (see Kuhn, 1964; Turner, 1981). Entering the maze indicates that customers are likely to remain in line and therefore enjoy the roller coaster. The maze is where customers often hear prerecorded messages and instructions from amusement park personnel. The line and maze represent a type of structure, that is, a waiting pattern, and such arrangements, specifically the maze, draw customers closer, constraining one's wait-options, interactions, and encounters (see Goffman, 1963). And thus, as the winding line moves, one keeps seeing the same people, recognizing that such people become less strange and more familiar; consequently, placing them in proximity for possible interaction and dialogue.

The structure of waiting then gets at social order, organization, formation, and cultural norms while waiting. The maze and other wait-structures are clear examples of how waiting is organized and experienced. Waiting is often normative in that there are order and rules to waiting. While conflict may occur, clashes are *rare* given our normative understanding and acceptance of formal and informal wait rules and values. "First come, first serve" along with appointments are often acknowledged and honored protocols to waiting (see Lipsky, 1980:95). We tend to conform to established wait-patterns. Once individuals understand wait-structures, for example, how persons wait for boarding passes or waiting in the doctor's office, we are likely to conform to perceived waiting arrangements. Moreover, our comprehension and anticipation of the wait-structures affect our waiting behavior, that is, whether to arrive early—to be first and avoid waiting, or bring work or play items—so as to remain occupied while waiting.

Formal wait-structures are more predictable, thus adding familiarity to wait formation and wait expectations, giving rise to less strain. Formal wait-structures, such as doctors' offices or certain restaurants, reflect social systems that maintain a history of waiting; the existence of formalized structures is designed to routinize one's wait, while at the same time, formalized structures potentially manage anticipated and unanticipated delays.[1] It follows then that industrialization leads to common forms of organization (Suzman, 1977): forms that guide and normalize our wait-behavior. Institutions with similar *structures* tend to induce common psychic reactions or regularities in the personalities of their participants (Suzman, 1977). In short, we eventually internalize how waiting should occur at the post office or supermarket, which may reflect how wait-structure affects our personality. That is, whether one is patient or anxious or whether one will wait at all. Overtime, emerging structures become formalized and waiting patterns then develop from specific social situations and certain needs of participants, allowing individuals to anticipate wait-length and wait-styles, that is, whether one will sit or stand while waiting.

Put simply, *wait-structures* are areas of wait, places where waiting occurs. Waiting for service and/or "waiting your turn" resembles formalized waiting, as in waiting for class to start or waiting for concert tickets. Waiting for friends or waiting for friends to call is informal waiting. *What* we are waiting for determines the nature of our wait, and more often than not, formal waiting is tied to institutions and situations having established wait procedures. Informal waiting is less normative. It is more casual. There is no wait-list, no wait-line, or wait-room. Here, one may wait in his car or in her house or on the phone. Moreover, one may find himself/herself waiting in the park for a birthday party or waiting for announcements and news to arrive. Waiting for furniture and appliances is more formal and could take all day, but it is clear that the *area of wait* depends on *what* we are waiting for, and the object of our wait is tied to the formal and informal nature of our wait experience. Again, it is clear that we wait on most everything, and thus, the wait-structure reflects *what* we are waiting for, recognizing that wait-structures are both formal and informal.

To what extent are wait-structures negotiated? Are they flexible? Might they shift and change? Are they stable? And to what extent are flexible structures stable? Symbolic interactionists generally contend that "any social system is a negotiated order" (Maines, 1977), individuals are active agents in social life, who interact, refine, and redefine structures. Structures are made real through our everyday involvement. According to House (1981), whenever an individual modifies the nature of expectations or behavior associated with a role, he or she is modifying an aspect of social structure. Such negotiation of social structure is an endemic feature of social life (House, 1981). Structures are negotiated, and renegotiated because at times, certain structures don't work; they don't fulfill or meet individual and group needs. Structures remain stable given our socialization and basic acceptance of societal values. In short, recurring patterns of behavior, such as waiting in line, is by definition an aspect of social structure (House, 1981), which in turn lends itself to modification. For instance, we are more receptive to amending wait-rules when the physically challenged are among us with no accommodations. We are more considerate and permit them immediate access given their condition. So individual and group flexibility are situationally desired in stable wait-structures.

Culture is a good indicator of one's perspective on waiting. For House (1981:542) culture is a set of cognitive and evaluative beliefs—beliefs about what is and what ought to be—that are shared by members of a social system and transmitted to others. Freud (1955) argues that we learn the values of our culture by identifying with parents and others who hold these values and hence take the values as our own. Additionally, social structures are persisting and bounded patterns of social relationships among persons or positions in a social system (House, 1981). But, it is culture that allows us to make sense of social structure, and without culture, structure may not exist or may appear confusing and anomic at best. "Wait your turn" becomes a very significant cultural value that guides waiting expectations and arrangements. Culture helps identify who is next and why persons are next; the belief system attached to "wait your turn" explains our wait-rationale and social behavior.

Many cultures maintain some system of line-waiting, and generally, waiting in line reflects the cultural value of consideration. Clearly there are wait systems in China, Russia, India, Japan, Germany, and other countries, and yet no system is identical. *What is similar is the wait.* Globally, waiting in line is quite common. But how is it done? Waiting may involve an elaborate system of space saving, queue jumping, or simple respect for others. Line-waiting maintains specific mores and folkway for each country. For example, Daniel Brooks (2018) explains that in Russia, "Someone might stand in two or three lines at the same time. It's possible to leave a line and come back to it later on . . . If a line is long, a place can be reserved in it by agreeing with the person in front of you (not behind you) to hold your place for a few short minutes." Japan wait-culture is more reflective of respect. Weller (2016) makes clear that "Japan's love of line-forming begins with the lessons kids learn as early as kindergarten: self-discipline, cooperation and respect . . . After many years

of learning this behavior—showing respect for the group by waiting quietly—the end result is a cultural custom that spans nearly all circumstances,"
including "standing in line for a comic book convention called Comiket." A
structural approach to waiting must account not only for persisting patterns of
social behavior, but also for the existence and persistence of shared cultural
values, beliefs (House, 1981), and norms. Whether Russian or Japanese, we
learn the specific wait-structure attached to our culture, and in most cases,
producing order and organization within society.

The structure of waiting also contains a racial component that manifest
itself in a perceived and actual privilege of whites, for example, African
Americans and Latinos *waiting for* and *waiting on* whites. Black–white interaction often reflects a power relationship where whites receive service first
and Blacks provide service for whites. In the latter case, Blacks have consistently performed domestic chores for whites, "*waiting on* them hand and
foot." Whether nursing them to strength, cooking and serving food, cleaning house, washing and ironing, running errands, and raising their children,
Blacks and Latinos have a service relationship with whites; a relationship that
identifies power and privilege in whites—at the expense of minorities. Whites
have little concern with Black–Brown sentiments and would not consider
changing the overt and covert "wait-system." For in their view, the system
functions well. It is normal. The U.S. society contains a racial wait-structure
in which whites have constructed and wish to preserve. During the Jim Crow
era and segregation, custom favored whites over African Americans. Jackson
(1993) recalls that the drugstore was extremely challenging during his young
life. Jackson explains that "my beef (with the drugstore and the system) was
that I was forbidden to sit at the counter." He complains:

> If any Black wanted service whether for himself or, like me, for those he worked
> for—he simply had to stand and wait until all the white folks were served. Those
> Blacks who went contrary to this were worked over something fierce, often by
> those mild-mannered Milquetoasts who looked as if they wouldn't hurt a fly. A
> fly, no; but an uppity nigger, in a minute.
>   Yet I went to the drugstore each morning with my order of coffee, cakes
> and whatever, written out and clutched firmly in my hand. And each time I
> was confronted with rows of white folks, seated at the counter and clamoring
> for attention. I did what I was expected to do: I waited, all the while hating it.
> (Jackson, 1993:4)

Jackson hated the system because it viewed him and other minorities as infe-
rior and invisible (Ellison, 1972). He recognizes that the U.S. wait-structure
is one that services whites first and African Americans last. Breaking down
an unequal wait-structure has often proved costly, for example, death, church

bombings, and jail, but it leads to a structure more consistent with American values, for example, "first come, first serve." This was the sentiment of the Montgomery Bus Boycott—that Blacks should board on a "first come, first serve basis," (King, 1958; Cone, 1992) and not suffer humiliation by boarding from the rear and after whites. Moreover, it was the goal of *freedom riders* who sought to change the separate wait-room policies of Southern bus terminals. Consequently, while Black and white wait-norms have formally changed, there are informal occasions where the previous wait-attitudes remain.

CONTEXT OF WAIT-STRUCTURES

The context of wait-structures manifests itself in the varying situations of wait; waiting is contextualized based on one's milieu, and such environments determine how waiting is organized. Wait-structures vary from situation to situation, but what is common about most wait milieus is that *structure in waiting* exists. Theoretically, we recognize that waiting is an ongoing process. We are always waiting on something or someone. For instance, one may be home working, yet waiting for a TV program or waiting to pick up children from ballet or waiting for mail or waiting to receive a phone call so that dinner plans materialize. Whatever the context, waiting is quite normal; yet, the environment determines wait length and wait utilization, that is, what we *do* while waiting.

WAITING PROPS

In most situations of wait, there are *waiting props*, consisting of rails, ropes connected to poles, floor markings (such as arrows and lane lines), floor signs, symbols, and signs directing people how, where, and what to expect while waiting. Put another way, wait-props are material objects that guide, instruct, and organize waiting. Amusement parks, post offices, banks, DMVs, Covid-19 car lines, and hospitals are often noted for *waiting props*. For example, one sign at Kaiser Hospital instructs: "Please have your health plan card & photo identification card ready. Payment is due at the time of registration: Visa and Master Card accepted." It follows that the purpose of *waiting props* is to guide waiting, to answer frequently asked questions, and to informally monitor others while waiting, so as to deter line-cutting and reduce delays.

Accompanying various rails and ropes, the Dermatology & Allergy clinic posts a sign that reads: "PATIENTS"—"Please form a line and wait to be called. Have your health plan card ready. Thank You." As one patient (Janet) was leaving, she proceeded toward the end of the line. The receptionist, who is currently servicing a customer, notices Janet, inquiring "checking out?" Janet: "Yes." The receptionist extends her arm/hand so as to reach for Janet's paperwork. Janet gives receptionist paperwork. Receptionist separates papers, returns an extra copy to Janet, and she leaves. This exchange takes less than two seconds while the receptionist resumes servicing current client, and seemingly, the current client is not bothered by the brief interruption. One's time is valuable, so why wait when service involves a simple paper exchange. It is important to note that Janet adheres to *wait props* and wait-rules; yet, the receptionist's acknowledgment of Janet redirects her wait-intention as they smoothly complete their transaction.

Given the sensitivity of "first come, first serve" and time considerations of others, persons are likely to observe the order in which customers arrive. While wait norms vary from place to place, *typically* wait props permit understanding of wait environments, particularly when wait modification is evident. For example, in the X-ray waiting room, the following sign appears: "Some patients may be X-rayed ahead of other patients because of the type and extent of injuries and/or medical status. We will make every effort to handle all requests as quickly as possible." Such a sign indicates that waiting for X-rays may not follow a "first come, first serve" procedure, but this department is conditionally more flexible in that one's wait depends on "the type and extent of injuries and/or medical status." Thus, though R-patient entered before B-patient, if B-patient is X-rayed ahead of R-patient, it is assumed, based on the sign, that B-patient's medical status is worse and a cause for more immediate attention. There is no need for explanation; the sign explains possible questions. In part, such signs are designed to eliminate verbal explanations and possible conflicts among patients.[2]

But what happens when *props* don't make sense, or are overlooked, or simply ignored? There are instances when misunderstandings occur and customers are not deliberately undermining wait-props and procedures. Similarly, there are moments when wait-props are simply ignored as a way to circumvent waiting. One posted prop instructs, "Please have your health plan card and photo identification card ready." This is an important sign and directive that allows lines to move faster and therefore shorten wait-time. In one instance, an elderly man, Hussein, apparently could not read well, hear well, or understand English well. After returning from lunch and greeting an established long line, one clerk said aloud, "Please have your Kaiser cards ready!!" When Hussein approached the counter, Jamal, customer service representative said; "Give me your Kaiser card!" Hussein looked through his wallet, pulling out a social security card. Handing it to Jamal, Jamal loudly objected, "No, I need your Kaiser card!"

Hussein mumbled, "This is the one I use."

Jamal demanded again, "I need your Kaiser card!!" As Hussein and a friend fumbled through his wallet, Jamal impatiently waved his arm, saying

"Step to the side!!" Eyeing the next customer, he asked, "Can I help the next member!?" As the Kaiser-member approached, Jamal held out his hand, requesting, "Give me your Kaiser card!" Jamal accepted and swiped the card. At that point, Hussein found his card, extended it to Jamal but Jamal held up his hand in a stop position and replied, "Hold on!" Jamal completed his transaction with the "next member" and then assisted Hussein. Theoretically, while *wait props* are designed to organize waiting and stabilize the process, *failure to follow signs and verbal directions could result in longer waits.* Officially, Jamal controls the situation by instructing Hussein to "hold on"— all in an effort to keep the line moving.

MAKING SENSE OF WAIT-STRUCTURES

When rails, ropes, and signs are absent, how do customers manage? How do clients make sense of wait-structure? The lack of *wait props* may present temporary *structural anomie*. A wait-area that is not clearly defined, as with rails, ropes, and poles, may lead customers to ask other customers whether they are waiting on service and/or "Where's the line?" *Structural anomie* may develop given ambivalent and vague wait-areas. One does not know where to wait, where to stand, or whether others have been assisted.

At McDonald's, one observes four African American customers (two adult females, two adult males) standing in a *wait prop-less* line to order food. Additionally, there were two males who had recently ordered and stood off-line, waiting for their food. The first female patiently waited to hear those magic words, "May I take your order please?" The wait was very normal and ordinary, until a white teenage female, Meg, drew their attention by barging in and proceeding straight to the service register. All who waited— gazed as she entered McDonalds, walking straight to the front line. As Meg approached the register, her head turned, making eye contact with those waiting, thereby, recognizing that customers were not only waiting but staring at her as she approached the register. With a smile, Meg quickly reversed her direction and said aloud, "I guess I have to wait, huh?" Without receiving verbal response, Meg voluntarily proceeded to the end of the line. The two males, who were at the end of the line, acknowledged her smile, as they made eye contact and smiled back.

Suppose Meg did not go to the end of the line? Now what? Presumably, there would have ensued comments about her "cutting" line; comments of rebuttal may have come from those waiting and possibly a reaction by cashier. To avoid confrontation, she went to the end of the line. And, why does she go to the end-line? As a society, we have learned to "wait our turn." Thus, she proceeds to the end-line for two reasons: the etiquette of waiting (again, going to the end-line was the right thing do); it is a cultural norm within the U.S. society, which suggests a certain order and organizations to waiting. "Wait Your Turn" is a standard U.S. folkway that is learned and internalized beginning at home and reinforced during daycare and preschool years. Avoiding confrontation becomes the second reason. In order to avoid conflict and respect an established folkway and the people in line, Meg's behavior reflects an understanding of the culture and a definitive social structure. No one said to Meg, "Go to the back of the line." But such comments were unnecessary, for she clearly understood the nonverbal language of customers. Noteworthy, in this particular McDonalds, there were no rails, ropes with poles, or signage guiding and directing one's wait. Customers simply lined up in front of an open register. In this case, only one register was open. Had there been rails and signs, it is unlikely that Meg would have gone directly to the front of the line.

One of the most confusing and potentially hostile elements of wait-structures is gas stations with no entrance or exit arrows. It is confusing because our wait-norms and expectations are frequently overlooked and sometimes dismissed. Waiting behind a stationary car does not mean that you will pump gas next. Identifying an open pump, someone may enter from the opposite direction and begin pumping gas that will prolong your wait and your ability to be next. The car in front of you is now finished but blocked in. Impatience and norm confusion may lead to hostility. Arguments may also arise when someone claims to be next but is not. So, while gas station wait-structure is potentially confusing and hostile, it is more likely that a structure naturally emerges out of shared expectations, socialization, and consideration. That is, customers become accustomed to the semi-structure of certain service stations and adjust their movements, reactions, and interactions accordingly.

Alternatively, a most vivid wait-structure is found in settings where number counters are posted and an electric screen indicates the number currently served. The order of such a system is unmistakable, recognizing that the next customer is never in question. At Home Depot's paint department, one is required to pull a number and wait; such a system is also apparent at other appliance, hardware, deli, and retail stores. One does not necessarily wait in line, but in the surrounding area—close enough to hear and see your number. Failure to respond when called results in another number being announced, and it varies whether a previously called number will receive service immediate, later, next, or whether pulling another number is required. Barring a line, the number system provides order, thus one is not required to determine "who is next," for the numbers accomplish order chronologically. Individuals pull a number, from the number counter machine, mill around, possibly shopping for paint supplies until called. Such a system seems appropriate when lines and rails are not available, or when rails and ropes are ineffective or simply preferring number counters. Such a system might remove attempts to cut in line. Yet, this same structure appears more relaxed in that the "next customer" is not "breathing down your neck," given our preference for distance and space when surrounded by strangers (Hall & Hall, 2005).[3]

INSTITUTIONAL AND INDIVIDUAL ARRANGEMENTS

The structure of waiting further gets at institutional and individual arrangements. The institution arranges wait-patterns by using rails, ropes, rooms, benches, number counters, and signs. Such institutional *props* tell us where, how, and when to line up and wait; these reflect social arrangements designed by the institution for more "efficient" service (Ritzer, 1993:122). But within social institutions, individuals frequently arrange themselves. For example, in a hospital waiting room or airport waiting area, patients and passengers take great care to keep safe distance. Given available spacing, persons are careful not to sit next to the other. Often a gap or chair separates strangers while markers (purses, book bags, reading materials, computer bags, etc.) are placed in vacant spaces to prevent invasion. Markers are reluctantly removed when spacing is limited, but self-arrangements within U.S. institutions often reflect cultural values of individualism, safety and privacy. Even when spacing is limited, our wait method is often privatized and distanced by sleeping, reading, computing, phoning, and pod-casting. Additionally, in order to avoid space congestion, one may simply choose to stand off to the side. In short, we wish to keep our distance and to ourselves.

Which wait-structures permit persons to wait by standing or sitting? Which wait method is most bearable, standing, or sitting? Which is most stressful? To what extent do institutions provide a combination of standing and sitting? Post offices, banks, supermarkets, DMVs, and amusement parks permit persons to stand while waiting. Hospitals, dental offices, airports, laundry mats, courtrooms, auto repair shops, and certain restaurants permit customers to sit and wait. While it is debatable whether one experiences shorter waits while standing or sitting, it is clear that waiting is tied to services we desire. For instance, waiting in line for a popular concert, theater production, iPhone, movie, or play-off game may in fact prove lengthy. In some cases, customers may develop "wait shifts," for example, "your turn to wait" in order to obtain desired service.

"Sit-waits" tend to require appointments of some type, while most "stand-waits" are appointment-less. One is not likely to visit the dental office without an appointment and the post office does not schedule appointments.[4] Those involved in "sit-waits" often occupy themselves by reading, social media, text/cell phone conversations, or home/office work; while "stand-waiters" were frequently observed viewing phone, watching other customers, watching monitors, and watching transactions between customer and employee. On the one hand, customer observation is wise in order to "keep your head in the game," that is to know when to move forward and when you are next. On the other hand, customer observation may prove invasive and uncomfortable to certain others. It follows that institutions might consider ways of privatizing transactions. "Sitting and waiting" then is typically linked to name announcement. A receptionist announces, "Tahara?" "Yes." "The doctor's ready to see you," informs receptionist. Sitting allows one to relax, enabling a sense of comfort, contemplation, and reflection. Conversely, standing may become uncomfortable, resulting in body and mood swings.

Bus stops and restaurants provide a combination of sitting and standing, for example, "combo-waiting." With such combination, individuals are frequently looking for an available seat; if one obtains a seat, he/she is now placed in the "sit-wait" category as it pertains to how one waits and comfort in waiting. But "combo-waiting" provides options in that individuals are not required to wait in the immediate area of service. One can wait outside the restaurant or at the bar; further, one may wait on the bus bench or underneath a covered area near the bus stop. The primary difference among "sit-wait," "stand-wait," and "combo-waiting" are the options involved in the latter.

Baggage claim waiting offers an interesting analysis of how order and consideration are assumed. Moreover, it is an instance of "stand-wait" in that customers are not standing in line; they are standing circular, around a luggage carrousel. Leaving the plane, customers either walk or ride to the baggage claim area; signage often directs customers, and when they arrive, people gather around the baggage claim area, awaiting luggage. Those arriving first typically assemble near the carrousel opening where suitcases, traveling down a conveyor belt, are released. As others approach, they naturally flow to open areas, although some squeeze in small gaps. There is an approximate wait of twelve minutes and the initial stages of wait are characterized by loose and casual behavior of passengers. The looseness is expressed by talking on the phone, greeting love ones, observing others, eating, and listening to music. As time passes, customers draw closer and closer to carrousel rail and thus each other. The flashing red screen above the carrousel reads "Flight #227," as the conveyor belt begins motion carrying and unloading passenger bags. Now, former passengers move closer to carrousel, and sometimes jockeying for position to get closer. Though distance is now nearness, our concerns about strangers have taken second fiddle to identifying and obtaining personal property. That is, the primary focus is baggage retrieval, not watching others, eating, listening to music, or conversing by phone. In short, the wait is almost over. The conveyor belt is moving and it's time for action; the act of obtaining property, one's bag. Physical distance resurfaces, yet during the "search and wait" process, proximity is less apparent, and while the possibility of assisting someone struggling with a heavy bag is evident, consideration of others seems normal in that someone usually grabs and lifts the bag for a child or a senior. Additionally, the one option available in this "stand-wait" structure is the possibility of waiting off to the side until the baggage carrousel is nearly vacant and the conveyor belt stops. Upon which time, one may retrieve her luggage. The above assumes that one's luggage will arrive. But suppose one's bag does not turn up? This experience raises waiting to another level, a level of anxiety and uncertainty.

STRUCTURE AND SOCIAL CONTROL

Whether *waiting props* exist or not, authority figures (Price, 2005) play key roles in waiting. At times, enforcing wait-rules requires that social control agents take some type of formal action. Structure does not simply exist—it is constructed and managed. Consequently, the presence and action of authority figures are crucial and advantageous to maintaining structure and social order (Price, 2005:45–47). In the case of Janet and the Dermatology department, the receptionist reduced her wait by acknowledging Janet and waving her forward. Conversely, Jamal's impatience with Farrad led him to call for the "next customer." Certain gas stations could reduce anomie by installing and enforcing direction arrows. Additionally, Phillip and Gene, Kaiser customer service clerks, recognize the importance of redirecting patients and therefore maintaining wait environments by alerting and instructing patients of wait-norms and wait-locations. For example, entering Family Practice, one's attention is immediately drawn to the bold lettered sign, informing: "Line starts here: This is the front of the line." The sign includes arrows to assist with direction. One lady, Lao, apparently does not read or understand "wait-sign" in that she acts opposite of the sign's instructions. Lao, who is elderly, proceeds to the clerk's counter area rather than wait line. There is only one clerk on duty, and he is currently servicing a patient. While this check-in station is built for three clerks, Phillip, the clerk, notices that Lao is standing directly behind his counter station, sensing that Lao is either inattentive or unable to understand "wait sign" instructions. Phillip then requests and points, "Ma'am, please go to the front of the line. Other people will come-in and line-up behind you." Lao complies by nodding and moving to the front-line, responding, "O.K." When Phillip calls out, "next," Lao advances in the opposite direction of sign instructions.

A similar incident occurred in the lab while patients await service. For example, entering the lab, one observes a line of customers waiting their turn for check-in and service. Often, a line full of customers is indicative of a certain wait process. Guadalupe, however, enters the lab and walks straight toward the front to the clerk's station. The clerk, Gene, also noticed Guadalupe's actions, so when their eyes meet, Gene points her to the end of the line, saying, "The line is over there." Guadalupe acknowledges his direction by walking to the line's end.

The comments and directions by each clerk reinforce that there is normative order to waiting. In these cases, the clerks become symbols of authority representing the institution (hospital) and the reality of wait organization, that is, how waiting is organized. Their positions and comments legitimize their behavior and the procedure itself, which everyone seems to follow. Failure to follow procedures and disobeying clerk instructions could incur conflict and protest by those observing and waiting. Presumably, Lao and Guadalupe recognize that an audience is watching, so their actions are potentially labeled deviant or normal. In short, authority figures are often found managing wait-structures; they become part of the "props" who on the one hand guide waiting and on the other reduce waiting.

Legitimate authority figures are not the only persons to confront and direct individuals who are inattentive, uncooperative, or unfamiliar with wait norms. Such guidance may additionally stem from regular, ordinary people who see that customers or patients are lost, unaware of where to go or intentionally uncooperative. Frequently, ordinary people declare, "the line starts back there" or "you have to wait like everybody else." By responding to wait obstruction, officials and ordinary people bring life to wait procedures that appear abstract and at times taken for granted.

Everyday people are accustomed to waiting; waiting is so routine that often an internal wait-structure emerges though wait-props do not exist. For example, arriving at the bank or post office early (before it opens), a customer is likely to wait by the front door. Those customers arriving next are likely to form a line behind initial customer. Waiting can be individual but a line requires more than one person. Hence, waiting is internalized when we adhere to norms without question, that is, they are automatic.

A small line of three began to form as customers waited for the bank to open. The first person, Tim, arrives at the time in which the bank is scheduled to open, 9:30 a.m. Peering through the door window, Tim begins to pull on and shake the door but the door remains closed and locked. Soon another customer (Judy) arrived and stood behind Tim. A middle-aged Black male, James, also showed up as he casually talked on his cell phone, standing behind Judy. Yet, within a matter of seconds, a line is formed and no one is verbally talking to the other. Still, there is an unspoken communication of line placement and line order, for example, an internalized structure. Finally, Nia arrives but she did not wait at the end of the line. Nia walks to a covered area near the line-front and waits. James suddenly asserts, "Excuse me ma'am but there's a line back here!" Nia looks up, recognizes the face and voice, walks toward James, and then they smile and embrace. After exchanging greetings, James resumes his cell phone conversation. For those watching, James' joking comment was discovered after a friendship relation was determined, yet Nia feels compelled to explain to the rest—why she is standing underneath the cover. She says: "I'm not cutting line. I'm just standing over here to keep from getting wet."

Whether Tim and Judy were looking for or expecting an explanation from Nia is not important. The key feature here is that Nia provides reason, and such explanation displays consideration (to those waiting), acknowledgment of unwritten waiting rules (see Harold Garfinkel's analysis of ethnomethology, *Studies in Ethnomethology*, 1967), and ways in which persons have internalized wait-structure. In such a short line and possibly long lines, those waiting are aware of who arrives first, second, third, etc. They know who is in front of them and who is behind them. Standing off-line and underneath a covered area did not bother Tim and Judy. Nor was the impression received, by Tim and Judy, that she was "cutting." Her "cutting" clarification was sparked by James' initial comments. Waiting norms imply folkways about waiting behavior; about how one should wait and about the order of waiting. James' comment, "there's a line back here" is very real and very important. In part, and like authority figures, regular-ordinary people become part of the area's *wait props*—who assist in managing wait-norms. Moreover, we expect those arriving after us to wait behind us, not in front of us. Those who break this rule are often sanctioned, frowned on, stared at, or addressed in another manner. The back of the line is where we all must start then work our way forward, hence cutting or somehow receiving an unfair advantage is rarely accepted, *though it is clear that everyone does not begin at "lines-end."* Nia explained that she was not cutting, or cheating, but taking temporary cover. Still her explanation was unnecessary for she stood off-line.

STRUCTURE AND WAIT-TIME

How wait-time is attached to structure examines varying considerations by individuals and institutions. Time is valuable and when institutions-for-service construct waiting procedures, the amount of customer wait-time is of major concern. One executive remarked, "One of the biggest customer concerns is the problems of queuing. . . . Anything a retailer can do to lessen the perceived wait is going to be a benefit" (Ritzer, 1993:122). Institutions are interested in both minimizing customer wait-time and/or providing a comfortable wait-experience. Minimizing customer wait-times gets at furnishing sufficient customer service representatives and offering alternatives to waiting in line. For example, a bank provides options to use ATM machines, online banking, or wait in line. Yet, there are some transactions that must be conducted face-to-face; consequently, banks are concerned about customer comfort and minimal wait. Banks then offer "free" customer coffee while waiting and viewing the latest news on mounted screens. For institutions, the idea is that persons become less concerned about wait-time and more interested in the latest news. Coffee and news are nothing more than distractions and are designed to erase our wait anxieties and wait awareness. The free-market emphasizes competition, and if another establishment advertises "less time in waiting" or "no waiting," then customers may switch banks.

As the individual interacts with wait-structures, one of her most immediate concerns is: "How long is this going to take? Or how much time do I have to wait?" Auto repair establishments appear well versed in estimating wait length, for they realize the difficulty in separating customers from their prized possession, their vehicle; and therefore, placing limitations on customer mobility. Often, wait-length estimation is so internalized by customer service representatives that they "automatically" provide time estimates, preventing customers from raising time-estimate questions and only allowing them to clarify, and in some cases, negotiate time estimates. For example, one customer returned her car to body shop for a minor adjustment on her trunk. As the auto technician took her car away for service, he promised, "It'll be about 10 minutes." Why did he say this? And does he provide a time estimate for all (return) customers? What is the significance of a time estimate? Returning suggests that one has already been there (body shop) and that individuals do not wish to spend much time waiting. Specifically, a time estimate suggests consideration and respect for one's time. When time estimates are maintained along with customer respect, it could lead to return customers and/or new customers. Such a comment was not prompted, for example, the customer did not ask "how long?" The estimate was volunteered seemingly because customers have become conditioned to receiving time estimates, and service providers are likewise trained to give wait estimates. In part then, the purpose of time estimates permits customers to make informed wait-decisions so as to wait at the facility or elsewhere.

Waiting is often frustrating when customers believe they are *wasting time* and possess little control of wait-decisions. Unlike wait-estimates, waiting is most aggravating when it is unexpected, with nothing to do, and thus a waste of time, a lack of productivity. Many customers will not wait upon discovery of long lines; they will return when lines are shorter or when lines don't exist and/or when time permits. It follows that customers generally believe that utilizing time is an important value that permits one to complete tasks and utilize skills. Additionally, one's inability to provide time estimates only "adds fuel to the fire." The "fire" is maintained and suppressed when time clarity arises. But it is this perceived *waste of time* that has troubling effects on business and customers, alike. For example, Amy was waiting in line to order coffee. Apparently, the persons currently being serviced, Judy and James, were taking too long in deciding on beverage selection; plus, the clerk offered detailed information on each possible drink. So, Amy, watching the "inconsiderate" transaction, stormed out in anger. Her storming out did not seem to bother the clerk or anyone else. Seemingly, the clerk was so entranced by assisting customers that she appeared unconcerned with Amy's wait-time. In fact, she appeared more concerned about attentive customer service. Now, while Amy is not likely to return, Judy and James appear quite satisfied. From an institutional standpoint, the question arises: How much time should be spent with customers? And at what point do clerks acknowledge those waiting? Part of the problem is that Amy was not acknowledged; she was ignored. It follows that Amy's time is valuable and not to be wasted, thus finding another coffee shop was a clear alternative.

Finally, the issue of time, as it relates to courtroom waiting, is tied to a system which is built on delays; a system that requires individuals to give up huge chunks of time; and a system where defendants might benefit from delays. For instance, if defendants are convicted, then they go or return to jail or prison; but if the courtroom is delayed, their "freedom" is lengthened. Structurally, one can literally wait in criminal courtrooms all day! Defendants are required to check in with bailiff at 8:30 a.m. It is not necessary for family members, courtroom observers, loved-ones, and witnesses to check in; still, many wait just as long as defendants who require check-in. Frequently, family members and others wait to hear specific cases. When the judge enters, he or she reads and identifies defendant names who have scheduled hearings. In short, she calls roll; she raises questions of those not present; she may ask lawyers about the status of their client. Vowing that "he should be here shortly," the judge declares to the attorney, "Your client will be in *contempt* if he has not arrived by 10 am."

Three African American defendants and two Latino defendants arrive at 8:30 a.m. yet were not serviced in the morning court session. One African American was instructed to return at 1:30 p.m., after lunch. It follows that one does not know when he or she will be called. And the judge does not know how long each case will last. At times, there are cases where defendants return the next day. Yet, they are to receive hearing priority. Given the criminal court process, these defendants and audience members must wait an unknown period. They are at the mercy of the court. Apparently, they come prepared to wait; they are prepared to stay until called; preparing simply means having patience and thus watching "the show."[5] Waiting is not only tolerated but expected by all. Waiting has become as much a part for defendants as it has for lawyers, judges, bailiffs, police, and others. In short, waiting is a crucial part of this environment. This does not mean that a person's time is disrespected; it simply means that a person's time is tied to a system where waiting is inevitable.

STRUCTURE, CROWDS, AND WAITING

To what extent does structure exist in crowds? Some would argue that structure and order are questionable as with lynch mobs (Litwack, 1998), spontaneous riots (Lofland, 1981), and spectator violence at sporting events (Dunning et al., 1986, 1987). Such crowd behavior, at times, is based on emotion and rumor (Turner and Killian, 1987). Alternatively, McCarthy and Zald (1977) cite a rational component to movement participation: the costs of participation are weighed against rewards. Historically, studies of crowd behavior have focused on protest, disorder, and violence, not enough research however emphasizes structure and organization among certain gatherings. Benewick and Holton (1987:201) highlight how peaceful crowds, which are leisure in nature (Lofland, 1981), "neither pose challenges to the preservation of public order nor threats to prevailing conceptions of social order within the community." The peaceful crowd has no particular goal, except to enjoy the moment; but they are all brought together by a curious interest that temporarily catches their attention. People gathering to watch street theater, a concert in the park, or a popular speaker visiting a college campus may reflect instances of peaceful crowds. Structure and organization are detected while the crowd waits for the main attraction; loud music and podiums announcement are also used to draw collectivities.

The wait-structure of a *Bill Clinton* gathering is unmistakable; he is a popular personality in which many hold interests. The event took place on the sculpture garden near McGown Hall at University of California, Los Angeles. The entire perimeter of the sculpture garden was railed and roped off. Only police, secret service, and other officials were permitted inside sculpture garden barriers. The crowd of students stood between McGown Hall and sculpture garden awaiting Bill Clinton. A podium was set up facing the crowd and many waited and gathered near podium. Police, in-and-out of uniform, monitored railings and barriers as to control, making sure no one jumped barrier. Given the status of former president Bill Clinton and the open environment, there is a heavy police presence; they are very visible, they are invisible, they are everywhere.

The media is present, situated in front of the stage with cameras and lights. Behind the podium and on the side of the platform, several poster-size signs read, "Yes on 87—Less Foreign Oil-Cleaner Energy," along with a display of an American flag next to podium. The event is outside and police are all around interior and exterior of garden. One officer is watching from the roof of Bunche Hall. The crowd is calm, socializing with one another as music from the 1960s and 1970s plays (James Brown, Aretha Franklin, Cool and the Gang, Stevie Wonder, BT Express-Express Yourself, and other artists); apparently, music that Bill Clinton enjoys, not college students. Clinton was to arrive at 9:15 a.m. but he does not arrive until 10:15 a.m. and actually speaks at 10:35 a.m. No one leaves—in fact, the crowd swells and waits; it has become an event.

While some police appear uptight, others are calm by talking and socializing with crowd members. One group, four white men in black suits, enters the roped off area and they are immediately meant by police. One officer questions them, and they explain their actions; the officer radios to verify their story. A short while later, their explanation is verified, and they are permitted entry.

As students, staff, faculty, and others wait in anticipation, time is passed by talking to one another, talking on cell phones, text messaging others, taking pictures with phones and cameras, walking to locate a better viewing angle, and paying little attention to music they cannot relate to. Hence, there is a noisy hum among crowd members, consisting of talk and music. The crowd hum suddenly stops as someone announces, "15 minutes." Vying for a better view of platform, several students take to the trees. The trees heighten their viewing level so as to see over crowd participants, having fewer viewing obstructions. "Taking it to the trees" seems innocent and even innovative as a way to avoid crowd conflict and crowd obstacle. But authorities don't see it that way. They view it as a control and security problem. Consequently, one uniformed officer yells, from his interior position, "Get out of the trees, Get out of the trees!!!" Several students climb down very slowly, while others don't leave (at all). Prompting an officer to threaten, "If you don't get down, I'll send officers to get you down!" The threat convinces some but not all tree viewers. Soon officers patrol on bikes, demanding of resisting students, "Hey! Get Down! Get Down!" The students comply and officers ride off.

Interestingly, there is no line, no entry fee. There is however a gathering, a crowd to see Bill Clinton. Before Bill Clinton speaks, two speakers address the crowd about campaign matters. The crowd grows impatient, jeering the first speaker, "When is Clinton going to speak?" The second speaker is noticeably rushed as the crowd bemoans her exclaiming, "Enough already, we came to hear Bill." She turns red, shortens her speech, and leaves the platform. There is a huge crowd roar as she completes her speech and exits the platform.

Given crowd behavior and dynamics, it is noteworthy how most crowd members were orderly and compliant. They were calm, composed, and willing to wait. There were no picket signs or protest chants; there was simply an interest in seeing and hearing an international and national personality, Bill Clinton. How did police presence affect crowd behavior? Moreover, how is wait order and structure internalized? Certainly, police presence is designed to deter deviance and control gatherings; we have (many times over) witnessed the consequences of those who violate norms in the presence of authority. Such stock of knowledge affects and explains how we internalize our own behavior, our own conformity. Part of the structure and order of crowd behavior reflects order and structure in everyday society, which transcends itself in our personal experiences. That is, to a certain degree the structure of waiting is internalized. When Mr. Clinton finally reaches the podium, the wait is over and loud cheers begin, the wait-structure is maintained through his address.

SUMMARY

This chapter, "structure of waiting," recognizes and acknowledges structure in waiting. There is clear evidence that structure is often "worked at" and managed by those in wait-environments. Structure of waiting gets at social order, organization, formation, flexibility, and cultural norms while waiting. It explores how *wait-structures* are areas of wait, places where waiting occurs, but within each wait-structure, there are formal and informal wait rules. The "structure of waiting" further recognizes that there is a process to waiting, evidenced by wait-props, authority figures, time and crowds. While each *wait-structure* presents a different set of concerns, it is the structure itself that guides our waiting. For example, waiting in a dental office is much different than at the bus stop. My concern with wait-structures suggests and explores a type of normative order within society, and when *structural anomie* exists, individuals often resolve problems and difficulties. At times, wait-structures are internalized, while at others, wait-structures are clearly constructed by institutions. Some establishments *instruct* customers to "STOP: Wait for Wash Ticket," while others are calm, telling customers, "Please wait to be seated." It is the structure that provides a sense of stability, predictability, and direction, allowing a relatively stress-free wait. Structure in waiting cannot be de-emphasized; if so, then we take a principle idea, and situation (waiting) for granted. Given that *all* experience waiting, it must be understood in light of *how* waiting occurs, and the *functions* in waiting.

Waiting in undesignated areas often signals red flags to others waiting, and those responsible for wait-management. Still, for the most part, waiting is orderly. It is not chaotic. Persons recognize the need to wait—that individuals cannot have their item or order *now!* Parents cannot pick up their children *now!* Motorists cannot rush through traffic. Structurally and culturally, we learn and adjust ourselves to wait-environments. Waiting implies a certain degree of cooperation. Charon (2004) argues, society does not exist without cooperation, and one's willingness and ability to wait implies cooperation, consideration, and community. Most situations in society are structured, whether it is driving (we drive in lanes), classrooms (desks, chairs, and podium), hospitals (appointments). Thus, *waiting* is no different. Social structure guides our behavior. It helps us make sense of our environment and therefore respond appropriately. Structure, or social patterns, is a key feature to our understanding and response to waiting.

NOTES

1. See *Wait Explanations* for a complete analysis of unexpected delays.
2. See Charon's (2004:57–58) analysis of signs and symbols.
3. In some cases, people tend to lounge on the counter, blocking access with those with next-number.
4. Except for passports, the post office does not schedule appointments. There are always exceptions, like the DMV, but most "stand-waits" are appointment-less.
5. "The Show" is explained in chapter 3.

Chapter 2

Waiting Places

An analysis of place reveals another significant feature of waiting. Within space and time, one generally waits, leading to several locations where individuals wait. Place then is examined to draw attention to, and connections between place and waiting. That is, what is the relationship between place and waiting? Our analysis leads us to think deeper about waiting and how we organize ourselves around place. Part of what we learn concerns individual wait-preferences; while architects construct wait-structures, individuals may resist such structures and wait outside the lines. Others are comfortable within the lines. And seemingly, designers of wait-structures are more considerate of groups, rather than individuals. We also learn about tolerance and conformity, that is, if there is no other place to wait, then most will conform as a means to an end. This then highlights the complexity of place and waiting; there is an ongoing negotiation between place (wait-structures and wait-locations) and waiting (the individual and the group).

In their investigation of "medicine and place," Aultman and Wear (2006) reveals how doctors become more aware of the whole patient. By leaving their place (hospital) and driving to the patient's place (home), the doctors' interaction, understanding, interpretation, and diagnosis of patient is more holistic. Within hospital settings, doctors clearly exert power and control (Zola, 1997). The hospital is an established institution that requires bureaucratic management. More often than not, patients make appointments, journey to medical facilities, check in, and wait in defined places. Doctors, however, are there; they are part of an institution that provides advice and treatment to patients. While patients are at the mercy of medical establishments, doctors receive a glimpse of patient history, usually through medical charts. Hospital doctors do not witness a patient's living conditions that could affect illnesses, and therefore receive a narrow view of patients.

Aultman and Wear (2006) recognize that home visits could change the structure and interaction process of patient and doctor relations; that is, it "might lead doctors to a richer, more complex understanding of their patients' experiences of illness" (2006:85). The doctor must first find the patient's home. Then, while patients usually inquire at hospital counters, doctors make inquiries during home visits, for example, "I'm here to see Mrs. Buckholdt?"[1] And while patients wait for service, doctors (now) wait for patients, for example, "take a seat; she'll be down in just a minute." While waiting, one cannot resist looking around the residence that brings identity to the patient. The patient is more than a chart. Displayed paintings, family pictures, pets, used furniture, odors, others residing in home, and locked doors provide an important window into the patient's world. Finally, the conversation that occurs in the doctor's office may not resemble that in a patient's home. In short, patients may ask more personal questions of doctors, offer them drink or food, and simply face distractions that do not occur in exam rooms. It follows that patients, during home visits, exercise a certain measure of control and autonomy (Aultman and Wear, 2006).

The changing of environments, among patients and doctors, could bring about new interpretations of place. Encounters change because situations change, and when one is outside his/her comfortable, normal environment, individuals are likely to experience anomie. Hence, in addition to signifying location and mental sensation, place also defines our roles and statuses, for example, a woman's place (Bottero, 2005), a patient's place, and a child's place. "Trading places" could strain relationships among doctors and patients, Blacks and whites, parents and children, women and men. The unequal place of women within society is without question. Sociohistorically, it was believed that a woman's place was natural. That is, given biology—a woman's place was "naturally" domestic. With the advent of women's rights, a woman's place became less "natural" and more diverse, providing more choices. Still, while the feminist movement provided increased challenge and more choices, their opportunities remained limited. Consequently, a woman's "place" or status suggests a combination of nature and choice—though it is evident that structural and economic arrangements have in part stagnated place for women (Bottero, 2005). Clearly, there is stratification among women and men, but to what extent is their unequal status reflected in societal stereotypes of a "woman's place" (her role) and a "man's place"?

Place becomes more fascinating as we examine its many usages. For example, no hiding place, marketplace, hiding place, Frank's Place, displaced, workplace, saving place, trading place, no place like home, right place-wrong time, place in history, no safe place, between a rock and a hard place, out of place, a good place, a bad place, a place in my heart, a woman's place, a place in line, save my place, and a sacred place. Ideas regarding place are constructed through symbols, language, location, music, and interaction. Stokowski (2002:372) writes, "People actively *create* meaningful *places* through conversation and interaction with others." Place then does not exist, according to Stegner (1992:202) "until things that have happened in it are remembered in history, ballads, yarns, legends, or monuments. Language then is central in the formation of a sense of place" (Stokowski, 2002:372). How we use language to understand, name, interpret, and define place is crucial; our various usages of place evolved from interaction and experiences that were formulated into meaningful language—a way to express our experiences. This in turn amplifies the social construction of place; place is a social construct that exists not only in our minds but also in reality. Place then is subjective as well as objective (Stokowski, 2002). Our ability to construct place or as Schneekloth and Shibley (1995) prefer "the making of places . . . not only changes and maintains the physical world of living; it is also a way we make our communities, and connect with people." So, the idea of place is powerful: a concept that is inclusive and exclusive; a concept that is diverse and intolerant; a concept that is broad and narrow; a concept that provides joy and pain; a concept that is objective and subjective, and yet, a concept that continues to emerge.

Whether the identity of individuals, groups, or communities, place is a process that helps us assemble and define ourselves: who are we? Identities are often tied to *place*. One way to determine one's image of self is by examining places in which persons spend lots of time, such as homes, dorm rooms, bedrooms, parks, mountains, stores, offices, cars, recreation rooms, work environments, personal libraries, etc. When Professor Martin retired, he sadly remarked, "I'm going to miss this place." Cleaning out his office was a major task for he had accumulated thirty-four years of "stuff." He spent more than two weeks organizing, discarding, packing, reminiscing, and moving. His pictures of Marx, DuBois, and Goffman, plaques, degrees, and certificates that covered his walls; his files, artifacts from France, Italy, and Canada, protest posters, books, and pictures of family and friends all defined Professor Martin. He spent hours in his office advising, researching, and writing. He frequently said, "I work better at school than home." He was even aware of custodians who changed his radio station and repositioned his trash can. In short, Professor Martin recognized that his office was *his place*. And, needless to say, his identity was caught up in his workplace; consequently, Martin sadly confessed, "I'm going to miss this place."

Much of our reference to place emphasizes specific locations, such as mountains, parks, beaches, golf courses, vacation resorts, baseball fields, banks, offices, etc. The physical landscape often brings about reminders of how place came to be—and the extent to which one wishes to revisit that place. What significant incident or experience occurred to define this site as

place? A homerun? A wedding proposal? A death? Desiring to revisit a physical place has much to do with our experiences. For instance, there are various
places that we revisit yet spend limited time. Alternatively, there are places
where we do not wish to go or return. When Henry Box Brown escaped from
slavery, he was not concerned about returning. Other fugitives recalled the
pain of plantation slavery (Blassingame, 1979; Bennett, 1993), for example,
public floggings, child abuse, rape, economic exploitation, lynching, castra-
tion, personal invasion, poor medical care, poor working/living conditions,
etc. and could not bear to return. Without question, some places develop
problematic encounters, becoming *bad places*.

Conversely, there are places that are *not place* but are places nonetheless.
Such places (*not place*) lack significance and are very ordinary; in fact, rarely
do we view them as *place*. Such ordinary, insignificant places include waiting areas in laundry mats, hospitals, courtrooms, airports, restaurants, bus
stops, classrooms, grocery store lines, and amusement park lines. Many such
places are routine because we have not experienced a significant encounter;
they have little meaning to us, except the everyday, and thus we take them
for granted. This then responds to Gieryn's (2000) comment about pursuing
place. He writes, "To pursue place itself is to ask what these places of varying scale have in common and how they differ" (Gieryn, 2000:464). Well,
place itself develops and maintains personal or community significance—and
location is often a key feature. "*Placelessness*" (Relph, 1976) is ordinary
and lacks significance. The commonality of *place* rest in its location, for
example, its physicality; your place is different from mine, but it is a physical
landscape. Moreover, place may be a mental thought or mental journey. Put
simply, place differs in how we experience it.

THE ORDINARY: WAITING PLACES

What is a waiting place? A waiting place refers to a certain seat or area in
which individuals wait. There are times that we prefer to wait at a certain table
(Duneier, 1992) or chair or area, but if such spaces are occupied, we adjust
and wait elsewhere. Additionally, waiting places get at the variety of venues
where waiting occurs, such as barbershops, beauty salons, dance studios, auto
repair shops, break rooms, subway stations, police stations, hallways, juror
assembly rooms, and several other locations. Waiting is something we *do* and
the places where we wait are often *ordinary*, everyday spots.

Waiting for children at a ballet studio is seemingly routine, lacking
interest. Typically, parents bring their children to a one-hour ballet class,
and many adults wait in areas provided. The studio lobby is where waiting
occurs and chairs are bolted to the floor, making chair movement impossible

or difficult at best. Chairs are bolted next to the other, so when one sits, one is in close proximity to the other. Usually, there are not enough chairs for parents, their children, and students arriving for upcoming classes. Consequently, many persons sit on the carpet floor or stand to watch their child's ballet class through an open door or window. When several parents observe class, comments are made about dancers, ballet instructors, and/or upcoming programs.

Ballet classes are ongoing and children who begin at age five progress through the dance program; such a program can take dancers through high school (and beyond), where ballet becomes extremely technical. Parents then develop a routine of bringing their children daily, three times a week, or once a week. While waiting, parents engage in a variety of tasks, like caring for children, knitting, conversing with others, watching class, reading, writing, watching others, texting and/or talking on cell phones. In this environment, the waiting area and persons become familiar to the point that parents prefer waiting in certain seats or certain areas within the studio. In short, one becomes accustomed to a *waiting place*. One's familiarity with waiting areas and places increases the likelihood of conversing with others while waiting, and decreases the stranger syndrome, that is, we can better anticipate the other's behavior. Hence, there is a higher level of waiting consistency[2] and familiarity among "ballet waiters" than "other waiters," for example, those waiting for dental, auto, and restaurant services. Consistency lies in the frequency that one waits in the same place with the same others. At times, waiting with the "same other" is linked to *saving place*, that is, certain parents are likely to save a place (a chair) for a late arriving friend.

The proceeding focuses on *mundane wait places*; there is no significance to the places described. The following simply analyzes the places we wait, for example, hallways, courtrooms, segregated bus terminals, etc., recognizing they are places where waiting occurs. Further, I develop distinctions among wait regions, as a way to guide our understanding of wait places. Put simply, the forgoing examines *ordinary wait places* and specific *types of wait regions*.

TYPOLOGY OF WAIT PLACES

There are three types of wait regions that reflect the sort of waiting one will experience. For instance, *wait rooms, enclosed wait sections*, and *open wait areas*. *Wait rooms* are best exemplified in hospitals where there are defined waiting rooms, leaving these rooms somewhat confined; airports, restaurants, auto repair shops, and dental offices represent examples of *enclosed wait sections*; and bus stops, metro stations, and subways along with places where waiting is outside and visible—characterize *open wait areas*. Unlike *wait rooms, enclosed wait sections* do not possess a defined room, but a prescribed wait area or region. Further *enclosed wait sections* and *open wait areas* frequently offer options in waiting. That is, persons may wait on the bus stop bench or individuals may wait near the bus stop vicinity.[3] Similarly within airports, one may wait near departure gates, in an airport restaurant and/or many feet away from boarding gates. *Wait rooms* provide fewer wait options and it seems wise to wait in hospital wait rooms rather than miss appointments. One important difference between *enclosed wait sections* and *wait rooms* is the former permits wait-audiences to view and hear conversations (typically business transactions) among clients and employees. For example, waiting in Johnson's dental office, one can hear and watch dental customers transact business with employees. The *enclosed wait section* is located in the same vicinity as the business counter, allowing wait-audiences to tune in. In one case, customer and clerk discussed business (amount owed and next appointment), family (educational and career goals of client's son), and dental matters (recommended toothbrushes). While the idea is to appear personal, a clear problem is privacy. The same is not true of *wait-rooms* in those conversations (business and medical) between patient and medical personnel occur in separate rooms or privately. Once in the *wait-room*, "wait-patients" listen for their names, for example, waiting to be called. Wait-audiences are unable to hear private conversations that occur in exam rooms and generally, appointments are often made by phone, computer, or in distinct areas.

Open wait areas are visible to the public. One may drive or walk down a street and witness "bus customers" waiting; the same is true for restaurants that provide outside waiting, parade waiting and those who waited hours for the latest iPhone or Harry Potter craze (see Jill Lawless, 2007; Sean Popke, *USA Today*, 2007). Such gatherings become public symbols of waiting, in that customers are seen waiting for the bus, a table, an iPhone, or a book; one's wait is public not private. Additionally, public waiting brings attention to those waiting, in that spectators' stare, wonder and inquire about the occasion, that is, what are they waiting for? Or, "I saw you waiting at Best Buy." At times, the "craze" is so pronounced that customers camp out to obtain the best position in line, thus ensuring product purchase. Conversely, *wait rooms* and *enclosed wait sections* conceal one's waiting, that is, no one (the public) knows that you are waiting, where you're waiting and why you are waiting. Anytime one can be seen waiting in public, it is considered an *open wait area*.

Unlike auto and restaurant waiting, traditional hospital waiting rarely offers alternatives to waiting. When medical appointments are scheduled and patients are awaiting service, one must remain present to receive service. One cannot drop off, leave and return, as is the case with auto waiting; moreover, one cannot call-in-orders and pick up, as is the case with restaurant waiting. Appointments are cancelled when patients leave, and rescheduling is usually initiated by patients, not the institution. Appointments that are rescheduled [still] require that patients wait for service. While pharmacies offer alternatives to waiting, it is doubtful whether patients awaiting medical treatment will ever experience this option.

Within our three major wait categories (wait rooms, enclosed wait sections, and open wait areas), there exist conditions upon which we wait. On the one hand, there is a contained wait, and on the other, there is a broadened wait. *Contained waits* refer to places where waiting is required; one feels "locked-in" and there is little choice involved as with air travel, doctor's offices, jury duty, and immigration. Receiving a citizenship appointment, an immigrant is likely to rearrange his/her entire day. The importance of citizenship leads to rearranging one's schedule, for one is "held-up" all day. Those desiring citizenship have little choice except to wait and conform. Similarly, passengers stuck on airport runways often have few options; still the law permits a three-hour wait maximum on domestic flights and a four-hour wait on international flights. Historically, there have been reports of passengers waiting up to twelve hours.[4] Refusing to wait could bring sanctions and/or longer waits. For example, the supervisor for the fifth floor jury room warned:

> If jurors leave early or miss several panels during the day, credit is removed for the day and they are re-summoned to start service over again. We make it very clear that we cannot hold them against their will and they are free to leave at any time. We then let them know there are consequences of leaving which may include being fined up to $1500 and they are still *ordered* to serve jury duty by a judge.

Broad waits reflect places where choice is a real feature. That is, options exist whether to "wait or not," for example, to wait at the establishment or return when service is complete; or return when one has more time and/or lines are shorter or nonexistent. Still, various companies provide wait-tolerance in that one's decision to wait is enticed by length of time, comfortable surroundings, and/or interesting dialogue with others. Most car repair shops, restaurants, barbershops, and post offices reflect *broad wait* patterns. One Honda dealer exhibits choice in order to entice waiting. For instance, while Honda wait area clearly depicts an *enclosed wait section*, it is portrayed as very relaxing and cozy. The wait lounge is roomy and spacious; there are three comfortable leather sofa-chairs and separate regions for TV viewing, reading (and staring out windows), writing, and a computer work station. The cashier and restrooms are located within wait area; the restrooms reflect hotel or restaurant restrooms in that they appear new, clean, and smell fresh. The floor is carpeted throughout and the walls are decorated with pictures and plaques—pictures of plants, snow mountains, little league baseball teams, and plaques that brag about superior service. Those waiting are spaced out, that is, strangers are not sitting next to others, yet those sitting close and talking (father and son, married couple) know each other.

After checking in your car, a service attendant provides customers with a brochure entitled: "Comfort Honda: Your Guide to Recommended Maintenance."[5] Inside brochure is a flier which reads,

> Thank you for choosing Comfort Honda in Concept Point for your car care needs . . . While you're *waiting*, we thought you might like to take advantage of some of city's eating establishments, recreational play parks or shopping centers. Our shuttle driver will be glad to shuttle you to your destination within 10 miles. If going off-sight is not something you want to do, then Comfort Autocars offers a Home Style Diner, a children's play room and a wonderful parts boutique and a very relaxing lounge with a work station equipped with wireless internet access. We know your time is valuable and we will do our best to get you on your way as quickly as possible.

Comfort Honda recognizes that customers wait for vehicle repair, and they are interested in making one's wait more comfortable. Thus, they offer customers activity options (e.g., something to do while waiting) and/or one may choose to wait in "a very relaxing lounge." Note that their description does not refer to waiting area as "waiting room," recognizing that "lounge" has far better connotations than wait-room. Wait-room may suggest that one is bored with little to do and that wait-rooms appear dull and uninspired; whereas a lounge clearly indicates that one is comfortable and relaxed. In short, Honda is making a clear effort to provide contentment so that customers not only wish to wait but also to return for service, for example, return customers. Additionally, Honda has placed an economic value on waiting, that is, "we know your time is valuable," and showing respect to customer's time is an important consideration. It follows then that *places* which are conducive to waiting are likely to persuade, entice, and encourage customers to "hang around," and such companies clearly indicate that they desire your business. This *waiting place* is tempting; it is comfortable and flexible to one's needs.

While not as comfortable, the post office offers another example of broad waits. It is the sort of place where people walk in, observe long lines, and in disgust remark, "I can't wait!" Later, the customer is likely to return, but those who stay, post office personnel attempt to move lines quickly. For instance, Jose, post office supervisor announced, "Is there anyone here who wants to pay by debit or credit card? Or is there anyone here with a pink slip to pick-up mail?" No one in line responds. Customers simply stare at Jose. Jose then urged, "Come on people, help me out!" One customer, George, informs, "I have a package I need to weigh." Jose, "Give it to me. I'll weigh it. You stay in line, don't lose your place." Jose goes to weigh package, and as Jose returns, he confirms, "The package is o.k. You have enough postage. I'll take it from here." Jose takes the package, placing it behind the counter. George raises his eyebrows and inquires, "Can I go?" In a loud tone, Jose announces, "Yes, you're free to go." It follows that flexibility in waiting exists at the post office in that no one is "required" to wait, yet one's wait-decision clearly depends on the urgency of what needs mailing.

HALLWAYS AS WAIT PLACES: COURTROOM, COLLEGE, AND HIGH SCHOOL

Generally, the hallway is a very commonplace to wait among court personnel, college students, high school students, and those who attend hearings at state and capitol buildings. Hallways are considered informal settings, where the atmosphere is laidback and unpredictable. Further, hallways are innovative places to wait in that there are no wait-signs or wait-instructions. While magazines rarely exist in hallways, TV monitors are frequently visible. Often, hallways are used as "time out" areas to get away (or take a break) from formal proceedings; they are used for transition (going from one place to the next); they are used for business advice, business transactions, social outlets, introspective escapes, studying and simply waiting for the next phase, for example, the next class, the next hearing, the next court case, or a return from court recess, etc. A hallway then provides a good example of *place* that is socially constructed (see Schneekloth and Shibley, 1995; Stokowski, 2002).

There is a noisy buzz in the court hallway; it is a long hallway of about 50 yards. When one opens a courtroom door, the outside chatter enters the courtroom. The buzz begins as people start to gather, before formal hearings commence. There are several benches along the walls of the hallway for seating, resting, and deliberating. All are not sitting. Many are standing and talking. Behavior ranges from sitting to standing to walking. There seems a constant buzz. Though as morning wears, the buzz dissipates for cases have been called, cancelled, transferred, and completed, allowing many to leave the court building. Diverse groups appear in hallways, such as lawyers, police officers (uniformed and plain clothed), detectives, witnesses, family members, babies in strollers, children with parents, court reporters, and youth.

Given the casual and unpredictable nature of hallways, lawyers take the opportunity to talk with clients. Lawyers take statements from clients. They advise and guide them by telling client what to expect and what to say;

some even attempt to calm their clients. Lawyers also talk to police and investigators, advising them, receiving evidence, and obtaining statements. And, while lawyers interview clients, they are likely to inform them of the possible outcomes. One district attorney (DA) stood in the hallway, outside her courtroom, advising, instructing, and obtaining information from police, detectives, and clients.

Frequently, while waiting in the hallway, lawyers (district attorneys and public defenders) exit courtrooms looking for certain individuals. They call out, "Officer Sanchez, Officer Sanchez"; other court personnel may shout, "Mr. Anderson, Mr. Anderson"! Such lawyers call out as they walk down the hallway looking for a possible response. At times, there is no response. On other occasions, someone may spontaneously say, "He's upstairs," or "He'll be here at 11." In short, the *business* of court spills out in hallways to summon police and others.

Additionally, hallways provide a *social* atmosphere of small talk, laughter, and reacquaintance. Two individuals, a lawyer and a police officer, who apparently had not seen each other for a while, made eye contact, greeted one another with a handshake & hug, and inquired about the well-being of the other. After the normal "I'm-doing-fine" exchange, they then began publicly discussing football. Lawyer, "Are you still playing football?"

Police officer: "Yes, it's still pretty fun."

Lawyer, "You better be careful, sometimes they throw those passes pretty high." They both chuckled, for it appears an inside joke.

In another case, one plain clothed officer recognized a friend and thus approached him, shook hands, and confessed "I haven't seen you in a long time." They began to dialogue about what brought them to court, and then discussed certain mutual acquaintances. Still, another observation illustrates two white police officers, wearing jeans and a dark blue jacket that read *POLICE* on the back, conversing with a Latina who sat amid these two. They seemed to enjoy their time together, for there was much laughter and motioning. Even other police officers who greeted them did not seem welcome, for they were having their own little party. At one point, one officer arose and began imitating someone by dancing. They giggled—seemingly getting a kick out of the demonstration.

Hallway scenes appear loose and spontaneous. Frequently, officials vacate their status to enjoy the moment. One might notice uniformed police officers and investigators standing in a circle, talking and laughing. And to the right, there is another group, presumably lawyers and clerks, laughing and talking about a party they attended. They were loud and carefree; in fact, they simply appeared to enjoy one another's company. Socially, one wonders whether hallway musing is a much-needed break from work, that is, lawyering, policing, clerking, interpreting, and investigating.

Finally, there are those who are not socializing with anyone or conducting business of any type. This group is spending quiet time in the hallway by reading a book or newspaper, by gazing at those who pass, talking on cell phones, looking to the ceiling, and thinking about their case or situation. It is an *introspective* way to pass time, and though hallway buzz is noisy, this group pays little attention to the hallway scene.

Thus, there is a *business, social,* and *introspective* dimension to this courtroom hallway. One can better understand the hallway buzz by recognizing the players. Such a diverse atmosphere allows individuals to wait with more patience and the social circumstances may "shorten" one's wait. The business, social, and introspective dimensions emerge naturally from this environment. No one tells the other to act businesslike, social, and introspective or simply "to be quiet." It is an atmosphere that helps individuals manage the long process of waiting. Further, it is an environment that recognizes perceived status. Those wearing suits are viewed as lawyers, some suit wearers are viewed as police and/or investigators; many police officers wear their uniforms or some other type of identification (badges, guns, handcuffs, jackets with *police* written on rear); and then there's the ordinary, everyday individual (often an ethnic minority) who is observed wearing sweats, jeans, worn dresses, baggie pants, and t-shirts. Those who interact—do so on the basis of known characteristics. That is, lawyers tend to interact with clients, other lawyers, and police while doing business. Police officers, lawyers, and clerks often socialize with one another while waiting. And those spending quiet time keep to themselves.

There are other hallways that are not as loud and social, yet maintain a significance of their own. Students frequently wait outside classroom hallways for several reasons, some of which include waiting for friends to exit classrooms, waiting to talk with teachers or professors, and waiting to enter occupied classrooms. While waiting, students chat with one another about class, YouTube videos, and/or social media sites, some study for upcoming exams, complete homework, and even share class notes; others are simply listening to iPods, talking on cell phones, text messaging, tweeting, thinking, sleeping, gazing at others, eating, and working on personal computers. Without doubt, high school and college hallways are interesting for there are limited chairs (if any). Most persons are standing or sitting on the floor, and like hallways outside of courtrooms, there exists a buzz as classes are released and several minutes before class starts.[6] But unlike the court hallway, the school buzz is not constant and high schools usually employ some type of hallway monitor. Here, the idea is to maintain a level of quietness so as not to disturb the class while in session.

Careful study of high school and college hallways reflects a similar social structure as courtroom hallways. For example, school *business* is accomplished by professors talking with and assisting students, students completing homework and studying for exams. *Social* dimensions are experienced as students discuss YouTube videos and upcoming events, such as proms, school plays, speakers, basketball and football games; finally, the *introspective* dimension of thinking to oneself, sleeping and listening to iPods are clearly evident in such hallways. Given the public nature of hallways, we are not likely to witness individuals showering, disrobing, or performing surgery. While such situations are private, we are, however, likely to hear outbursts of joy and pain in hallways. In both cases, hallways become a spontaneous *place of wait*, a place where one is awaiting a formal occurrence, for example, court or class.

Generally, hotel and dorm hallways are not considered places of wait. Hotels and dorms provide lobbies and lounges for waiting; or persons simply wait in someone's room. But standing or sitting in such locations is often considered "out of place" or odd. Waiting outside a hotel room, one is likely to wonder or be asked, "What/Who are you waiting for?" The same is not true when waiting in court or college hallways; certain assumptions are made when waiting in such areas. Moreover, the extent to which one waits for formal occurrences, like class or court proceedings, outside of dorm and hotel rooms is unlikely. Hotel and dorm hallways are transitory. People go from one place to another. It goes without saying that waiting places emerge in certain hallways and not others.

Finally, while every hallway is not a place to wait, all hallways possess a transitory dimension along with wall postings that often display monitors, pictures, information, and/or direction. Hallways function not only as guides but also as information sources during our transitory or waiting processes. In particular, school and court hallways often reveal much about our wait-status. School hallways reveal whether class is cancelled, delayed, and/or room changes; courtroom hallways often reveal the location of certain judges, times that court proceedings resume and courtroom changes. Such information is valuable allowing participants to make informed wait-decisions.

OTHER WAIT PLACES: WAITING IN CARS, LAUNDRY MATS, AND SEGREGATED TERMINALS

Waiting is often taken for granted because it is so much a part of what we do; we wait without thinking; we wait because it is necessary. Waiting in one's car is likewise unnoticed and a rare point of investigation. It is rare because we put little thought into "car waiting." We simply wait in our cars as situations (traffic, appointments, etc.) emerge. For example, there are times when individuals wait for significant others in cars rather than entering stores, gyms, or hospitals. Parked in a hospital parking lot, Juan waited for his wife, Carmen, in the driver's seat of his Toyota. As she left the car, Juan reclined and calmly closed his eyes; he used his wait time to rest. At the close of swim practice, there are several occasions when parents wait in their cars instead of the pool lobby or pool deck, as their children shower and meet them in the parking lot. "Car waiting" may provide opportunities to complete phone calls, office work, or listen to one's favorite radio program or CD. And waiting in cars after school is a common scene among parents who are required to proceed through a car line. Such a line is equipped with school officials who religiously enforce rules and speak to anyone inhibiting progress. Automobile traffic is yet another case where we wait in our cars. Predictable traffic, like driving to work, presents less stress than unpredictable traffic, for example, viewing a wreck while driving to Sunday matinee. Presumably, controlling emotions and situations is more probable in predictable traffic, and we routinely arrive to work within sixty minutes. Conversely, when one encounters unexpected traffic, not knowing traffic reasons or how long one is stuck, such anomie could stir up impatience, nervousness, and even road rage. Emotionally, one is unprepared to wait; but wait in the car they must—in order to arrive at the matinee.

Unlike hallways, waiting in cars is unique in that cars provide a sort of privacy that is not evident in hallways. It is difficult to conceal behavior in hallways, but cars are enclosed and windows can be tinted, so hiding contraband and behavior is easy—seeing inside could prove difficult. Many are attached to their cars, constructing them in ways that reflect their identity. It is a *wait place* where one spends hours in traffic, and long periods waiting for loved ones to depart schools, hospitals, and/or swim practice. Consequently, whether text messaging, talking, reading, working, watching DVDs, or listening, it is important to possess such amenities to enhance and ease our "car wait" experience. For these reasons, many would *rather* wait in their cars.

Like other wait places, laundry mats are temporary locations where cleaning and drying garments are key activities. It is a place where many visit weekly, and the routine of washing and drying has produced *preferences* for specific machines. In addition to waiting for one's wash or dry cycle, some customers wait for certain machines. It is clear that some machines wash and dry better than others; moreover, regular customers are familiar with the length of a wash or dry cycle. Time is important for it determines how long customers wait for the availability of occupied machines and even the amount of time doing laundry. When asked about cycle length, without hesitation, one customer revealed that it takes "about 25 minutes" to complete a wash cycle. Those waiting for machines, sit near various washers, and machines in-use are often "marked" by items on top of machines, for instance bleach containers, dryer sheets, tide, laundry basket hangers, and plastic bags.

Waiting in laundry mats is uneventful but necessary given societal hygiene norms. Without question, class and gender elements are evident, since more women frequent laundry mats than men, and women are often accompanied by children; whereas, men typically arrive alone. Upper and middle-class families can afford washers and dryers, yet it is quite common to observe working class, students, and minorities spending time in laundry mats. Though as a place of wait, it is an environment where customers are aware of their surroundings and strangers rarely talk. Still, persons are often pleasant and friendly.

Wait places are frequently observed in churches, classrooms, meeting rooms, and so forth. That is, parishioners, students, and committee members prefer to sit and wait in specific areas. One respondent, Jane, revealed that "I have to sit on the left side of the table because I have problems with my right eye." So "sitting on the left side of the table" becomes her waiting place: a place where she not only waits for meetings to start, but given her medical condition, a practical place in order to see better. Arriving early may prove necessary to obtain one's usual place. Overtime, students and parishioners develop favorite waiting places, sitting in the same area or place each time services or class meets. It has become *their* waiting place: a place where there is a sense of comfort, a place that is preferred over other locations in the same room. Interestingly, those who frequent the same locations generally spot individuals in the *same* place. How and why we develop our waiting places depend on various situations, for example, medical conditions, personality, coercion, etc.

An analysis of place recognizes that some locations are more desired than others. Some places possess exciting and meaningful qualities, while others are very dull and drab. Some places are only accessible by social class and others determined entry by race. Powerful and race conscious whites, within the United States, developed *dejure* (Plessy v. Ferguson, 1896) and *de facto* rules designed to keep Blacks and whites "in their place" and on their side of the tracks.[7] Thus African Americans and whites were designated specific places (or locations), ranging from hospitals to parks to neighborhoods to schools to churches and even waiting rooms. Anyone challenging place was severely beaten, jailed, or lynched.

Historically, segregated wait rooms have existed in Greyhound and Trailway bus stations and various airports, including the Greenville, South Carolina airport (Morris, 1984). White wait rooms generally contained more amenities and comfort than "Colored wait rooms." White wait rooms were more accommodating in that they were located near terminal exits and regularly serviced. Often, one could find restaurants, restrooms, spacious rest areas, magazines, games, water fountains, newspapers, and comfortable seating. The Greyhound terminal at Rock Hill, South Carolina was in part "filled with pinball machines played by white youths," becoming more or less their "hangout" (Branch, 1988:415). "Colored" wait rooms were cramped, restricted, and neglected; Blacks wanting food placed their orders at the back door of bus terminal restaurants and ate inside Black waiting rooms or outside. At times, there were limited chairs to accommodate those waiting. Compared to white wait rooms, Black wait rooms were less attractive places, appearing drab and dreary.

Many of those wait places and facilities became targets of protest. After the 1960 Supreme Court case outlawed segregated facilities at bus terminals, the Boynton case (Raines, 1977), it was decided that on May 4, 1961, two small integrated groups would ride a Greyhound bus and Trailway bus from Washington, DC, to New Orleans to test whether buses and terminal facilities were segregated (Morris, 1984:231). James Farmer, national director of the Congress of Racial Equality (CORE), explains:

> The strategy for the "Freedom Ride" was that whites in the group would sit in the back of the bus. Blacks would sit in the front and refuse to move when ordered. *At every rest stop, Blacks would go into the white-only waiting rooms and try to use the facilities.* "We felt we could count on the racists of the South to create a crisis so that the federal government would be compelled to enforce the law." (Williams, 1987)

Earlier, in November 1959, CORE made plans to sit in at the "white" waiting room of the Greenville, South Carolina, airport. The protest was organized to boycott the fact that the first African American major leaguer, Jackie Robinson was ordered to leave the white waiting room a few days earlier (Morris, 1984:191). Such examples get at inequality and distinction in wait-places. Why are certain wait places separate? And why are others more valued? While CORE recognized stratification among particular *wait places*, they sought to expose contradictions and ultimately eliminate "white and Colored" wait rooms (see Bottero, 2005). *Switching places* proved effective given the outcomes of court rulings. CORE viewed segregated wait rooms as unnecessary and one comfortable wait place was sufficient for both groups.

DEVELOPING WAIT PLACES

Under what conditions do formal wait-places emerge? What conditions and situations bring them into existence? In certain cases, there seems an absolute need for a wait area, and one wonders why wait rooms were overlooked in the first place. Working in family court, Judge Sanders explained that he hears many custody, domestic violence, and child abuse cases. Having no one to babysit, many parents bring their children because they cannot afford childcare; thus, children accompany parents to court and often misbehave. Some parents have little control over their children and others refuse to discipline. Judge Sanders conveyed that during family hearings when both parents are present. Frequently, their encounters are argumentative and distasteful. Judges have few friends during custody hearings since "someone is usually upset following our decision, and our judgments sometimes heighten confrontations among parents." Given outbursts and parent/children battles, the courtroom and court hallway were so loud that it was difficult to conduct courtroom business. Judge Sanders and his colleagues were also concerned about the "moral issue of children watching their parents' fight." Growing tired of overt family feuds, Family Court-Judges, presiding at L.A. Superior Court, discussed the idea of developing a wait room for children. Consensus was swift and construction soon followed. Their resolve was so sincere that Family Court-Judges not only convinced city officials but also paid for constructions and childcare staff who work with children.

One's immediate impression of the children's wait-room is that of a daycare facility, a room that is filled with life and potential. Monica, Site Manager, was clear in making distinctions between daycare and the children's waiting room. One important difference is fee requirements in daycare, while child waiting rooms are free. Additionally, day cares are license, and waiting rooms are not. In day cares, parents are permitted to visit children and inspect facility. Parents do not have these privileges in court wait-rooms. Finally, daycare parents bring cupcakes, cakes, punch and goodies bags to celebrate their child's birthday, but child wait-rooms do not permit such celebrations.

There are several rules connected to children's wait-rooms. First, it is a facility for *the public* who are involved in court business, namely defendants and those present for hearings. The children's wait room is located on the second floor of the L.A. Superior court building and *family court* is on the same floor where domestic violence and child custody cases are conducted. Access is a central reason why the children's wait-room is on the second floor. Court employees (lawyers, attorneys, judges, jurors, clerks, secretaries, janitor, bailiffs, and sheriffs) are prohibited from using children's waiting room. *The public* must initially check-in by reading the policy, completing and signing a consent form. The form provides rules and regulations of the facility and failure to follow rules disqualifies violators *forever*, according to Monica. Parents may leave their children for five minutes or five hours; but if parents leave superior court building (for any reason—no matter how brief), they must take children. Leaving and failing to obtain children from waiting room is an unforgivable sin (Monica says, "I'm very strict"). If wait-room staff members need to contact parents, and they are not in established location, again, it is a violation. The waiting room staff will not give medication or provide lunch. They are closed for lunch, for example, 12:00–1:30 p.m. Their hours of service are 8:00 a.m. to 12:00 p.m. noon, and 1:30 p.m. to 4:30 p.m. Snacks are provided, and they have an academic program for children. Potty training is a requirement and children must fall between ages 2–1/2 and 13 years. Children who become a problem for staff are sent to parents; if parents are not available, sheriffs are asked to intervene. Unhealthy and sick children cannot use wait-room, for their condition is unacceptable—in that the possibility of infecting other children is very real.

Again, viewing the children's wait-room closely resembles a day care center—equipped with colorful blue and yellow carpet, pictures and paintings on walls, computers for children, play stations for climbing and playing, toys for children, arts and crafts on walls (butterflies, flowers, trees, etc.). Parents are forbidden entrance because of privacy and protective issues; consequently, seeing inside is difficult because the room is fully covered and shielded. The door is opened from inside to admit children. They are very concerned about the safety of children; that is, children should not be used as revenge for someone else's problems.

The children's wait-room has become a cozy wait-place; away from parental feuds and court bureaucracy; a place full of imagination and possibilities, a temporary getaway. In the traditional sense, children do not view it as a waiting room but as a playroom to engage in arts and crafts until retrieved. Some even wish to return. Interestingly, it is a wait-room for children only, not parents—who are occupied doing family court business. And such wait-rooms are not for parents and children as is the case with the pediatric wait room. It is a wait-room with specific directives from judges.

While there is a clear distinction among child's waiting rooms and day cares, one also recognizes a similar distinction among adult waiting rooms and children's wait-rooms. Put simply, children's wait-rooms are more spirited, more radiant, and seemingly possessing more life and potential. Adult wait-rooms are quite drab, lonely, and lack meaningful interaction. It follows that adults often arrive prepared to wait by bringing books, computers, cell phones, tablets, and newspapers, whereas, children are virtually entertained. Therefore, when developing wait-rooms, what is one attempting to accomplish? In short, when developing wait-rooms, *designers should have specific wait-goals*. Judges were motivated by multiple issues, including the ability to conduct family court business, parent-child separation during hearings, and protection of minors. Judge Sanders believes their aims were accomplished prompting other court facilities to model similar wait-rooms.

"THINGS ARE NOT WHAT THEY SEEM"

"There is certainly a whole lot of waiting going on here at the Clara Shortridge Foltz Criminal Justice Center, formerly the Criminal Courts Building . . . On any given workday at 8:30am, anyone can go to the third floor and see literally *hundreds* of people—defendants, police officers, civilian witnesses, defendants' families, defense attorneys, prosecutors, others—all waiting. One can go to the jury rooms here in the courthouse and see hundreds of prospective jurors waiting too . . . One waits and waits and waits. It seems as if waiting is part of the culture here."[8] Courthouses are wait-areas for many persons who typically wait for the judge's arrival or to conduct some type of court business. It follows that the place of wait often determines what we are waiting for, that is, court proceeding or court business. Similarly, waiting at a bank suggests that one will engage in some sort of financial transaction; waiting at the post office indicates that my objective is mail related; and waiting in line at 31 Flavors, Coldstone's or Ben & Jerry's implies a desire for ice cream or a cold beverage. Generally, one is not likely to wait for carpet at a dental office, and one is not likely to wait for sentencing at an airport. It is more common to wait for doctors within hospital wait-rooms and buses at bus stops. But is this always true? Does waiting at the bus stop really mean that one is waiting for the bus? Or does waiting in a restaurant mean that someone is going to eat? While in most cases this is true; it is not always certain that customers are waiting for services provided in the vicinity, by the facility, or at the bus stop.

Take, for example, a group of gentlemen who waited at a Pasadena bus stop; their body language clearly signified a desire to ride the bus. Yet, after waiting and shifting positions for more than an hour, and after watching passengers board and de-board, three potential passengers never boarded the bus. In fact, they left separately, walking in varying directions. Why sit at a bus stop and not board? Why wait at a restaurant and not eat? This is unclear and the reasons vary. But clearly, waiting at a bus stop does not mean that one is waiting for the bus, and the same is true when waiting at restaurants. The assumption is bus riding and eating will occur, "but it ain't necessarily so." One could accompany someone to lunch, or restaurants may facilitate meeting places for others. Likewise, bus stops may furnish hangouts for youth, ways and places to pass time, and a legitimate place to check on others or receive a signal. But whatever the reason, it is clear that our waiting may not be linked to services provided.

It is as if our roles consistently match our behavior and that our actions reflect our words. A police officer abusing a child is inconsistent with his/her role and priests molesting children is certainly incompatible with theirs. We assume and anticipate predictability but often "things are not what they seem"

(Berger, 2007). For Peter Berger, such a statement gets at the first wisdom of sociology, recognizing that some sociological investigations are deceptively simple and obvious. He urges us to look beyond the routine or the obvious and explore certain hidden and deceptive encounters, for example, critical thinking. Waiting for the obvious is likely to occur at "controlled places" and not others. For example, purchasing an airline ticket, hassling through the check-in and search processes and arriving at the boarding gate is a good indicator that one is waiting to board the plane; yet, waiting outside a classroom, in the hallway, does not mean one is going to attend class. Natasha indicated that she was "waiting for a ride home." She was outside the classroom waiting for her friend's class to end, so she could get a ride home. And unlike the airport, the class corridor presents far fewer controls. So, *how* does one determine whether one is eating or meeting, attending class or not; also, *how* does one determine whether one is riding or hiding? While controls narrow our wait-choices and assumptions may prove helpful, sociologically there is little certainty whether one will board the bus or not, except to investigate "the obvious."

WAITING DISTRACTIONS

People are often bored by waiting, and long waits, as in DMV lines and airport tarmacs, are often frustrating and may produce conflict. Long waits are more taxing when explanations are not provided, not possible to give or unbelievable. Consequently, various industries go through certain measures to ensure that customers are distracted. For example, slot machines in airports, TV monitors in banks, and magazines in grocery store lines are designed to take your mind off of waiting. A pleasant distraction designed to entertain as one waits. Wait-distractions also occur when something unusual, spontaneous or attention getting happens, as in police activity during traffic or loud vendors as spectators await game entry. Such distractions and unusual events are considered *natural distractions* because there is no script, while industry planned manipulations are *calculated distractions*.

Hospital wait-rooms represent *calculated distractions* in that they are equipped with televisions, magazines, and soft music. The local news, soap operas, or talk shows are usually channeled into these rooms. Conversely, those who lack television interest may thumb through magazines for a temporary distraction. A well-lit room having soft wall paint and wall pictures that display flowers, plants, mountains, forests, sunsets, blue skies, snow-covered mountains, mist, and morning dew are all intended to enhance pleasant experiences during our wait. Carpeted floors with sufficient space and cushioned seats along with fake flowers and plants adorn such rooms so that we might relax.

Natural distractions are more spontaneous, grabbing our attention in ways that spark emotion and thought. Additionally, institutions have little control of *natural distractions* for they just happen; they are unpredictable. Before judges arrive, the courtroom is relatively quiet though soft talk ensues in deference to courtroom etiquette. The bailiff is standing and soon announces, "Please turn off cell phones and pagers." Initially, he instructs in English, then in Spanish, but not in Korean though Korean defendants are present who need an interpreter. When the judge arrives, the bailiff instructs: "Rise, court is in session, the honorable Judge Titus presiding."

The first thirty minutes of court is greeted with *cell phones* ringing. The first phone belongs to a lawyer and the second to a Korean defendant. As the first phone sounds, the white lawyer, who is seated in the audience, scrambles to reach in his top coat pocket to turn off phone. The court is caught off-guard by the ring and all gaze in his direction, including the bailiff who stares him down. The second phone belongs to a Korean defendant, again, bringing notice to his area, causing all to gaze in his direction; he too scrambles to turn off his phone. Interestingly, the Korean is dressed in an expensive tailor-made black suit, which leads to stares. Most other court attendees, excluding lawyers and employees, tend to dress down. And seemingly, those who dress up bring a certain attention to themselves; a type of curious interest, for instance, who is that person? What is his profession? Is he wealthy? Is she an actress? Is he a celebrity?

Other than the ring, the most important action here is turning off the phone. The action and motion of turning off the phone indicates that one has inadvertently left his phone on and apologizes by quickly turning off phone. Though late, he is complying with formal courtroom guidelines by immediately silencing phone; and everyone observes that he has violated court protocol. Still, imagine such persons answering their phones and conversing. Certainly, the court's attention is not only captured but judges are likely to confiscate and fine violators. There are noticeable signs outside courtrooms that read: "Turn off all pagers, cellular phones and alarm watches. Subject to confiscation and/or fine by Court." One's motion to turn off phone is linked to this rule and the possibility of formal sanction. Similarly, cell phones that ring during church services, classroom lectures, seminars, and theater performances annoyingly capture our attention, and the same apologetic scramble of silencing phones is performed, receiving an informal sanction (dirty looks) for an overt violation. Yet, cell phones that ring during theater performance are not wait distractions; they are natural distractions without the "wait" component. Cell phones that ring during court proceedings are natural distractions in that many are awaiting cases and such distractions become a spontaneous part of the "courtroom show." Within wait areas, however, the *natural distraction* is crucial for it diverts our attention; it engrosses us and temporarily takes us to another *place.*

SUMMARY

Of all wait-places, juror assembly rooms seem most conducive to facilitate waiting. For example, the TV is strategically placed in the rear of jury assembly rooms. One may sit and watch all day or sleep and "watch." There are desk corrals (as in libraries) for persons to sit, spread out their materials and work; there are books and magazines atop of desk corrals for leisure reading. In the middle of assembly room, there are pay computers for work, e-mail, and/or games; those who are not using computer terminals are advised to sit elsewhere. Finally, there are vending machines and restrooms located inside assembly room for juror convenience. These items along with comfortable chairs are provided for jurors, not to mention the items that they bring to keep themselves busy. But such items illustrate a type of sensitivity to jurors waiting, attempting to make their duty bearable.

During orientation, jurors receive valuable information about juror expectations and "how to wait." The juror administrative clerk instructed, "Your main function is to sit in this room to see if your name will be called." She indicated that calling names are random and if jurors do not get selected for panels, they remain in the jury assembly room the whole day. This then gets at a *culture of waiting* and how jurors develop a "mentality of waiting." Unlike courtrooms, there is a soft buzz of jurors talking to each other. Some are making and receiving calls; others are writing, knitting, and eating. Conversely, courtrooms demand strict adherence to rules, which include no eating, talking, newspaper reading, and cell phone talking. Spectators and clients may leave after preliminary hearings but jurors remain all day.

While certain places are conducive to waiting, others are not. For example, bus stops and waiting in line at MCJ (or detention waiting) are poor facilities for waiting. *Theoretically, when waiting conditions are poor, persons are likely to search out better, more bearable conditions.* Detention waiting is a case in point, especially on hot days. Many in line will escape to shaded areas while loved ones keep their place. At bus stops, the three-seat bench cannot contain and cover those waiting in rainy or hot weather, so a Churches' Chicken awning or a shade tree is used as a temporary wait-place. *How and where one waits largely depends on conditions.* When wait conditions are relaxing, as in Comfort Honda, the possibility of waiting is enhanced, producing far more comfort.

Waiting places are locations where queuing occurs. They range from mountains to hallways, from hospitals to courtrooms, and from airports to grocery lines. They are ordinary places and sacred places; they are physical places and mental places; places of refuge and distain. But waiting places develop their own definitions and interpretations of *place* and *how* to wait. *Wait rooms*, *enclosed wait sections*, and *open wait areas* emerge from places and conditions of wait. One's wait experience is often distinct—so human interpretation of identical places is quite varied. For instance, segregated bus terminals conjures up negative experience for some and positive for others. And while waiting in laundry mats are usually experienced by lower and working classes, there are occasions when "things are not what they seem." That is waiting in a laundry mat does not mean that individuals are waiting to wash; and likewise, waiting at the bus stop does not mean that he/she will board the bus. It is assumed that we are waiting for bus or laundry service, and often, that is the case. But too frequently our assumptions are incorrect, clouding our sociological imagination (see Mills, 1959; Hoffman, 2006). Finally, distractions may function as pacifiers; they help us get through waiting and sometimes enhance our wait. But waiting places are many and varied. The amount of time spent waiting is connected to location and situations. The social fact that we all must wait is without question; the *issue* is *waiting place*, that is, we must wait somewhere, some*place*.

NOTES

1. See Haskett (2002).

2. Waiting consistency is experience among groups with regular wait patterns, such as "ballet waiters" and those who convene regularly at specific spots to wait.

3. Waiting for the bus in the rain presents one major challenge, for example, how does one stay dry while waiting? The bus stop wait-area was equipped with a covering over bench seats, yet only three persons could sit on the steel bench. One person sat and later another individual joined him; they seemed to know each other for they engaged in conversation. Soon, four men arrive and attempted to stand underneath covering to avoid getting wet. They were unsuccessful thus relocated to a "Churches Chicken" establishment, directly behind the bus stop wait-area. This establishment contains an awning, and thus those arriving and waiting for the bus could stand and wait in that area, managing to stay dry in the rain.

4. Fortunately, laws have changed regarding the amount of time passengers wait on tarmacs.

5. While the brochure and flier text are consistent, the Honda name and location are fictitious.

6. While in class, students tend to identify certain locations, *a place*, and remain there throughout the term. In short, students get accustomed to waiting for

their professors or teachers in a specified seat or area of the classroom, *a waiting place.*

7. See Stokowski's analysis regarding Politics of Place, in "Languages of Place and Discourses of Power," 2002; and see Thomas Gieryn's Place-Making, in "A Space for Place in Sociology," 2000.

8. Quote by Juan Mendoza, Attorney at Law-Deputy Public Defender.

Chapter 3

Wait Utilization

Things People Do *While Waiting*

Waiting in line at the Department of Motor Vehicles (DMV)[1] or *waiting* for immigration interviews is often extremely boring; a tedious process and yet one that is required. It is sensible among persons who wait, or *waiters*, to keep busy while waiting. This chapter examines *how* people wait; that is, what people *do* while waiting. Given one's need to meet deadlines, what persons *do* with wait-time is significant. *Doing* or *not doing* gets at one's preparedness to wait. But what is meant by *doing* and *not doing*? For our purposes, *doing* refers to engagement in an intentional act; *not doing*, if such is possible, refers to not doing anything and simply not knowing what to do which leads to boredom. The act of *doing* keeps one occupied and less bored; seemingly, time moves faster. Getting work accomplished while waiting is functional; one is pleased with his/her achievements. Conversely, *not doing* results in wasting time, a lack of productivity. The U.S. society values hard work, a Protestant ethic approach to one's daily routine. There is frequent admiration for those who use time effectively and efficiently. *Doing nothing* is potentially perceived as laziness or indolence in that one makes little or no effort at progress. *Non-doing* then is viewed as loafing.

There are situations when individuals encounter unexpected waits. Such circumstances could prove most problematic in that one does not prepare, and boredom and frustration are potential consequences. No one can ever anticipate being stuck on the tarmac for seven hours, and the frustration among passengers was enormous (see Delta the Worst Airline, 2009; Martilli, 2009).[2] Additionally, unexpected delays for medical lab results have caused many to adjust their plans. Such delays conjure up an *anomic ambiguity* in that there is uncertainty about holdups. Customers receive little definitive information and officials are either unwilling or unable to divulge further reasons for delays. The result is often aggravation leading to a waste of time and a clear case of *non-doing*.

Wait utilization then focuses on *doing*. How does one utilize his/her time while waiting? Time is valuable and taking advantage of wait-time is rewarding in that completing tasks or elevating one's business plan is beneficial. One high school teacher exclaimed, "When I wait, I take along my crossword puzzle to keep me occupied. People around me get mad, thinking 'darn-it, I wish I would have brought something to do.'" Another teacher remarked, "When I wait, I prepare myself. I take books, papers, magazines, and crochet. I really get prepared." For these teachers, it is important to have something to do, to utilize their time, either by pleasure or work activities. Wasting time seems irresponsible given their time demands. Thus, in that same way, teachers expect preparation from students, imposing the value of preparedness onto themselves and students. Indeed, while waiting for class, students are often completing assignments, preparing for exams, or viewing social media.

How one waits may reflect one's environment. For example, it is unlikely that smokers will smoke while waiting to deplane and doubtful that moviegoers will read books while awaiting the main feature. Smokers may rush to deplane in order to smoke and moviegoers find it difficult to read in the dark. The environment simply influences how they wait. While these examples are sensible, the point remains clear and yet simple. Some activities are clearly prohibited and difficult to accomplish but many more are possible and feasible in a variety of wait-environments. For instance, *waiters* have been found to engage in talking on cell phones, talking to others, computing, doing homework, office work, drawing, staring, sleeping, knitting, praying, writing, playing board games, eating, observing, watching TV, reading, listening to others, and listening to music. This does not exhaust the list of wait-activities, yet these appear most common.

Having wait-options, that is, being able to do a variety of tasks within various environments is significant. It may provide continuity to writing or some other activity; having wait-options may further produce fresh ideas given one's surroundings. But most importantly, such wait-options give individuals opportunities to explore and engage in some meaningful tasks that is gratifying or useful, or both. If one is prepared, like the aforementioned teachers, boredom is virtually eliminated and the span of waiting seems minimized. The lack of wait-options is similar to being unprepared; one is not only bored, but seemingly, the wait is prolonged. The wait experience is imposed, producing strain and a sense of idleness.

INSTITUTIONS AND FIXED WAIT ACTIVITIES

Over the years, institutions have become more and more sophisticated. They are far more technical and institutions consistently perform surveys to understand customers. Further, surveys are designed to maintain and recruit additional customers. How one waits often reflects certain measures within surveys. For example, upon close observation some institutions and businesses strategically influence how individuals wait. While waiting, some institutions are interested in informing, and others are concerned with distracting customers. The DMV uses video monitors to inform customers of required documents before reaching line's front and consulting with customer service representatives. Similarly, institutions of higher learning use instructive materials as students wait in line for registration, financial aid, and transcript requests. By informing customers of required and official documents, such institutions influence how customers wait and conceivably reduce wait-time. Other institutions are less interested in enlightening customers and more interested in distracting them. For example, beauty salons and barbershops maintain TVs for diversionary purposes. Popular programs serve the dual function of entertainment and distraction.

It follows then that TV monitors are the most common objects used by institutions to manipulate wait-patterns among persons. Juror assembly rooms, supermarkets, banks, auto repair wait-rooms, car wash wait-areas, hospitals, restaurants, bars, airports, barbershops, and so forth often contain visual viewing devices, for example, TVs and/or video monitors. Most often, channels and programs are preset, discouraging customers against tampering, probably to prevent damage. The TV has become part of our wait experience, and watching it—is simply part of what we *do*. Preset channels and videos are instructive in that one's *doing* is further facilitated by the institution.

Some institutions provide more than TVs. That is, waiting in pediatric departments, hospitals have clearly thought through the importance of providing board games and toys for children. Some parents arrive for appointments with more than one child, that is, an infant and toddler; and thus, while parents are feeding, changing diapers or walking infants, toddlers are involved with board games and/or toys. The same is observed in various financial and correctional institutions where board games and toys are used to occupy children while parents conduct business or wait to visit inmates. The play area, which may contain a toy phone along with cars, dolls, small tables and chairs, crayons, paper for coloring, children's books, and sesame street toy characters (Telly, Cookie Monster), maintains their attention far beyond the wait; in fact, several parents were observed separating children from toys and nagging them when time to leave. By far, the most popular wait-gadget for children was video games. Observed primarily in barbershops, certain pre-teens were so engaged that they permitted other customers to go ahead of them in order to complete their game(s).

With the use of slot machines, adults have their own version of video games. Observed specifically in Las Vegas Airport, slot machines have a mesmerizing effect on gamblers. Such machines allow gamblers to extend their gambling or get an early start, for passengers are confronted with slot machines when arriving and departing. Recognizing that air travel is typically late, slot machines are placed throughout the airport, especially by boarding gates. Slot machines clearly give travel customers something to do—beyond watching TV, costly shopping, eating in expensive restaurants, and drinking pricey coffee. Such machines distract customers long enough to keep their mind off of plane delays and losing several hundred dollars. Moreover, such *doing*, playing slot machines, further contributes to the economy of Las Vegas. So, the importance of facilitating one's wait also has economic value.

While certain institutions provide and maintain fixed activities, various establishments instruct customers on what is prohibited. For instance, at men's central jail, there are signs on walls and pillars giving direction and information, for example, "mailing address," "inmate booking number information," and visiting area rules. Additional signs indicate "no cell phones," "no recording devices," and "no video cameras." Those who possess such items are asked to secure them in lockers. Similarly, courtrooms have several regulations, though they do little to facilitate waiting. In either case, failure to comply results in swift sanction. Correctional and judicial institutions are more likely than others (banking, medical and educational institutions) to maintain *wait-prohibitions*.

Institutions that provide fixed wait activities are interested in certain outcomes. For example, while waiting on the main feature, moviegoers are often entertained by trailers. Such trailers inform customers of upcoming events and movies, consequently, advertisement and returning to the theater is the motive. In the case of children, one outcome is to contain their behavior; giving them *something to do* decreases their potential to act out or meddle; whereas in the case of adults, who are sidetracked by slot machines, restaurants and shopping, fixed wait activities provide economic enhancement for communities. Finally, in the case of the everyday waiter, wait-devices such as TVs simply function to divert our attention and ease our wait.

ASSESSMENT

Shortly, I will introduce a chapter entitled "Waiting with Strangers." Assessment of strangers is examined in that concerns with security and safety are critical reasons for such evaluation. Further, we discovered that stranger assessments occur both verbally and nonverbally. The current section however examines assessments of a different type; here, the interest is in assessing one's ability, one's progress, one's fairness, and a comparison between cases. Whether employee or product related, major institutions are constantly involved in assessment. The concern is "getting it right" and improve performance. Employees receiving high marks on evaluation reviews are often rewarded; in contrast, low marks are penalized. In both cases, employees and supervisors convene and converse about employee performance, receiving feedback on how to improve, and praised for creativity and success.

While waiting, assessment is also occurring—though not in the formal sense but clearly less formal, and there are ways that sanctions and reward are applied. For instance, watching and evaluating swim lessons are done by most parents. They frequently appraise swim teachers, pool environment, other swim students and other swim classes.[3] Parents make mental and verbal notes of individual swim-student progress by assessing, "He's coming along well," "He swam a longer distance today," and "She's a pretty good teacher"; "She really knows how to get them to float." Opposite appraisals are also wedged by commenting, "She seems overwhelmed," and "Lucy is having a much harder time with backstroke." Additionally, parents assess rapport among swim teachers and students, or whether teachers spend more or less time with little Juan or ambitious Matt. In part, the purpose of assessment is to make decisions and adjustments, often involving honor and/or castigation. That is, whether to maintain or change swim teachers; whether parents should instruct children or leave them alone; whether to discipline unruly children or wait until class ends; and whether to confront teachers or complain to officials.

In restaurants or fast-food settings where cooks are observed, customers often wait by observing and assessing their behavior. Customers express interest in cleanliness, cooking styles, and portions. If the meat falls on the floor, how is it handled? Do cooks wear hats or nets? Are hands consistently washed? Given dietary concerns, some are worried about cooking styles and food preparation. For example, is food fried or broiled? Is meat fresh or frozen? And is soup micro-waved or heated? Finally, portion amounts are evaluated while watching and waiting. At Lucky Boys, a popular fast-food restaurant, customers inadvertently make requests, saying, "That's too much cheese," "a little more cheese," "no onions please," and/or "no sour cream." With an empathic attitude, cooks frequently oblige customer requests. And while there is a general understanding of cleanliness, cooking styles and portions, individual assessments are personal perspectives; one's assumption of how food should be prepared and personal taste. Like any entrepreneur-client relationship, restaurants are interested in pleasing customers and therefore maintaining their business. Assessments then assist individuals in making sense of the current situation, leading to principled possibilities, like recommending others, giving large tips and/or personally complimenting chefs or cooks.

Comparing and contrasting is another way to assess individual's behavior and situations. Reviewing "ratemyprofessor.com," it is clear that students compare and contrast professors; it is also clear that employees compare supervisors and their decisions; children compare and contrast parents; and those on the dating scene, compare and contrast men or women they hang out with. Comparing and contrasting judges and their decisions are also open to assessment while waiting in court. During court, attendees watch judges, lawyers, and defendants discuss and negotiate their particular cases. Attendees often provide quiet commentary and display emotions after sentences are rendered. For example, Kwame walked into court with his mother and sister. After the proceedings with judge, lawyers, and defendant, the judge sentenced Kwame to three years in the state penitentiary for a drug-related offense. Disappointing moans were heard in the immediate area of Kwame's mother and sister. In fact, they began visibly wiping their tears as Kwame was taken into custody. When another gentleman, Don, was sentenced to eighteen-month probation and required to return in that time to show completion of Canterbury Institute Drug Program, one lady remarked, "Hmm, he got off lite."

It is abundantly clear that courtroom audiences do not watch and wait passively; many are very attentive as they stare and comment on court proceedings and decisions. Within the confines of courtroom procedures and etiquette, observers quietly make assessments. Unlike assessing swim teachers, cooks and dry-cleaning establishments, the judgments of courtroom audiences have little or no value, for defendants are locked into a formal court system and if so ordered, defendants must return within eighteen months. In truth, the only meaningful assessment is that of the judge or commissioner. Rarely do courtroom-audience-members engage in outbursts that evaluate and even challenge a judge's decision. For example, during my observations, no courtroom spectator (ever) openly accused a judge of bias, unfairness, sexist or racist behavior. Such evaluations are usually contained and quietly conveyed to one's neighbor or within one's immediate space. Courtroom-spectator assessments are real, having intrinsic meaning only to the assessor, and yet it is what spectators *do* while waiting on their case of interest.

WATCHING AND LISTENING

Standing in line at the post office, one is likely to hear several conversations among customers, employees, and customers/employees. Customers discuss a range of topics including stamps, operating hours, boxes, the length of the line, and so forth. Employees often inquire of one another whether the post office stocks certain stamps or the existence of various zip codes. And employee/customer interactions are very normal pertaining to postal transactions, yet other conversations are simply odd and possibly embarrassing.

For instance, at the close of their transaction, Dick asked a postal clerk: "Are you Korean?"

"No, I'm Chinese." Smiling, Won Ji continues, "People always ask me if I'm Korean."

Now, quickly gathering his materials and turning red with embarrassment, Dick is apologetic, "I'm sorry, I shouldn't have asked." With head somewhat bowed, Dick leaves looking around to see whether anyone observed their transaction and conversation. The encounter was observed by those waiting, yet their glances shifted as Dick turned to face customers.

In public wait-areas, such as banks, post offices, dental offices, grocery store lines, and wait-lines for patients, it is not unusual to see and hear conversations between client and institutional representatives. Such settings are referred to as *enclosed wait sections* (see typology of wait-places), and interactions are visible and audible to those present. Here, customers are either waiting in line or seated in wait areas. The exposed structure reflects a lack of privacy, containing many strangers awaiting similar service. Such settings are designed to process customers rapidly, and yet personal and sometimes embarrassing information is often conveyed. In either case, others may witness transactions and assess encounters, for their *observation* of the transaction is what they *do* while waiting. Hence, those who bring nothing to *do* or find themselves in situations where waiting is brief, often engage in watching and listening.

Part of watching and listening is simply paying attention to *your* turn, that is one does not wish to miss his or her turn, and awareness allows individuals to receive important information. Whether in post offices or fast-food restaurants, customers are watching for the next available customer service agent. And within juror assembly rooms and men's central-jail-wait-room, individuals are listening for specific information. The waiting area of juror rooms and men's central jail is characterized with a buzz of conversation, yet when announcements are carried over intercom, noise and talking subsides. In the case of men's central jail, visitors are listening for the names of loved-ones because failure to respond could forfeit one's visit. Sheriffs are dogmatic, vowing to read names two times, for example, "I will only read names two times!" In juror assembly rooms, potential jurors are listening for their names to determine whether they have been assigned a case. Here, the attitude is not one of "us against them," but clerks freely and frequently announce and repeat names for juror panels.

While paying attention is a major reason for watching and listening, there are other reasons why *waiters* engage in this activity. That is, some customers are simply nosy, intruding into the business of others. An interracial couple, Black/white, was doing business at the counter and most waiting in line were intently watching and listening. The intensity of certain customers watching

and listening was amazing; four customers witnessed the entire transaction—
and their attention did not waver, as if in a trance. The diversity of the couple
seemed to spark their attention, along with the clear and distinct speech pattern of the African American male appeared to maintain their gaze, staring at
them even as they left the counter.

Watching and listening raises important concerns about privacy and
security; privacy pertaining to one's medical condition, and security by
openly asking and revealing one's phone number, name, e-mail address,
medical record number, or social security number. Patients feel differently about their medical condition in that some experience embarrassment
when clerks reveal the nature of their appointments, while others care less
whether strangers know of their gynecology or vasectomy appointments.
Since everyone experiences this information differently, it is sensible
among clerks to exercise more discretion in public wait-areas when gathering confidential information. Now at the counter, the intake clerk, Richard,
was discussing various scheduled appointments with Beatrice. The computer indicated that Beatrice had two appointments on the same day. "You
have a gynecology appointment at 9 am and a physical at 2 pm." Beatrice
seemed puzzled, wondering, "Really! I don't remember making a gynecology appointment." Richard insisted that it was correct, "Yes. It's right here
on my screen," and attempted to change the appointments so that they were
closer together. Beatrice appeared to go along with his assessment, until
Richard finally took a closer look at the name. In discovery, he shouts,
"Oh No! You're not Maria Lopez! I'm glad I looked at that." Those watching and listening began laughing due to his obvious mistake. Meanwhile,
Beatrice smirked, commenting, "And just look at me; I was just going along
with it."

As humor and laughter are ways to reduce stress and save face, Beatrice
seemed puzzled about her gynecology appointment. It is customary that
clerks inquire about the nature of patient appointment, yet the volume at
which their exchange occurs seems to "put her business in the streets." For
these reasons, those waiting are asked to stand a certain distance from counter
and remain in line until called. The signs that make these requests emphasize
confidentiality of patients. Beatrice appears more baffled and less embarrassed about the gynecological appointment though such wondering causes
Richard to take a second look. Seemingly, the exchange could have occurred
in a more discreet and professional manner.

To what extent do customers know that they are being watched? There
are varying degrees to which counter-customers realize they are being
observed. For example, the lady, Francis, who takes too long at counter,
and Dick, the man who asked, "Are you Korean?"—feel a certain gaze by
those waiting. Francis experiences guilt because she is taking too long and

others wish to complete their transactions and leave. Francis is somehow stalling progress. Dick experiences discomfort by being wrong about making his cultural inquiry. As ways to express their frustration, *waiters* make eye contact with Francis; and yet, no one returns Dick's glance, for they do not wish to be a part of his embarrassing moment. But the customer with a regular transaction is less cognizant of being watched, that is, interracial couple. They are more concerned about completing their transaction, not "who's watching me?" Sometimes, Uncle Sam is watching, and possibly listening to us all. Whether at the counter or waiting in line, the surveillance cameras are watching and recording our every move. And like the casual transaction, customers pay little attention to post office, store, parking lot, and bank cameras.

On other occasions, customers often listen without watching, as when customer service agents inform customers of car problems or medical scheduling problems and make recommendations in public view. Such an exchange frequently occurs in the presence of others, yet those others will not turn to view the encounter. "Those others" are very cognizant of the situation, and therefore concede that staring and eavesdropping are rude, particularly if caught.

It is doubtful whether watching and listening are reciprocal while waiting in line. Put simply, it is difficult to watch and listen to wait-clients while being serviced by institutional representatives. But in other situations, waiting and watching is reciprocal. For example, waiting for the bus, passengers often watch car-drivers stopped at red lights or pass through red lights; and drivers stopped at red lights often wait and watch potential bus passengers and those crossing. Each is simply observing their environment. Tommy reports that he experienced the reciprocal gaze of car-drivers and passengers while waiting at the bus stop. He shares, "As I waited at the bus stop, I watch the car traffic, people walking across the street and I'm aware of other passengers waiting for the bus. But as I continued to wait, I would hear someone walking with heels; the footsteps and heel noises were very determined, though I did not turn around. Sarah, a longtime friend, walked around where I was standing. She tapped my arm."

I turned around and she said, "I thought that was you! Where are you going? Come on, I'll give you a ride!"

Tommy: "No, no. It's o.k. I'm not waiting for the bus; I'm waiting for someone to arrive on the bus. My car is right over there," pointing in the direction of his car.

Sarah: "My son said, 'mom, don't go picking up some strange man!!!' But I thought that was you."

Tommy: "Yeah it's me, and I really appreciate you stopping to check on me. Thank you very much!"

Sarah: "O.K. bye."

Again, such an encounter verifies that *drivers* also watch and listen to those at bus stops, that is, those waiting for the bus. The watching appears reciprocal, especially when drivers are waiting at red signal lights. But more importantly, watching and listening is a significant part of what one does when waiting, given that watching people is an everyday occurrence. Situations are often managed by watching people, and in watching people, one may recognize a friend or family member. Watching and listening may prove informative, discovering valuable information while waiting; one further makes qualitative and quantitative assessments while waiting; and still others are tempted to eavesdrop. There are other cases, however, where watching and listening proves entertaining, which distracts or amuses one's attention and thus keeping their mind off of waiting. The next section examines "the show," which analyzes how persons are entertained while waiting.

THE SHOW

Watching and listening tends to occur any place where one is waiting, yet *the show* usually takes place in an auditorium-type setting. Further, *the show* resembles a certain element of entertainment and information, where audience members are either passive viewers or *show* participants. The courtroom resembles an auditorium-type structure, and while persons wait for their specific cases, they are often engaged in *the show*. That is, they watch *the show* while they wait, becoming entertained, amused, and even frustrated. Any show needs an audience or it would not be theater. At L.A. County courts, the courtroom audience typically consists of defendants, witnesses, casual observers, researchers, family members of defendants, lawyers, and police officers. Having power, the judge maintains the central area of the stage, and when decisions are reached, audiences are tuned in. Some characters are well-defined and others are not. For instance, those in obvious costumes, for example, robes, uniforms, jumpsuits, and business suits seem guided by their status, while undercover police officers are more difficult to detect.

As persons begin to gather and find seating, the courtroom is relatively quiet though there is soft talk in deference to courtroom etiquette. Lawyers are reviewing files and talking to clients while stenographers are turning on machines and shifting documents. The bailiff is standing and soon announces, "Please turn off cell phones and pagers." Initially, he instructs in English, then in Spanish, but not in Korean though Korean defendants are present who need an interpreter. When the judge arrives, the bailiff instructs, "Rise, court is in session, the honorable Judge Titus presiding." Her introduction and entrance—denotes her role as main character.

Like live theater, critical observation reveals that some *shows* are boring while others are intriguing and interesting. Some scenes are exciting, others are sleepers. Yet, in viewing the courtroom show, the emergence of "main features" and "side shows" is clearly evident. Lawyers advising custodies-clients, lawyers talking to other lawyers, clerks talking to lawyers, audience outbursts, bailiffs talking to lawyers and custodies, cell phones ringing, lawyers talking to interpreters, and the constant human traffic that walks in and out of courtroom represent "side shows." The "main feature" occurs when judges or commissioners, who use microphones, proceed with the business of the court, by questioning and confronting attorneys, questioning clients and custodies of attorneys, confronting custodies and in some cases, scolding and talking down to custodies. The judge is always the main attraction in that court sessions and operations are difficult without judges. While side shows pose an element of distraction, noteworthy is the fact that main features and side shows frequently occur simultaneously. The importance of side shows gets at preparation and even rehearsal for main features. For example, attorneys consult with clients, either before the judge arrives or during court. Essentially, they are preparing to present their case. Also, side shows determine the extent to which rules are followed. For example, if audience members are too loud or cell phones ring, court officials are likely to remind and encourage violators to obey rules. While *side shows* happen, they are contained and main features usually trump side shows (see Goffman, 1959).

One of the most significant scenes of main features is when criminals enter courtrooms for sentencing. They have been detained in L.A. County Jail and transported (see Price, 2005; Emerson, 1981) to courtroom by L.A. County Sheriffs. During court, the sheriff or bailiff guards a locked room in which criminals are held. The criminal holding room is located near the courtroom front, where judges and attorney may view and/or consult with criminals. When ordered by judge, the bailiff unlocks holding room door and brings criminal into courtroom. The criminal is handcuffed, ankle cuffed, and dressed in a bright orange jumpsuit, which reads "L.A. County Jail" on the back. At this point, the entire courtroom looks in the direction of the hand/ankle cuffed criminal; the audience is curious as to what will happen or whether anything unusual takes place. The proceedings begin and all present, especially loved-ones of criminal, stare with interest. Loved-ones of criminals also express more emotion, for when Carlos was sentenced to five years in the state penitentiary, mother and daughter sobbed openly, wiping tears as they flowed.

Not all scenes of main features are emotionally painful—some are downright funny, amusing, and simply entertaining. For example, in the case of Leroy Johnson who was also assisted by sheriffs though seemed not to have loved-ones present, he complained loudly about not understanding why he was in jail. In response, the judge asked, "How long have you been in jail?"

Leroy answered, "About one or two weeks."

The judge smiled, questioning "You don't know!? If it were me, I'd know to the letter!"

Leroy: "I don't know, I think about two weeks."
Judge: "I don't know either; maybe you'll know in two weeks." A collective laugh was expressed, as the Judge instructed, "Next!"

In another scene, one defendant was detained for failing to acknowledge a warrant that was mailed to his house. During proceedings, George, the defendant, claimed that "the notice never came to my house." According to Judge Titus, George also failed to pay a $10 per month restitution fine. Judge Titus' facial expression wrinkles and eyebrows raise as to convey doubt that George had not received warrant; she also expressed disappointment that the fine had not been paid. She discloses, "George I see that you haven't paid fine! Why?"

George: "Because I didn't have the money."
Titus: "This fine is minimal, $10 a month. That's like not having McDonalds for a week." The audience bursts into laughter.

If interesting, *main features* sustains one's attention; the audience is fascinated by the performance and concerned with outcomes. At the same time, *side shows* have the ability to distract; it is like persons arriving late to theater performances. The movement of late comers grabs our attention, and adjusting one's position so late comers can squeeze through aisles, further takes us away from main attractions. Unlike theater performances, side shows are frequent occurrences at L.A. County Court. While they are not a part of court business, side shows deflect and at times interrupt court proceedings. For instance, two cell phones[4] sounded as the judge announced her caseload. The first phone belonged to a lawyer, the second to a Korean defendant. As the first phone sounds, the lawyer who is seated in the audience scrambles to reach in his top suit pocket to turn off phone. The ring draws the attention of the court and all look in his direction, including the bailiff who stares him down. The second phone is from the Korean defendant. Again, the ringing brings attention to his area, thus all in court gaze in his direction; he too scrambles to turn off phone. Interestingly enough, the Korean is dressed in an expensive black suit, which leads to extended stares; most other court attendees, excluding lawyers, simply dress down. In short, further attention, a type of curious notice, is granted given his attire.

The most important action here is *turning off the phone*. The action and motion of *turning off the phone* indicates that one has inadvertently left his phone on and apologizes by quickly turning off his phone. Though late, they are complying to formal courtroom guidelines and everyone observes them recognizing that their options are limited. Still imagine if these persons answered their phones and engaged in conversation. Certainly, the court's attention is captured and judges are likely to fine rule violators, possibly making this into a *main feature*. There are various signs outside courtrooms, instructing those who enter to "Turn off all pagers, cellular phones and alarm watches. Subject to confiscation and/or fine by Court." One's motion to turn off phone is linked to this rule. Similarly, cell phones that ring during religious services, classroom lectures, and theater performances; and while our attention is sidetracked and annoyingly attained, the same apologetic process of silencing phones is performed. Again, the incident represents a *side show*, a distraction from the main feature.

Finally, certain women are skilled at gaining our attention by their attire, demeanor, certain noises, and perfumes. Spending long hours in court, our attention is easily distracted by women who are attractive and who stage their attire and entrance. One female attorney dressed in a short white top, black skirt (which fell right below her knees), no nylons and black pumps. When she strutted in and out of courtroom, her heels made a distinct sound, drawing everyone's attention. Her black skirt was worn in such a way that displayed her legs and many courtroom observers scanned her physical features. She fashioned long brownish-black hair that was well groomed and frequently flinging it as not to cover her face. Here again seemingly to draw the attention of others, including Judge Patterson. Conversely, most other female attorneys seem less interested in entertaining the court by attire; often they adorn themselves in dress or pants suits, with comfortable shoes for lengthy work days.

Why is the above important? The courtroom *show* has produced such theater that it can no longer confine itself to court. It has literally gone "Broadway." The media regularly broadcast TV Court, including Judge Ephriam Mablean, Judge Hatchett, Judge Mathis, Judge Joe Brown, and others. Such shows are in fact designed to entertain, for it is difficult to stay on-air without solid ratings. And as in conventional court, TV Court retains an audience attending to the main features of performance, yet *side shows* are typically rare. What is it about conventional court that makes its way to TV? Seemingly, many within U.S. society are enticed by confrontations, whether legal or not. And while courtroom confrontations emit many emotions, for example, stress, joy, and pain, there are real consequences. To Judge Brown, "Creative sentencing is far more effective in some cases than sending someone to jail." For example, in one case, "a convicted burglar was required to invite his victim into his own home so that the victim could choose any item he wanted to take away" (see Turley, 2005). Additionally, Court TV is cognizant of informing the public about the law. One viewer asserted that her knowledge of the law was more pronounced after viewing a landlord and tenant dispute. And Judge Sanders believes that audience members and viewers should be informed of law—"so they know their rights and how we arrive at justice."[5]

Essentially, watching *the show* is what one does while waiting on their particular case. *The show* is specific to certain waiting environments,[6] and once cases are heard, loved-ones are likely to leave *court theater*. There is no charge for watching court theater, though it is a very structured and formal mechanism of people watching. Conventional theater temporarily removes life's worries, as do certain scenes in court theater. But usually loved-ones attend court for specific scenes and not to escape their problems. In fact, fantasy has no place in real situations where one is forced to face cold hard facts. The entertainment of court is a by-product and an unintended function of waiting. Additionally, viewers, whether on TV or not, get wrapped up in certain cases, appealing to one's sense of justice. Therefore, while judges make formal decisions, audience members and viewers come to their own conclusions, and even critically evaluate the judge's decision, demeanor, and punishment.

"MOST WILLING TO WAIT FOR"

What one *waits for* may further help to explain wait-utilization. It is clear that waiting is relative and everyone is not willing to wait for the same item; yet, most are willing to wait for *something*. Why then is one willing to wait for one object and not another? Individuals possess different wait-interests for distinct reasons, and the object of concern may reflect how waiting takes place. For instance, one open-ended question raised the issue of "what are you *most* willing to wait for—and why?" This question examines the hierarchy of waiting in that it is stratified and circumstances that are most significant receive higher priority. It implies that there is a choice in waiting, thus discovering that respondents are significantly concerned with families, children, relationships, education, and careers. Respondents also recognize that *choice waiting* is a process and could take several years; but during that process, *doing* must occur in order to achieve wait-goals. *Choice waiting* is carefully thought through; rushing to accomplish goals is unlikely though reevaluating and/or revisiting strategies is probable. Ultimately, *choice waiting* gets at life's necessities and views such essentials as possible and obtainable.

Again, what one *waits for* is often tied to the importance of an object, person, or occasion. Such waiting ignores ordinary levels of waiting, like waiting at banks, bus stops, or supermarkets. "Most willing to wait for" gets at a sense of values that holds significance in one's life, and one is therefore committed to that object of wait. This type of waiting is more or less a choice and not an obligation, though later, it may appear obligatory. Consequently, from one's own life experience, he or she has been socialized to value certain objects, persons, or occasions—and their sense of values then reflects their willingness to wait.

In an open-ended survey to college students, the following question was asked: "What are you most willing to wait for—and why? In other words, what is *soooo* important to you—that you are willing to wait hours, days or years? Thoroughly explain by providing examples and explanations." Given this type of survey, the responses and explanations varied, yet each idea naturally emerged from respondents. The categories that formed include family, careers, education, entertainment, health, food, cars, happiness, death, attire, vacations, immigration, pets, and religion. A miscellaneous category surfaced given the vagueness of certain responses. For example, several respondents wrote replies that reflect the following statements: "I will wait for anything that I know the outcome to," "I am willing to wait for anything worthwhile," "I'm willing to wait for important things, like life impacting decisions, because I think that they are worth waiting a long time for," and finally, "I'm willing to wait for the inevitable; those goals which I've set for myself and know for certain I will accomplish. I can wait patiently for a predetermined outcome, or results I know beforehand." All such responses are vague and lack specifics, yet 23 percent of the sample issued vague answers.

From the categories mentioned above, family emerged as the most important grouping worth waiting. Thirty-four percent of sample appears to have an intense commitment to family; they are willing to wait and sacrifice for family. Broadly speaking, family includes marriage, children, relationships, love, brothers, grandparents, and other extended family members. One respondent confessed, "I will wait a long time for the right person to marry and have kids with. Since it is so important to be ready and prepared for that kind of commitment, I am willing to wait my whole life for love and family." Another person wrote, "What I am willing to wait for is my family. They are everything to me, because they are always there for me. I would wait for them as long as I need to." Seemingly, this next individual has had much experience and counsel in relationships, she writes:

There is a quote, "the best things are worth waiting for!" There are only a few things that I would devote such time to wait for. One of these things is love. Love needs patience and patience needs time. When it comes to love, I am willing to wait. You cannot rush into a relationship with someone and not wait to find out if that person is right for you. Rushing into marriage is one of the biggest mistakes a person can make. It is also the same to rush out of love. When you love someone with so much heart, you need to be patient and wait. Things may go wrong, there might be bad days, but waiting and giving it time will definitely save a relationship. I take my time and wait with love whether its hours, days, weeks, months, or even years.

Family is a primary group that one is emotionally and physically linked. While family drama is real, this group typically cares and sacrifices when nobody else will. When waiting at airports, schools, hospitals, and extracurricular activities (club swimming, volleyball, gymnastics, etc.), one usually waits for family members. In short, much of our sacrificial and extended waiting includes those who are primary.

While no one is surprised by family being first, it is worth revealing the status of other categories, keeping in mind that such categories emerged naturally. From highest to lowest, categories emerged in the following order: career, education, entertainment, health, food, and car. Death, attire, and religion received the same status; immigration, happiness, vacation, and pets received the lowest rankings. In short there were fewer respondents who identified these categories as important.[7]

WAITING, REMINISCING, AND THINKING

What one does while waiting depends on what he is waiting for. It is clear that wait-utilization recognizes the variety of activities that one may engage in while waiting. Adventurous, pleasurable, and work-related activities are utilized to pass time and the type of activity could accelerate or lengthen one's wait. While everyone waits, parents in particular are no strangers to waiting; they wait long hours for medical appointments, appliances to arrive, and children activities. One parent acknowledged, "Everywhere you look you will find us 'soccer moms' ferrying our kids to sports practices and games and whiling away the long hours of waiting by eagerly comparing accessories and trading songs with other baby-boomer moms" (Gong, 2005:14). This parent is referring to her iPod and how it has enabled her to reminisce. She writes, "This little treasure has enabled me to revisit my past and groove to the present; it has provided me with an ever-evolving soundtrack for my life" (Gong, 2005:14). As they wait, "comparing accessories and trading songs" seems pleasurable, that is, music brings back nostalgic memories for soccer moms.

Sentimental recollections allow soccer moms to *think* about their past, while lyrics along with melodies potentially take them to previous *places* and events. Consequently, *thinking* is one key activity while waiting, recognizing much is written about *critical thinking*; it is a type of thinking that requires reflection, analysis, and questioning. Critical thinking entertains and challenges varying perspectives and diverse ways of pondering problems. Still critical thinking is not the only type of thinking. *Casual thinking*, for example, refers to recollections about events or persons, along with impromptu thoughts about loved-ones and situations. *Tactical thinking* considers planning and strategy, for example, how one intends to accomplish a task or develop a design, or defeat a rival. Such a typology is useful when examining thinking and waiting, for the mode of one's thinking may have consequences for later activities, recognizing that waiting provides opportunities to reflect and that all three types could merge when waiting.

Interestingly, *thinking* and waiting are closely intertwined. For example, buying gas is a routine occurrence among drivers, and while drivers wait their turn, it is clear that a variety of thoughts emerge—thoughts like dinner plans, content of office meetings, travel plans, tax returns, family concerns, political issues, and outrageous gas prices. Thinking is something we do along with other activities like watching TV, listening to music, teaching, or knitting. Additionally, thinking may provide a type of clarity to our situation. Kevin, a bank manager, revealed that thinking was his major pastime while waiting. He says, "I think a lot. I don't think about the end. I think about the outcome." "What's the difference?" "The end is like death and I don't think about death. The outcome is like the result of something. Now my wife tells me, I *over-think*. And I do over-think. I analyze everything. I could be watching a TV program and think about the intelligence of the actors. I also think about my daughter, who's in foster care and I cannot find her." Christina is another who thinks while waiting. She writes, "I wait calmly by using that time to think about what I am going to do later that evening or recap the next day's plan. I think about what I have pending, such as bills, homework, home chores, etc." And finally, tennis star Venus William receives clarity during rain delays— for it is here where she sits, waits and therefore contemplates her game. She shares, "I feel like I achieve clarity actually when it rains. The longer I have to sit and wait. The clearer my game comes to me" (Robson, 2007:11c). Reviewing her game and strategizing next moves are major activities while waiting. Athletes achieve more by figuring out how to improve their game.

In the above cases, thinking is a key feature of waiting. Thinking allows us to reminisce, review, analyze, and strategize. For example, certain songs could spark pleasant adolescent and adult memories; similarly, recapping a business conversation may occur when stuck in traffic. Our wait and our activity lead us to *think* about other things. There are times when our thinking has no relevance, as when we think—just to think[8]—and sometimes even our own thoughts scare us. We think about whether the clerk likes her job or how the waitress maintains her composure. Strategic thinking is most useful. Such thinking is designed to improve our situation; how one might improve his ability or how one can defeat her rival. Our thinking varies based on our environment and what persons wish to accomplish, but it is clear that our waiting involves a fair amount of thinking.

SUMMARY

This chapter has examined *how* people wait, that is, what people *do* while waiting. Given one's busy schedule and lack of time, wait-utilization focuses on *doing* and how persons are productive, entertained, or bored by waiting? Additionally, how one waits is linked to one's environment. For example, while flying from L.A. to N.Y., one is likely to read, sleep, watch TV, or watch other passengers. There are other environments where a variety of wait-options are possible. Waiting in line for concert tickets, one is likely to observe persons talking on cell phones, talking to others, watching others, texting, smoking, writing, and even surfing the web. In short, some environments permit more *doing* while others are restricted. This chapter has examined *institutions and fixed wait activities, assessment, watching and listening, the show, "most willing to wait for"* and *waiting, reminiscing, and thinking.* Each category provides an interesting and unique analysis of *doing* while waiting.

Institutions and Fixed Wait Activities examines how gadgets are intentionally placed in wait areas to entertain and distract customers. That is, through survey research some institutions have discovered items and gadgets that comfort and distract one's wait; strategically, various institutions have manipulated how individuals wait. Placing board games, TV monitors, magazines, slot machines, food, computers, coffee, plaques, pictures and certificates on walls may in fact guide our wait-patterns. As a wait-distraction, TVs are most common objects used by institutions; though when waiting in pediatrics, board games and toys for children are most popular. Slot machines in Las Vegas Airport have done a marvelous job of mesmerizing and baby-sitting travelers as they wait for flights. Hence the wait-environment often reflects a *fixed wait activity.*

Assessment is another activity accomplished through waiting. That is, persons assess and evaluate officials and control agents in various wait environments. It follows that one's assessment is far less formal than otherwise, yet the consequences are just as real. For example, parents transport children to swim lessons and watch; their watching is mixed with evaluation. If assessments are good, swim teachers could receive compliments from parents, an offer to conduct private swim lessons, additional referrals, recommendations, and gifts during Christmas. Conversely, poor assessments lead to complaints, request for instructor changes, and/or leaving the swim program. Clearly then an indirect or informal assessment has consequences for more formal appraisals. But assessment is what we *do* while waiting.

Watching and Listening is frequently done simultaneously, yet it is not necessary to watch in order to listen, humans can clearly listen without watching. There is no need for eye contact though in many Western cultures such eye gesturing is polite; it assumes one is attentive. More often than not, one is listening while watching, yet the extent to which one is hearing is debatable, in fact one may be daydreaming while making eye contact. The current chapter does not examine the reciprocity of watching and listening; it is more or less a one-way view, a single person analysis of an encounter. For example, in public wait-areas, such as banks, post offices, dental offices, and retail store lines, it is not unusual to see and hear conversation between client and institutional representative. Watching and listening is what we *do* while waiting and much of it (watching and listening) is paying attention to our environment so one does not miss his or her turn. But there are other objects that we see and hear while waiting, some of which include gossip, important institutional knowledge, and private information.

The Show customarily takes place in an auditorium-type setting; *shows* are characterized by entertainment and information, where audience members are either passive viewers or show participants. Within *courtroom shows,* main features and side shows are integrated. Main features sustain our attention but side shows distract us, it is like persons arriving late to theater performances. Waiting in courtrooms resembles watching a *show* or *courtroom theater* in that judges are main characters and defendants, lawyers, bailiffs, audience members, and others are supporting cast members. Court proceedings start only when judges arrive and their decisive power and status are recognized and respected by all. If the judge is late, court theater is delayed. If judges fail to show up, courts may receive replacement or court proceedings are postponed. The same is true with conventional theater. Consequently, audience members entertain themselves by watching the *courtroom show* and thus leave court when their case of interest is addressed. Recognizing court as a *show* is not new in that high-profile judges have left conventional courtrooms pursuing careers as TV Court Judges, and now their livelihood depends on ratings and thus their ability to entertain. And in many cases, conventional court has a similar entertainment feature.

"Most Willing to Wait For" is tied to the importance of an object, person, or occasion. Such waiting is less concerned with delays in banks, gas stations, or restaurant lines but more interested in family, career, and education. "Most willing to wait for" gets at a sense of values that holds significance to one's life, and one is therefore committed to that *object* of wait. This type of

waiting is more or less a choice and not an obligation, placing a hierarchy on wait-options. That is, some respondents place great emphasis on relationships in that they are willing to wait for the right person. While waiting, individuals continue to date, attempting to determine compatibility. Marriage and family are highly valued, thus rushing into marriage is unwise given the possible consequences. Respondents are also willing to wait on careers and education in that both require time to achieve, and while acquiring one's career and educational goals, each is worked at until accomplished. So ultimately, *wait utilization gets at doing*, how one passes time while waiting.

Waiting, reminiscing, and thinking explores our *thought patterns* while waiting. That is, while waiting for soccer practice to end, some parents listen to music leading to fond memories from certain songs. Without question, thinking is one key activity while waiting, pointing out significant distinctions among *critical, casual, and tactical thinking*. Thinking allows us to reminisce, review, analyze, and strategize. Thinking is an activity that few can avoid, in fact, our thinking frequently invades our sleep.

NOTES

1. Department of Motor Vehicles, DMV.

2. As of April 2010, U.S. Department of Transportation requires that "airlines must return planes to the gate & let passengers off any time a flight is sitting on the tarmac for three hours."

3. This is true of other parents who wait and watch their children learn new activities, such as gymnastics, skating, diving, track and field, baseball, ballet, piano, golf, and so forth.

4. This cell phone example was used in previous chapter, "Waiting Places," to illustrate *natural distractions*. This same example is currently used to demonstrate *side shows*.

5. Judge John Sanders is a retired judge, who worked at L.A. Superior Court, Family Court Division.

6. The analogy of *the show* maybe applied to other "stages" where attention-getting-behavior seizes our interest.

7. Regarding survey participants, 311 students participated in the open-ended questionnaire.

8. Here, philosophers may disagree.

Chapter 4

Waiting for Service

Life is not always microwavable, sometimes you must wait.

Waiting for service examines the process of waiting in line or elsewhere for an organization's service and/or goods. The typical picture illustrates standing in line for movie tickets or a morning cup of coffee. The primary focus is on the *nature of the wait*; that is, as customers wait, I concentrate on what they see, how they feel, what they experience, and how they define and interpret their observations and experiences. Further, *waiting for service* gets at a condition; for instance, under what conditions do customers wait? Do customers wait in rain, snow, humidity, or noonday heat? Do customers wait in waiting rooms, or the privacy and comfort of their vehicles and homes? Do customers wait in early morning, overnight, or even in shifts? The process and condition of waiting varies by organization and desired product. One is not likely to wait for play-off tickets in a hospital waiting room; just as one will not wait for surgery in financial institutions. Thus, while waiting for service is a common situation, our wait often reflects a desired product and specific venues.

ON CUSTOMER SERVICE

To what extent does organizational culture enhance the quality of customer service? Dunnett (2007) believes that organizational culture plays a crucial role in customer service and therefore customer satisfaction. For example, organizational culture emerges as employees within Kwame's Books develop a "pattern of shared values and beliefs that help individuals understand organizational functioning and thus provide them norms for behaviors in the organization" (Deshpande and Webster, 1989). Common experiences at Kwame's Books may lead employees to pervasive attitudes and sentiments about accepted behaviors and normative responses to specific situations (see Dunnett, 2007). Each organization may develop its own culture, and cultural interactions with customers have consequences for the overall operation of organizations. Yet, how such culture affects service is significant. Complimenting customers on attire and/or taste in books may become routine before service is rendered. It may also produce a mood that is conducive for service and therefore more sales.

Most organizations, even nonprofit ones like libraries, possess a marketing orientation toward obtaining business; and often, the focal point is customers. Deshpande and Webster (1989) suggest that a marketing philosophy is in fact an *organizational culture*, giving "the whole organization a particular value system that places the customer at the center of all activities" (Dunnett, 2007:42). Still, it requires work to develop this organizational culture, and since frontline employees maintain contact and interaction with customers, it is important that employees receive incentive and training. Certainly, incentive and training are formalized within organizational settings—still the employee's *heart* must connect with customers. Hence, the humanization of service (Gronfeldt and Strother, 2006) is strategic; it must be planned; and eventually, it must come naturally; so, as customers wait for service, they can sense and observe employee sincerity in customer service. Sincerity in service gets at one's ability to utilize an organizational culture and personal skill to enhance customer service.

Service is a concept that is fundamental to libraries, just as it is to hotels or hospitals, and library users are the center of library service. It is also clear that the library is a service-profession that must determine what customers want and use this information to create satisfying products and services (Miao, 2006). Customer service is more efficient when organizations know the needs of their customers. Clients use libraries for specific reasons just as individuals reserve hotels for specific reasons. Libraries are fulfilling specific needs, and customers arriving for service should not be taken for granted. Consider, for example, why should one return to your hotel or library? As they wait for service, do customers witness mistakes and poor professionalism by librarian or hotel staff? Does the library contain sufficient volumes of books, journals, and other materials? Does the library maintain adequate library technology and self-service for checkout? And does the library environment (lighting, study rooms, desks, computers, quietness, chairs, and sofas) invite individuals to stay and study (Miao, 2006)? All such issues get at the organization and its culture, and how such culture is conveyed to library users. *Waiting for service* then is improved, maintained, and even tolerated by the organizational environment.

Yet, service itself is difficult to standardize, for it is the *human factor* that leads to unpredictable actions and reactions. Customer service encounters at banks and department stores may appear routine but the process of each encounter varies by individual situations, relationships, attitudes, and duration. While customers are waiting, they observe and learn from ongoing encounters and often expect similar treatment given similar circumstances. The extent to which similar treatment occurs depends on the context of the situation, and even then, rarely are circumstances and treatment identical. Service to customers is more of an art (see Gronfeldt and Strother, 2006) in that it is difficult to reproduce identical encounters for every customer, and having unique personalities, employee interactions with customers is clearly diverse. But the art of service, that is the art of kindness, patience, and one's ability to read, understand, and interpret customer needs/wants is a skill that is not easily developed. It must be worked at; it is learned through experience; and finally, employee willingness to learn and provide *service as an art* is crucial to customer satisfaction.

So, while customers wait for service and interact with service providers, they actually become part of the organizational culture. One's frequency of patronizing certain establishments further submerges him/her into the organizational culture. It is clear that organizational culture emerges among employees; it is also evident that a certain culture develops among customers who patronize beauty salons, coffee shops, barbershops, and other businesses. In short, while two separate cultures are emerging, and clearly, one is more dominant than the other,[1] a culture also develops among service representatives and customers within a said establishment. For when regular customers undergo an extended absence, customers and employees alike inquire, "Where have you been?" Hence, the need to expand our analysis of organizational culture is significant; that is the inclusion of customers broadens our perspective and it heightens our awareness of customer influence.

Customer service becomes an integral part of an organization's delivery system and therefore a part of its culture. Customer service gets at customer satisfaction or dissatisfaction. Clients come to realize what they should expect from restaurants, and consequently, the perception of their experience is actualized by tip amounts. Thus, in the broadest sense, customer service is whatever enhances customer satisfaction (Davidow and Uttal, 1989:19). For Zeithaml and Bitner (2003), this definition appears somewhat elusive in that it fails to operationalize customer service. Zeithaml and Bitner (2003) sharpen our focus by distinguishing between services and customer service. Services include a wider range of industries such as plumbing, dry cleaning, auto repair, catering, health care, banking, and so forth. Similarly, customer service is typically provided by all industries, but it is the service provided in support of an organization's core product (Gronfeldt and Strother, 2006:25). Thus, customer service representatives are often found answering phones, providing direction, answering questions, addressing complaints, and adjusting bills. Customers then are usually not charged directly for customer service (Gronfeldt and Strother, 2006: 25), they are charged for the actual service.

My analysis of *waiting for service* includes service and customer service aspects of waiting. Waiting to be seated in restaurants, ordering food, waiting for food, and paying for meals get at the two ideas of service and customer service. If service is unsatisfactory, waiting to complain and/or posting a negative rating is another twist in the customer service cycle. Thus, whatever the case, one is waiting for service, whether assistance is free or charged.

This chapter focuses on waiting for service, that is, how we wait for service in *ordinary*, routine settings—and how we wait in *extended*, unusual situations. *Ordinary waiting* examines the routine process of waiting. It is a typical process investigating how individuals wait in line for service; an individual may sit in a hospital waiting room or stand in a grocery line or even wait at home for delivery. Waiting becomes ordinary because it is done frequently and even routinely. Habitually, it is taken for granted in that we expect to wait, and waiting is built into our daily activity as well as our consciousness. Such ordinary waiting often becomes normative in that there is a structure to waiting, for example, rails & ropes and number counters, and overtime, waiting principles evolve, for example, "first come, first serve," "please wait behind the line." So many who wait routinely develop expectations and anticipations of what should occur during the wait process. The more we wait, the more we are conditioned to wait, developing an internal clock regarding satisfactory wait-duration. Wait-duration varies by institution and situation. For instance, we are likely to possess longer internal clocks at post offices and car repair shops than grocery and bank lines. It follows that each wait-occurrence normalizes our wait-experience and expectation.

Conversely, *extended waiting* is linked to an unusual and sometimes unanticipated wait processes. As a precondition, extended waiting occurs infrequently and wait-duration is typically several hours; moreover, it is not uncommon for additional delays to occur. Typically, waiting norms are honored, but given unusual and unanticipated circumstances, waiting norms could be aborted; sacrificing wait norms and emergence of new rules is probable. Moreover, anxiety is heightened as a consequence of wait-durations and infrequency of extended waits. For as wait-duration ends, the excitement and anticipation of receiving a product is magnified. Additionally, the anxiety of not receiving service is also relevant, that is, waiting hours and not receiving service or product could draw out the worst. Extended waits often require more preparation, which may involve physical and/or mental grooming. For example, if one is waiting for the latest Harry Potter book, one is likely to begin waiting several hours before stores open (Lawless, 2007). Individuals are also likely to wear appropriate clothing and bring appropriate equipment, like chairs, air mattresses, tents, food, and drink. In short, extended waits may require planning by individuals, and extended waits that are unanticipated often expend more mental anguish.

Waiting for service is an area of study that has received little attention; examining this process releases another page in the sociology of waiting. Its significance lies in our direct learning from customers; we place ourselves in the position of clients and we examine what they observe and how they interpret their observations. The significance of waiting for services further unveils diverse situations of wait, disclosing concrete dialogue among customers, emotions, and revealing innovative strategies and shortcuts on how to wait. Such an analysis assists organizations in their service delivery systems; firms are now brought into the real world of customers. Moreover, we learn how customers themselves assist with customer service—that is, showing fellow customers where to locate store items, sharing information about products and assisting seniors with heavy packages. In such situations, we learn how waiting-for-service has active and passive components (active waits may appear shorter, while passive waits seem longer). Finally, when waiting for service is experienced collectively, persons recognize that "we are in this together" and making the best of our wait experience—becomes a common aim.

WAITING FOR SERVICE: ORDINARY WAITING

Waiting to deposit a check; waiting for car repair; waiting for medical attention; waiting for maid service; waiting for towing; waiting to order fast food; waiting to speak with an operator; and waiting for customer assistance at Nordstrom's are all such examples of *waiting for ordinary service*. Waiting for service is a daily and necessary occurrence; it has become routine and wait-expectations by customers are predictable. That is, waiting is necessary because simultaneous service to all is impossible and such waiting reflects a type of civil-order within society. Moreover, those customers who anticipate waiting often occupy themselves by reading, watching TV, texting, conversing, etc. But *what happens* while we wait for service? What *emotions* are experienced? How do customers respond? How is *customer service managed*? How do *problems* develop? And do employees know problems exist? In short, how do we make sense of *waiting for service*?

Typically, while standing and waiting, customers search for open and available clerks. When a window opens, the clerk announces, "Can I help

the next person in line!?" The wait has ended and the "next person" proceeds forward as service begins. This procedure occurs throughout the day
to customers waiting in service-oriented organizations. If customers appear
at service window with incomplete forms, clerks may request that customers
"step aside" and return directly to window after completing paperwork. This
prevents another cycle of waiting and allows line fluency. Such a system is
common at banks, post offices, hotels, hospitals, DMVs, and other service
institutions. Those waiting are aware that "Ms. Partial" is completing forms
and acknowledge it by an uninhibited return to service.

In one case, a customer began sneezing while being serviced; she left
the window for about two minutes and then returned. The clerk continued
attending her business, thus did not call for "next customer," recognizing
that "sneezing customer" would come back. Given the line's length, some
customers felt that clerk could have serviced another customer. One customer
actually breathed a loud sigh as the window remained vacant. Still, no one
approached the "open" window for a signal was not gestured, and those waiting recognized that the clerk and "sneezing customer" had not completed
their transaction. The "sneezing customer" was allowed time to step away
and attend to her condition, not to mention various germs she might have
spread. Seemingly, customers understand that there is structure to waiting and
at times, episodes occur while waiting for service. Since a call was not made,
no one approached the window—in short, our *conditioning* revealed that we
are not likely to move forward until called (see Milgram, 1963; Aronson,
2004).

Imagine a customer approaching the window who had not been called. The
clerk may say, "I'm sorry ma'am, I did not call you, please go back to the
line," or "I'm sorry sir, I have not completed my transaction with sneezing-
customer, you'll have to wait." In this instance, such a "mistake," intentional
or otherwise, is cause for embarrassment (see Goffman, 1963). And given that
most chose to avoid embarrassing situations, we are not likely to approach
window but wonder why the clerk is without a customer. Seemingly, most are
willing to wait additional time to avoid uncomfortable situations.

While waiting, customers observe others standing in line and processing
transactions; one is waiting his or her turn for service. Customers know who
is in front and behind them; anyone who arrives without waiting is visually
scrutinized, and most are aware that newly arriving customer did not wait.
Customers search for signs as to how "cutter" is linked to someone waiting,
for example, family member, friend, etc.? Did someone hold his place in line,
or did he abort the process? The circumstances of how individuals are linked
are revealed during interaction. Aborting wait-process suggests that one has
violated the "first come, first service" norm, and such violations are more difficult to ignore when lines are long. In one case, a line of ten customers waited

patiently as customer service appeared slow because of few bank tellers. One individual, James, invited his arriving friend to stand with him in line; this disturbed certain customers in that they had been impatiently waiting, yet James did not acknowledge those behind him. Here is a person who comes in the bank, notices a friend, and begins waiting near the front with James. The two talked and when it was James' turn, James and friend went to bank teller together; the teller handled each transaction separately. While no one verbally confronted them, the stares and glares were apparent by two women frowning at them as they conducted business and left. The extent to which tellers were aware of customer-cutting is unclear; tellers appear too busy; and it is difficult to monitor and service transactions. Hence after completing a transaction, tellers automatically announce, "May I help you?" while occasionally looking up.

Given our wait-socialization, certain emotions emerge when there is a lack of waiting, for example, norm violations. Line-cutters spark negative emotions for they have aborted the wait process. Though bank tellers are unaware of "cutters," do firms remain responsible? Or do firms depend on customers to maintain informal wait-norms? Seemingly these questions are determined by customers as they wait for service and a firm's willingness to *learn* from their customers. Brady and Cronin (2001) contend that the "firm that hopes to excel in the 21st century must become a *learning organization*." They must develop ways of responding to needs and concerns of customers, for example, a customer-oriented service culture.

Conversely, customers are happy and somewhat surprised when there is no line at ticket counter, and persons are not required to wait. In short, when individuals go to the bank, the market, post office, car wash, barbershops, salon, and airport, they expect to wait. Persons even arrive early to allow *wait-time*. It is a pleasant surprise when one expects to wait, but does not. Consequently, our waiting for service is frequently tied to cognitive and emotional experiences.

Other emotions are also evident when one assumes a short wait-time, though it is longer than expected. Frustration emerges; and by all accounts, one does not expect to wait long when you are the only person in line or there is one person ahead of you. Employees usually cite technical problems and beg your forgiveness. At times, however, there is reciprocity in emotions. For instance, conscientious service representatives may become anxious when customers wait too long. Janet, bank teller, was observed rushing to complete a task. As she works, she comments apologetically to delayed customers, "I'm coming, sorry to keep you waiting." Why is she anxious? In part, Janet is considerate of customer time, and viewing the faces of customers suggests a variety of messages. If avoidable, Janet, managers, and possibly other customer service representatives do not want customers to experience long waits, recognizing that they may patronize other establishments if customer service is insensitive. Seemingly though, customers recognized Janet's service sincerity and desire service from her. While other bank tellers are not as concerned, Janet's representation of the organization is likely to keep customers from searching for other banks. Further, Janet's behavior reflects Mead's (1934) classic analysis of "taking the role of the other." She places herself in the role of customers; she feels and responds to their sensitivities. In short, customer service behavior-CSB (Rogelberg et al., 1999) may influence emotional components and wait perspectives among customers.[2]

Waiting-for-service could prove problematic when formally defined wait-structures do not exist. For example, there is no defined line or number counter to clearly identify next person. So, who is next? And who keeps track? Do customers keep track or employees or both? Rather than inquiring, "who's next?" as was done throughout the congested morning, a senior Winchell's employee, Guadalupe, began servicing Jack who was *not* next. Jamal objected by exclaiming, "No! It's not his turn, it's mine!" Guadalupe and Jamal made eye contact, though Guadalupe continued servicing Jack. Jamal stormed out in anger and disgust. Clearly, Jack and/or Guadalupe could have halted their transaction, by recognizing and correcting their mistake. It follows that neither acknowledged the error, continuing their "service encounter" (Shostack, 1985). Though he objected, Jamal remains *invisible* and is pained by the encounter. He leaves as a way to protest and recognizes that other institutions may acknowledge Jamal's presence. The significance of structure cannot be overstated; wait-structure is designed to answer questions without being asked, thereby preventing conflict, confusion, and racism.[3]

By storming out, Jamal is clearly displaying dissatisfaction with customer service behavior. Among other reasons, customer dissatisfaction results from insensitive and conflictual encounters between employees and customers. The customer assumes certain responses that are inconsistent with product delivery; while avenues are available for bailout, employees refuse the bait. Rogelberg (1999) maintains that employees are significant to success at the "moments of truth." They are valuable links that retain or release customers; they are conduits that make customers happy or sad. This "moment of truth" is a customer's breaking point; it heightens or reduces emotions. It is what customers see while "waiting for service." Consequently, the *human factor* remains crucial in that "employees differ in the extent and frequency with which they correctly identify and fulfill customer needs in a timely, ethical and courteous way" (Rogelberg et al., 1999:422).

There was no sense of satisfaction by Jamal, no connection between Jamal and employee; in fact, Jamal was violated. How then is customer satisfaction produced? According to Liljander and Strandvik (1995), customers must develop positive emotional responses toward individual contact employees, and thus the relationship between employee and organization is stronger. But how are "positive emotional responses" developed? And how might customers develop stronger relationships among employees and their organization? *Fairness! Attentiveness! & Politeness!* Customers are interested in even-handed and courteous treatment by institutional representatives. Mistakes are probable—though acknowledging errors could smooth "moments of truth" that are observed by all. Hence, poor "service encounters" (Shostack, 1985) may lead to customer dissatisfaction, decreasing customer's desire to return, poor ratings, and increasing customer likelihood of complaining. Jamal experienced poor customer service, expressing a type of "consumption emotion"[4] (Westbrook and Oliver, 1991) that exhibited anger and disgust; such a reaction then is consistent with various studies (Schweitzer and Gibson, 2008; Allred, 1999) that examine the consequences of fairness-violations in service interactions.

Waiting for service is further problematic "when you can't find anyone to help you or check you out." Seemingly, service representatives are hiding and one could leave with unpaid items. When representatives are located, they are often found servicing other customers, thus prolonging one's wait for service. Such a situation caused one respondent to become very frustrated, exclaiming, "I'd rather pay the extra dollar so I don't have to wait." Expecting to find customer service representatives is reasonable; but ideally, customers assume that employees will locate and inquire of them. As in the case of Jamal, it is quite probable that certain situations lead individuals to change their shopping patterns in order to obtain better service.

Our conditioning, which is part of our socialization, is evident throughout our interactions. We are conditioned to wait our turn, and then proceed when called, and expecting others to work by the same general principle is not unreasonable. When norms are aborted, overlooked, or violated, emotional responses may ensue; one's sense of self is diminished. The *conditioning* of waiting is real—as are emotions resulting from wait-infractions. On one level or another, the emotion affects all involved and sends messages, containing values judgments, to all observers.

How customer service representatives handle incidents reflects the overall nature of the institution and what they are attempting to accomplish. Is this truly a customer-oriented firm? A customer-oriented culture? For example, service employees may experience close supervision at banks and post offices, and such climates may require exams, degrees, certificates, and training as a condition of employment; promotions and demotions are often tied to customer evaluations. Customer sensitivity then is valued by certain institutions, for they are attempting to portray a positive public image. Conversely, institutions that engage in quasi-screening, lack specific employment requirements, and loosely supervise employees have more difficulty with "customer service behavior" (Rogelberg et al., 1999) by employees. Employee commitment and loyalty is questionable and turnover rates are high. Such work is often unskilled and low paying. Therefore, sensitivity to customer waiting is weak, and seemingly, employees are more interested in themselves than customers. The latter case may in fact lead to more problems with customers and employees. Examples of such institutions may include Winchell's, Walmart, Target, K-Mart, Big Lots, Walgreen, Duane Reader, and other similar institutions.

Waiting for Service: Restaurants

Waiting for service is unpredictable and may take on an interesting twist when waiting-for-service at restaurants. Discovering that one can dine at the bar or bar tables may modify one's presumed wait plan. In short, it provides customers with *wait-options*, as to whether one waits for conventional seating or a more immediate and less personal space, for example, the bar area. Regarding conventional seating, some restaurants may offer free coffee and cake to distract waiting, other restaurants provide reading materials; purchasing drinks is another way to pass time, and even people watching could prove intriguing while waiting for service. In some cases, there is no waiting. How do we make sense of waiting-for-service in restaurants? It is clear that restaurants wish to get us in and out quickly, while at the same time, restaurants desire that persons enjoy their experience while not feeling rushed. Comfort in dining is a general goal of most restaurants, yet before dining there is likely a *wait*, which is filled with various distractions.

Generally, restaurant customers enter eating establishments, inquire about wait-time, and place their name on wait-list. Such encounters provide customers with a sense of time and atmosphere. Meanwhile, customers locate and move toward wait-regions so they might begin waiting-for-service. Wait-areas may provide comfortable seating in and out of restaurants. When seats are filled however, standing is the final option. Our waiting appears longer when standing and customers often become restless. In order to dissuade customers from leaving and recognizing that wait-comfort is not guaranteed, Mimis' Restaurant offers *free* coffee, punch, and sweet cake to make one's wait more comfortable and bearable. Offering customers coffee, punch, and sweet cake connotes a feeling of receiving "something for nothing," something at the expense of restaurant. More importantly, customers sense that this restaurant has carefully considered customer waiting. This sentiment makes waiting more tolerable and one is likely to wait longer without noticing.[5] These snacks may take one's mind off waiting and presumably hunger pangs are reduced. After twenty minutes, the customer is called, and if customer does not respond, hostesses will announce several times before cancellation.

Conversely, the bar area is clearly an option when food/coffee distraction is not successful. At one popular Pasadena restaurant, the hostess conveyed, "There is a 50-minute wait before we can seat you." It was crowded and customers stood wherever there was space, for example, near the bar, near checkout and even outside. Standing near the bar, one employee informed, "You can eat at the bar tables if you want. They (pointing towards a group about to leave) are near finished and you can take their table." Unfortunately, a group of five had been waiting; they were standing near the bar table awaiting the group's departure so they could slide in.

During crowded occasions and when waiting for a bar chair or bar table, aggressive behavior proves beneficial. Customers tend to stand in the bar area viewing and searching for seated customers who will soon depart. Such departure becomes evident when seated customers are preparing to pay bill and/or preparing to move to dining area. The waitress arrives, informs them of their house table, "Your table is ready," and assists by taking their drinks and appetizers to their new location. Observing this behavior, waiting-customers are likely to move closer and claim seats when "seated bar-table party" has left. At times, waiting customers may ask seated bar-table customer, "Are you about to leave?" They might respond, "Yes, in a few minutes." The waiting-customers remain near the table so that they might immediately lay claim after "seated bar-table customers" depart and before table is cleaned; additionally, such behavior indicates to others that they will occupy table. In other cases, there is no dialogue, customers simply move toward the soon-to-be-vacant table, as a way to inform others that they will occupy table next. All the while, such customers are talking, drinking, watching TV (usually ESPN), people-watching, and searching for table vacancies.

As Peter and Mary were about to leave, two females approached them asking, "Are you about to leave?" "Yes, after we get change." These women drifted near the bar allowing Peter and Mary a measure of privacy. Meanwhile, a male/female couple inquired about their table, "Are you almost finished?" Peter, "Yes, but those two ladies already asked about our table." The male/female couple politely said, "O.K. thanks," and honored Peter's response by looking for another vacancy at the bar and/or bar tables. Peter's response suggests that he became an unofficial hostess or control agent. Peter and Mary were not required to convey that someone had already approached. But it was the right thing to do. Not only the couple's compliance indicates conformity and consideration, but also they are adhering to an unwritten cultural rule of "first come, first serve," as is the case with official restaurant seating. After receiving change, the women approached Peter and Mary saying, "thank you." In part such a response indicates that Peter and Mary maintained credibility.

Waiting for service may require aggression and assertion; customers cannot solely depend on customer service representatives, who are very busy during crowded periods. Talking and negotiating with hostesses, waiters, and even customers may prove beneficial. One could save time by observing, inquiring, and learning acceptable norms of certain restaurants. Certainly, there is reciprocity in waiting for restaurant service; just as there is reciprocity in most business establishments. Customers are concerned about wait time, and institutions wish to facilitate one's wait by shortening customer waits and/or distracting customer-waits by offering comfortable seating, TV viewing, and free snacks. Still, such assertive behavior is usually played out in crowded restaurants.

Waiting for *self-service* has become a viable option in other type restaurants and businesses. Typically, customers are required to serve themselves, and at times, there is a short or medium wait before seating. At Hometown Buffet, customers wait in line to pay, locate seating, and then serve themselves. At Souplantation,[6] patrons dish their salad, pay the clerk, and search for seating. Though the process is different, the main idea of *self-service* is clear and buffets provide an excellent example. In part, the buffet is designed to nearly eliminate waiting for food. Still, there is some waiting, especially when popular food items are consumed, as chefs prepare additional servings. Customers who dine at buffets are not interested in *free* food enticements, captivating ESPN viewing, or aggressively seeking bar tables; this group is interested in minimal waits and servicing themselves. Their dining gratification is more immediate and less controlled. Sociologically, one can make more independent choices, and eat as much or as little as desired. Generally, *self-service* has emerged in our society to forgo waiting-for-service; individuals determine the type and quality of service; while employees are reduced to facilitators, they remove dirty dishes, bring clean ones, and assist with checkout.[7]

WAITING FOR SERVICE: EXTENDED WAITS

I found out that what you're waiting for—makes the difference.

Under what conditions do *extended waits* take place? Conditions may range from predictable to unpredictable situations. For instance, arriving at JFK, waiting to check-in, and finally reaching the counter, one discovers that his flight is delayed. "Jet Blue" representatives anticipate a three-hour delay, so customers pass time in restaurants, bars, lounges, and sleeping near the boarding area. After three hours, customers return to board—yet they are told of engine deficiencies, causing further delays. Customer service representatives apologize and inform customers that within two hours engine should be fixed and boarding will begin. In the meantime, several customers become agitated and begin complaining; thus, prompting Jet Blue to offer complimentary food and alcohol vouchers to all clients during flight. Seemingly, the offer of food and alcohol will reduce complaints, and thus giving customers something to look forward to. More predictably, when the final installment of Harry Potter, *Harry Potter and the Deadly Hallows,* was released, several bookstores reported that customers waited hours for stores to open. Baptista and Rajamanickam (2007) noted that "fans young and old started queuing in Harry Potter outfits and even in their pajamas." The event sparked excitement and maintained a festive type atmosphere. And the anticipation of receiving, reading, and completing *Deadly Hallows* set off a desire to wait for service and secure *Deadly Hallows* rather than risk a short-fall of books by local bookstores.

Extended waiting gets at delays that are prolonged, in that clients tend to wait hours for service. Moreover, waits may be unusual and unanticipated, as in Jet Blue and therefore produce emotional frustrations. At times, *extended waits* are predictable and often festive; one is waiting for an anticipated item or event; thus, preparation is often a consequence of predictive and festive events. In part, it is extended because such events are rare, often drawing media coverage, and yet recognizing that at times *extended* events are cyclical as with the Rose Parade and Black Friday. In order to make better sense of *extended waiting*, it is useful to examine several cases so that waiting-for-service is not only magnified but clarified. Berger (2007:6) argues that "things are not what they seem." Waiting for service within *extended* situations certainly falls in this category. As such, this analysis is intended to "peel away the layers" so that extended waiting is clearly examined and revealed. Three significant cases will occupy our analysis, for example, *iPhone waiting, Black Friday waiting, and Lunch Counter waiting.*

iPhone Waiting

Like the iPad, the arrival of iPhone caught the attention of national and local news. Both media outlets posted stories on their newscasts and websites. In the case of one local news station, ABC, they posted a story on waiting in line for iPhones. Among other angles, ABC (L.A. local news, Channel 7, June 26, 2007) news interviewed a person who was waiting in line, not to buy a phone but to sell his spot for $200. This gets at the innovative ways waiting is used, namely as a commodity. How long does one wait to earn $200? And who is willing to pay? Are such waits worth it? The real question is what are you willing to wait for? Rose parade, car sale, escrow to close, movie tickets, PS3, bus to arrive, someone to buy your space, or the latest Apple technology? After announcing the available date and sale of the long awaited iPhone, crowds of iPhone enthusiasts waited in line many hours for the privilege of owning this new technology. The scene was repeated and experienced nationwide at Apple stores; many wanted first dibs at owning this phone. By 9:00 a.m., more than eighty persons waited outside Pasadena Apple store; the line was positioned along the sidewalk curb so that passers-by could proceed without blockage. Walking and shopping along the path, many gazed with interest, inquiring of the iPhone crowd, and questioning whether they, themselves would wait in such a line. Their wait would conclude at 6:00 p.m. when iPhone sales began.

Today is Friday, yet the first person in line has waited since Tuesday. Many cite possessing advanced technology as their reason for waiting. Others have not waited as long, for example, a family of four, mother and three sons, have waited since 7:00 a.m. Near the end of the line, this family sat in portable chairs, snacking, and people-watching as they queued. Jim, nineteen-year-old college student, was most expressive, mentioning his primary reason for waiting was status; he concluded by waiting and obtaining an iPhone, his social "status among women would move up several notches." He also declared that "I am not bothered by the wait," rationalizing that "everyone has something they are willing to wait for."

Another respondent, Fred, twenty-six-year-old business associate, revealed that he was waiting on behalf of his brother in Iraq. Fred's brother, who is twenty-one-years-old, has been deployed for twelve months, and is scheduled to return in July 2007. He was fulfilling his brother's request, believing that *waiting for service* is "a small price to pay," a small sacrifice, given his brother's military service. Bringing food and books to keep him occupied, Fred arrived Thursday at 5:00 p.m. and is currently seventh in line. While customers were limited to buying two phones, Fred was further driven by technology, commenting that "this is real sophisticated technology and I don't know if we'll see this again. I want to be able to say that I have, that I possess this new form of technology and I was one of the first to buy it."

It follows then that there is a type of community that develops among persons who spend *extended* time waiting-for-service. It starts by strangers familiarizing themselves with immediate others. This may take the form of facial recognitions, property ownership, space allocations, and finally conversation. It may further actualize itself in voice recognition, body movements, and body art. *Theoretically, the longer strangers wait in close proximity, the development of community is probable.* Community goes beyond facial and property identification; community is also realized when values and norms are honored and maintained. When by-passers arbitrarily converse with certain "iPhone waiters," other community members often watch their interactions, and when possible, listen to their conversions. Their curiosity has everything to do with the status of by-passers. Are they somehow connected? Will they join the community? Or is this simply an inquisitive spectator? In Fred's case, he came with a friend, Hector, who was working but would return at noon. Hector's chair contained folded covers and pillows. Next to Hector's chair sat community members John (age nineteen) and Raymond (age twenty), who sat working on his laptop computer. Fred and I conversed about someone cutting in line, and such a topic drew the attention of John and Raymond. John chimed in recounting, "This guy said he would pay me if I let him cut in front of me. I said no way! All of these people would get so mad at me!"

Raymond warned, "no-way man, you'd just be asking for trouble."

It follows that extended waiting draws immediate others into conversations and such communication could lead to familiarity. For instance, John mentioned that "I've been talking to this guy, Fred, all night," and was proud to have learned all names of his immediate community. Moreover, Fred acknowledged that "when I need a bathroom break or to go buy food, these guys will watch my stuff for me. We'll watch each other's stuff."

For Fred, the community may extend beyond the *apple store, iPhone wait,* in that he was networking. "I have my own business, so I've passed out my card."[8]

In November 2006, a similar scene was played out with Sony's PS3. That is, the anticipation of Sony's latest video games, advanced technology, and bragging rights led "gamers" to wait overnight in front of Pasadena's Best Buy (see Solis, 2007). Unlike Colorado Boulevard, where the Apple Store is located, tents were permitted, offering more comfort and overnight privacy. Still, community was evident as gamers conversed, "surveilled," and ate during day and evening hours. Those conversing late into the night were also attentive to their surrounding community and possible encroachments on their village. Such a community however is temporary; they are not meant to be permanent. That is, while norms and values are inserted from the larger society, such communities disband when doors open. Tents and chairs are folded; food and garments are stored. And while "community members" may greet one another in the store, they are not likely to meet and greet again. *Waiting for service* is the focal point of this short-lived community.

Black Friday

For some, Black Friday has become routine or more like a ritual. Historically, getting up on Friday after Thanksgiving is part of the weekend holiday. If stores open at 6:00 a.m., many shoppers are willing to arrive by 4:00 a.m.

and earlier. More recently, Black Friday begins on Thanksgiving Day. The overnight is less necessary, yet arriving early is crucial. Given the crowds, confusion, and aggressive rudeness, many shoppers have abandoned Black Friday all-together, opting to shop online. The purpose of Black Friday is to take advantage of sales and merchandise that is often limited and provisional. It signifies the beginning of the Christmas shopping season and the possibility of obtaining merchandise at bargain prices. It is a yearly occurrence throughout the United States, and by planning one's purchases, it is an occurrence that many await and look forward to. Waiting an average of two hours does not permit a community-type development, as witnessed at Apple and Best Buy, yet some of the same principles of watching immediate others, preventing cuts and small talk with strangers are clearly apparent. The Black Friday customer is generally armed with store advertisements, warm clothing, and hot coffee.

A numbness hovered the crowd as customers waited in line; the feeling one experiences when first waking—a drowsiness, that is, a feeling of incomplete consciousness. No one appeared excited, just waiting, waiting for Target to open. While waiting, customers observed others; they talked and watched two young girls play tag. The assembly's attention was drawn to their game of tag, for they seem ill-affected by the morning chill; they were alert. As time passed and the line stretched around the corner, our attention was shifted to Target employees who brought out several store carts filled with red "goodie bags." Outfitted in "target red," customer service representatives strolled carts to the front of the store, where they remain for twenty minutes. In anticipation, customers wondered whether Target would give "goodie bags" to waiting customers and whether there were enough bags for all. In fact, all customers received a "goodie bag." Receiving a "goodie bag" made the wait seem shorter and worthwhile, as the mood of the crowd changed. They now appeared perked up and joyous. Receiving a free and unexpected gift often puts waiters in a cheerful and jolly mood. Customers were smiling more, laughing and talking aloud as they examined the bag's contents. A crowd-chatter emerged that was not there before. One employee mentioned that "giving away 'goodie bags' was Target's way of thanking its customers." She mentioned that it was a "worthwhile promotion" in which Target gave away 500 bags.[9]

Target employees, along with Target security, managed and controlled the line. When lines curved incorrectly or when customers lined up in wrong spots, employees guided customers to proper places. Employees even took time to announce to customers that certain "ad" items were not available and instructed customers on where to find specific store merchandise, that is, "the TVs are up the escalator—to the left; and the microwaves are on the main floor to your right." Generally, one received a feeling of respect, concern, and care for customers. The "goodie bags" clearly influenced crowd mood and behavior, and such crowd respect, resulting goodwill in the customers' minds—was transferred to employees as they informed and instructed customers. While there were no police patrolling, K-Mart retained police to deter any possible line or waiting infractions. One patrol car was clearly visible near the K-Mart entrance door, and various policemen walked and talked to those near the front of the line. However, unlike "Target," there was no "goodie bag" distribution. Needless to say, police presence deterred possible infractions, yet customer service suffered given the impersonal nature of employee-customer interactions.

When doors open, customers *rush-run* through the entrance door sprinting to their area of choice. If controls are absent, stampedes could occur as in the Long Island Wal-Mart (see Gould et al., 2008) and *Brandsmart* in Coconut Creek, Florida (see Kovacs, 2005).[10] Electronics and appliances appear most popular. Many customers dash to electronics, and once there, another line forms. Target and K-Mart permitted all customers to flow in responsibly, often instructing, "Be careful, there's enough for everyone." Initially, employees of San Diego's KB Toy Store allowed fifty persons entrance, and twenty additional customers awaited entry. KB is relatively small, so employees monitored the line, giving customers shopping bags and ad papers. On Black Friday, customer entrance varies by store size, crowd size, product advertisement, and crowd demeanor. As *everyday-people* plan for Black Friday, the anxiety of *waiting for service* and making certain that specific items are obtained explain the *rush-run* behavior of Black Friday crowds. And while caution is urged, the strategy, the wait, and the outcome result in a worthwhile experience, for they have saved money by acquiring items at bargain prices.

Lunch Counter Waiting

Lunch counter desegregation, voter registration, bus integration, and doctor office visits proved challenging and certainly dangerous during the heart of civil rights movement. Customer service in "five and dime stores" and various department stores were almost nonexistent for African Americans. Going to and through the back door was custom. As in contemporary times, Blacks endured gazes, stares, and suspicions of white employees and security officers. Treatment was hostile and rude; cutting in line by whites was common and "first come, first serve" norms rarely applied when servicing African Americans. Southern Blacks could not try on garments or return damaged merchandise. This "separate but equal" system ranked African Americans as second-class citizens and whites as privileged Americans.

Other Americans (Asians, Latinos, Puerto Ricans) were encouraged to model and emulate white Americans, for this was the standard. And while attempts were made to emulate whites, it was difficult to "get it right." It was difficult to look, dress, and walk like whites; it was even more difficult to talk, dance, and sing like whites. Some even tried to pass as white, for it was thought that if "others" simply became white the race problem would disappear.

Recognizing that Blacks could never become white, and vice versa, and realizing that difference was an asset and not a liability, many decided to protest for equality and fairness. Through workshops, participants of Student Nonviolent Coordinating Committee (SNCC), Congress of Racial Equality (CORE), Southern Christian Leadership Conference (SCLC), and other civil rights groups were trained in nonviolent direction action strategies. Students' enacted hostile situations were given advice on how to handle demeaning remarks, physical violence, and intimidation; generally, Blacks were trained in patience and civil disobedience (see Aldon Morris, 1984). In short, "orderly" protests were designed to be "ideal." Dr. Jacquelyn Jacobs, who participated in the Montgomery Bus Boycott and various other demonstrations, recalled several incidents of waiting-for-service. "When we decided to exercise our right to service at food establishments and lunch counters, we waited in line to be served. It was *really scary*. I remember a lot of scary situations because while we were waiting, we waited in an open area, and waited in the same lines with whites. Lots of them taunted us, and questioned our being in line. They shouted, 'What are you niggers doing in line.' In some instances, whites just came and got in line in front of us. We were told not to push, but if somebody just forced themselves, not to get violent but just stand; and keep moving as best we could—because there was some friction there, It was lots of friction! Even after we got the food, I remember sometimes we would be so *nervous*. I had a friend who ordered a club sandwich, and these sandwiches would be real tall with let-tuce, tomatoes, bacon, and stuff. I remember sometimes that the contents of the sandwich would just begin to fall out because—after you got to the lunch counter, from all you went through to get there, you really couldn't eat, but we did it anyway."

While Dr. Jacobs recognizes that friction is probable, protests are rarely orderly or "timely." They do not fit neatly into our schedules and calendars. King was often admonished to wait and change would evolve; wait because the time is not right; wait and problems would solve themselves; wait and life will get better. In Birmingham 1963, King was accused of being in to much of a religious hurry and that the timing of such demonstrations was ill-advised and "unwise" (King, 1963). Critics rationalized that perhaps the timing of the Birmingham campaign could be reconsidered. King's response was swift and direct. "For years now, I have heard the word *'Wait!'* It rings in the ear of every Negro with a piercing familiarity. This 'Wait' has almost always meant 'Never.' We have waited for more than 340 years for our constitutional and God-given rights. The nations of Asia and Africa are moving with jet-like speed towards the goal of political independence, and we still creep at horse and buggy pace towards the gaining of a cup of coffee at a lunch counter" (King, 1963:81). In short, waiting for service has limits in that time and waiting is often connected; one is expecting some type of service and the absence of that service brings about actions. Additionally, when the amount of wait-time is unknown or knowingly compromised and abused, waiting could lead to outbursts and other emotional frustrations.

For example, Dr. Jacobs recalls another instance of *extended waiting* while visiting the doctor's office. That is, doctor visits and exams could prove torturing and problematic though "healing was our primary purpose." Many shared similar experiences, and thus visited doctors only when absolutely necessary. "Doctors' offices were segregated and we experienced a lot of anger, frustration, and hurt; you see, we only had white doctors in some of the little towns; the town I lived in. You could go to the office, and they would have a little partition between where the whites could sit and African Americans. Still, we could see each other, 'cause they didn't have separate waiting rooms per se." Jacobs continues:

> Doctor's office was another time we waited. It was very tense because we would be looking at the whites and they would be looking at us. They wouldn't give us appointments and even if you had an appointment, whites could come-in without an appointment and doctors and nurses would service all of the whites before African Americans. So, you could get to the doctor's office at 7 O'clock in the morning and may not leave until 5 or 6 pm. Sit there all day in misery and whites could come in and out. The doctors would go to lunch and everything, and you just had to wait if you needed to see them. So, we experienced a lot of anger and frustration and hurt feelings; you understood that you really didn't matter. And when you finally saw the doctor, you were so upset until your pressure and others things would be all out of whack because the frustrations you suffered.

While this *extended wait* was time consuming, it sparked a movement to create and solidly consider fairness. Whether at doctor's offices or lunch counters inequalities and alienations frequently lead to grievances followed by social movements; and such demonstrations are not only for service but also for normative service. That is, "first come, first serve" must apply to all. In part, extended waits magnify and exemplify injustice and ideologies within one's social structure.

SUMMARY

Extended waiting takes on an interesting twist in that it involves situations where customers experience lengthy waits; and such "waits" range from joyous, surprising, communal to frustrating. But the wait is atypical, it's different in that it may not occur daily and usually draws media attention. Additionally, extended waits are memorable experiences in that the process of *waiting for service* often exposes individuals to unforgettable and unusual events and encounters. It is difficult to forget a communal occasion, or receiving an unexpected gift, or the taunting of segregationists, or always being last and second-class. Given our biological makeup, it is unclear whether persons could manage back-to-back instances of extended (or extraordinary) waiting. For many, whether joy or pain, such back-to-back waits may prove unbearable, and for these reasons, they are viewed as extended and many times, extraordinary.

Ordinary waits provide an everyday picture of how waiting-for-service is experienced. It is a situation that occurs routinely and such an experience is not limited to class, race, age, geographical region, or gender. Everyone waits—it is connected to a universal culture. Unlike extraordinary waits, "ordinary waiters" are less likely to pay someone to stand in line and such waits usually involve less time. The frequency of ordinary waits allows "waiters" to anticipate wait-durations and service encounters. To some extent, waiting becomes internalized; individuals become conditioned to wait, developing internal clocks as to appropriate wait-times. Waiting for service suggests that persons become anxious and fidgety when expected wait-duration expires. So, waiting for service is valuable in that individuals' take-in their surroundings, and often, experience a range of emotions.

The crucial question is under what conditions might ordinary waits become extended waits? When one expects to depart in twenty minutes, yet the airplane remains on the tarmac for hours? When unexpected blizzards cause sudden delays for airports, trains, and cars in strange cities? When children of divorced parents expect a *circus outing* then falls asleep while gazing out the window, awaiting a father who never arrives? When mothers, wives, and children are promised a return date, yet one's military tour is lengthened? Such examples illustrate how ordinary may become extended waits and how such delays possess unforeseen consequences. The same is not true of extended waits, that is, extraordinary waits are not likely to become ordinary waits. Extended situations are typically experienced occasionally and endure considerable time. Black Friday occurs once-a-year, and it is difficult to anticipate the next electronic craze. Yet, our attention is drawn to extended waits, for there is something different, something unique, something out-of-the-ordinary that makes persons focus on unusual events.

Customer service is an interesting feature of waiting-for-service. Here's where "waiters" observe and sometimes participate in employee/customer transactions. An organizational culture manifests itself while waiting, allowing customers to anticipate their service encounter. Moreover, waiting for service could expose one to various incidents, like cutting, fighting, stealing, disrespect of customers, stampeding, and violations of wait-norms. How are such incidents handled by customer service representatives? Or are they handled at all? Waiting for service in ordinary situations and extended situations is revealing; it brings to light something about our society, about ourselves, about others, about specific organizations, and certainly about the services we are awaiting.

NOTES

1. The organizational culture among employees is most dominant; here, policies are developed, maintained, and changed. The organization often requires personal information from customers that defines the nature of their relationship.

2. Other customer service representative expressed similar sentiments in that Patricia, who works at CVS admits that she is sensitive to customers who wait longer than necessary. She states, "I'm always apologetic, saying 'I'm sorry, I'm sorry you had to wait.' And if I'm working in Photo, I'll give them a discount because they had to wait." And Tanya, who works in a bank, confessed, "I get a little nervous and start working faster—so I can hurry-up and get to the next customer."

3. See Timm's (2008) analysis of customer turn-offs.

4. Consumption emotion refers to the set of emotional responses elicited specifically during consumption experiences (Westbrook and Oliver, 1991). Consumption emotions have been conceptualized as distinct categories of emotional experiences and expressions, such as joy, anger, and fear (also see Wong, 2004).

5. "Freebies" may emotionally bind the customer to the wait; while the anticipation of desirable restaurant experiences could lead to wait toleration by customers.

6. Souplantation is no longer in business.

7. The idea of *self-service* is also covered in chapter 8.

8. On April 3, 2010, Apple began sale of iPad. Similar crowds and behaviors were observed outside of Apple stores.

9. What's in the "goodie bag"? A small package of ground coffee (cinnamon vanilla nut), an apple cinnamon raisin breakfast bar, a small box of animal crackers, and a stuff animal-mascot (dog)—"Bulls-eye." (Bulls-eye: Limited Edition Series One, Black Friday 2007) (18,794 of 75,024)—Made in China.

10. In Long Island, an employee died and four shoppers were injured after being trampled. In Florida, seventy-three-year-old Josephine Hoffman was knocked down and stepped on as she got caught up in the human wave that rushed into a *Brandsmart* store.

Chapter 5

Wait Explanations

Attention: Alaska Airline flight number 007. The cabin crew is still cleaning. We will board in just a few minutes, and thank you for your patience.

Wait explanations give reasons for delays; they generally explain why one is waiting. There are times when individuals are stalled and long to know why. "What could be taking so long?" "Why am I held-up?" "Why did he get his food before me?" Wait explanations provide a basis for standstills. They offer cause and understanding for delay and stoppage. Such inquiries suggest that persons are attentive while waiting; they are attentive to time and order, thus when there is discrepancy, customers may confront those in charge. For example, Jose (restaurant customer) confronted Miguel (restaurant manager) when Shaka received his food out of order. "Why did he get his food before me?" Working the register, Miguel explained, "Your food takes longer to prepare, plus you ordered more." Satisfied with Miguel's response, Jose returns to his seat. Granting a reason to customers assists them in making sense of transactions and assures them of their significance and place in line. It follows that wait explanations are generally offered by institutional representatives, and still there are times when *ordinary others* offer explanation. Both angles are examined in an attempt to more fully comprehend wait explanations. Admittedly, most of my data stem from institutional representatives, recognizing that when customers are delayed, they seek answers, usually from institutional representatives.

Additionally, wait explanations are sometimes accompanied by apologies, attempting to patronize and appease customers, for example, "I'm sorry, the cook misread my handwriting, but your order should be out next." The apology is another feature of wait explanations; it makes the explanation work, that is, it possibly convinces a customer. The tone of apology is usually sympathetic and sincere, for the idea is to please, calm, and maintain trust of customers. Presumably, customers receiving excuses instead of explanations are likely to complain and/or never return. When delays are apparent, customers simply want answers, and if explanations are offered without prompting, interaction is not strained but possibly enhanced. In short, customers sense that employees are attentive to their situation.

Specifically, explanations, on the one hand, provide reasons, clarifications, and at times proof; excuses (see Scott and Lyman, 1968), on the other hand, may be viewed as lies or somehow "stretching the truth." They sometimes sound like pleas to the hearer, possibly prompting additional questions by hearer. While it is difficult to verify explanations and excuses, the motives of explanations and excuses appear different. Seemingly, explanations intend to convince while excuses appear to deceive.[1]

Further, explanations appear to contain promise and hope, promise that service will soon materialize. And hope that service or product is *worth the wait*. There is nothing more disappointing than to wait for unsatisfactory service or disgusting outcomes. Conversely, the promise is something individuals anticipate and carrying out the promise determines whether the original explanation was accurate. For instance, "I'm sorry, the cook misread my handwriting, but your order should be out next." After lengthy delays, customers count on their order being next. Inconsistencies could lead to distrust and credibility concerns. Hence, explanations not only remind individuals why they are waiting, but such explanations suggest that institutions are considerate and conscious of their time.

Assessing blame is often another attribute of wait-explanations; reasons for waiting may imply blame. For example, "a shortage of cooks has caused your order to be delayed," or "the carrousel is experiencing technical difficulties, bags will load shortly." Albeit rare, when some persons are confronted with delays, they acknowledge responsibility, for example, "I'm so sorry! Forgive me for omitting your party, we will call you next." Blame distribution is an important piece of explanation, for blame assigns fault; generally, customer service representatives blame someone (or something) else so that one's credibility and competence remain in-tact. The waiter or company now mediates the resolution of waiting. Those who accept fault save face and repair their competence by offering quick remedy.

It follows that each wait-situation is unique, allowing wait-explanations to emerge from specific contexts. What then is the best strategy to deliver a wait-explanation? How does the context determine the plan used in delivering a reason for delay? How does the context influence who provides the explanation? It is clear that we live in a *culture of explanation*, and when delayed, we want answers. How does the context determine the nature of that explanation? That is, when waiting for class to start and the professor is late, are there times when ordinary persons (students, not clerks) provide explanation? Are explanations given by institutional officials only? These theoretical issues and others are the focus of this chapter, all in an effort to make sense of *wait-explanations*.

The concept *wait* is used in varying forms to communicate a variety of situations. For example, when giving instructions or directions, certain signs or individuals tell us: "Wait Here!" Advertisers urge us *not* to wait or deals may expire, for example, "What are you waiting for?" or "Why wait?" And usage of waiting is reflected in important decisions like college admissions, medical results, promotions, draft picks, and judicial conclusions. Such decisions are clearly tied to emotions. Yet methodologically, it was useful to read and collect wait-information that focused on advertisement, instruction, and significant decisions. It presented a variety of options and analysis that one could pursue. To be sure, all waits do not involve delay. For example, after a lengthy (eight months) O. J. Simpson trial, the case finally went to the jury. The jury deliberated for nearly four hours—then signaled to Judge Ito that they had reached a verdict. Judge Ito informed the court and the nation that he would *wait* until morning before announcing the verdict. In this case and given Ito's announcement, waiting does not involve delay. In short, his reading of the decision is not late or delayed; it was scheduled for a defined, objective time. Stress may arise while waiting, but one is not delayed. While this wait/delay distinction is important, my primary focus is on the *explanation*; hence, there are occasions where I use wait and delay interchangeably.

My analysis of wait-explanations begins with explanations provided by *institutional representatives*, followed by *ordinary others* and *inanimate objects*. First, regarding institutional representatives, *explanation strategies* focus on approaches used to deliver explanations, followed by *social status* and its effects on explanation. Next, I investigate how *lies* are used as explanation, followed by institutional representatives who provide *no explanation*. Then I shift to explanations offered by *ordinary others* and *inanimate objects*. Here, this analysis departs from one's usual understanding of explanation, that is, it explores how explanations are given by regular-ordinary people (*ordinary others*), not institutional representatives, and how signs, symbols, audio recordings, etc. (*inanimate objects*) are used as mechanisms for explanation. This chapter concludes by considering the *functions of wait explanations*. Why are wait-explanations necessary? What role do they play in calming, facilitating, and/or correcting situations?

EXPLANATIONS OFFERED BY
INSTITUTIONAL REPRESENTATIVES

Explanation Strategies

Lawyers, military commanders, and baseball managers are very strategic when planning to overtake opponents. They often study adversaries to determine weakness and strength; thus, it is not unusual to incorporate several approaches and angles to defeat opponents. In order to win, planning and experience are key assets. Lacking sufficient knowledge and experience could prove detrimental; the line of attack is rarely spontaneous. Those providing wait-explanations experience a similar dilemma, that is, what is the best way to explain a customer's delay? Which method is most convincing? After all, the goal is to offer a *convincing* and *satisfying* explanation. But how is this done? What strategy is used?

While the definition of winning is broadly defined, military commanders, baseball managers, and customer service representatives are interested in success. For military commanders, lawyers, and baseball managers, defeating opponents means winning; likewise, convincing customers is clearly a form of winning and therefore success. While customers are not defeated (although they may be manipulated by explanations), they frequently accept explanations. Consequently, each environment defines winning somewhat distinctly and all employ various strategies to obtain success. *Explanation strategies focus on approaches used by customer service representatives (and others) to deliver and convince customers of wait-explanation.* They are strategies that reflect organizations and what they wish to accomplish. Among the strategies uncovered are *showing, eye contact, and making an appearance.*

Showing

Showing is a strategy used to convince customers of wait-explanations; it is designed to remove customer doubt allowing individuals more receptivity to explanations. Suddenly, clarifications make sense and institutional suggestions are seriously considered, though persuading and convincing clients are the first steps. Those who are waiting can actually observe the "wait circumstance." For example, one male clerk appeared in a hospital wait-room and announced, "Those of you waiting for X-rays, I just want to let you know that X-rays are backed up. As you can *see*, it's pretty crowded in here. There's only four techs." While patients could not see or count all four "techs," patients could witness the crowded wait-room and such a crowd *may* confirm what they don't see. At issue is the large number of patients waiting for service. Supply does not meet demand. The same is true at crowded restaurants. Mother's Day crowds typically delay service. Within the hospital wait room, the clerk places emphasis on the crowded room, which is designed to convince patients of "X-ray back-ups." But given the crowded room, how much convincing is needed? He continues by announcing, "There's only four techs," which patients *cannot see*. Patients do not need to see "the techs" to know that it is crowded. Seemingly, "techs" were used as an add-on to convince patients of his explanation. It follows that evidence (crowds) makes explanations easier to accept and further permits clients to make informed wait decisions.

An interesting case of *showing* occurred at "Sears" auto repair waiting area. A middle-aged white lady, Anne, seemed troubled as she arbitrarily glared at certain customers; while other customers were eating and viewing TV, it soon became clear that her real interest was "Sears" auto repair representatives. When Rosa, "Sears" auto repair representative, entered wait area, Anne's eyes became fixed and anxiously attentive to Rosa's words.

With a slight accent, Rosa drew near updating, "Nothing has been done to your car yet. The part hasn't arrived."

In shock and surprise, Anne replies: "Why??!! It's been two hours!!!"

Rosa explains that "I was just out there and the technician has not started. The manager is going to come-out and speak to you."

Anne is so flustered and agitated that she asks, "Should I go see the manager in *his* office?"

Rosa quickly objects, "No, no. *She* is busy with somebody. It will only be a couple of minutes."

Rosa leaves to continue her work though Anne begins pacing the wait-room floor, and for about ten minutes, every auto employee who enters receives stares from Anne, for she does not know the Sears auto manager. Finally, the manager arrives and warmly greets Anne. The attractive manager is white, female, blonde, and about forty years. Beth, the manager, introduces herself and immediately apologizes for the delay and mix-up. For some reason, this seems to tame Anne's anxiety and anger. And though Beth offered a similar account—her explanation seemed more acceptable to Anne.

Anne wanted to know why car repair had not begun. Beth explained that repairs have started but there was a mix-up in communication between Rosa and auto technicians. Beth explained that they were waiting for parts to arrive and could not proceed until parts were delivered. Beth then took Anne to the garage area to *see* her car and further explain what the technicians were doing. Beth spent additional time reassuring Anne, eventually supplying her with a business card. Then, instructing Anne to "call me if you experience any more problems." Beth provided another apology and left. Such a strategy calms Anne, for she is no longer pacing but seated and enjoying the game show.

In this case, showing is a form of convincing and validating their explanations. Proving tends to remove suspicion. Given Anne's two-hour wait, she found it tough to believe that technicians had not started; she had difficulty accepting Rosa's explanation. Consequently, the unusual nature of the manager caught her off-guard. Receiving a white female manager in a predominantly male industry was just as shocking as uncovering that the part had not arrived. Seemingly, Anne related to Beth better; her story and strategy appeared more credible. While Beth's calm and apologetic demeanor was affective, to what extent does status, gender, or race of person delivering explanation influence explanation acceptance? This question naturally emanates from this encounter, and whether one believes wait-explanation has much to do with how explanation variables are constructed and received.

Eye Contact

Eye contact is another method used to convince and validate wait-explanations. It is a nonverbal technique that varies from culture to culture. As a way to communicate, the U.S. culture accepts and encourages eye contact; it suggests that persons are engaged and attentive. Conversely, traditional as well as (certain) contemporary Asian cultures frown on eye contact between youth and adults; such eye contact suggests a type of disrespect. Even within the U.S. culture, nonverbal behavior requires interpretation. For example, the language of the eyes ranges from stares, gazes, quick looks, glares, winks, peeks, eye-sparkles to glances. The context of eye behavior assists us in defining the situation, whether one is experiencing a stare, a sparkle, or a soft glance.

We use eye contact to invite social interaction, as when men are introduced to women and wish to extend their interaction—often both maintain their gaze and continue asking and answering questions. They are inquisitive; they want to know. Such interaction implies curiosity and while the introduction generates contact, the language of the eyes sustains or suspends contact. It is *the exchange* that reveals *something* about the other. Yet, eye contact is often supplemented with additional body gestures and words. For example, soft gazes along with smiles and pleasant words indicate appeal and a desire to maintain interaction. Alternatively, eye shifting may raise doubt, just as holding stares too long and quick looks. Taken together, it is very possible to detect sincerity in eye expression.

Restaurants are common places of wait. Individuals wait for tables; they wait to order, and finally the food arrives; hence a normative wait-cycle that diners anticipate. Waiters and waitresses can ease the process by pleasantly informing customers of unexpected delays. For instance, as Angela topped off their water glasses, she *gently* looks toward Latoya and Isaiah expressing, "Sorry about the wait, the kitchen got backed up." The couple nods and Angela continues, "It's crowded tonight but our cooks have a very good reputation." They thank Angela as she wipes water drops from their table. With an *empathetic* look, Angela softly conveys, "Hopefully, it will not be much longer." Seemingly, the eye contact gets at the sincerity of her explanation; it was natural and uninhibited. The explanation was volunteered and not triggered; the couple was occupied with one another and enjoying the ambience of the restaurant, when suddenly Angela appears. Experienced waitresses can somehow sense that the arrival of food is taking too long, thus ward off problems by accounting for delays. Waitresses are aware of kitchen/cook situation and telling customers without prompting could prove promising.

The type of social interactions that exist among women who are interested in men is dissimilar than that of restaurant customers and waitresses. The goals and motives are different. Often, in the case of restaurants, employees initiate social contact by greeting, informing, and instructing customers. All the while, customers are interpreting employee words and gestures; even when waitresses are at a distance, customer may observe their movements and behavior. Are movements sincere or false, quick or slow? How do we know? It is important to look for consistency. In similar situations, does Angela provide *soft gazes* to diners or is her interaction abrupt? As a strategy, the use of eye contact can be most effective; it can soften interactions, making them more personable. And ultimately, effective-delicate eye contact could increase rewards.

Making an Appearance

Celebrities in high demand often make brief appearances for charities, galas, and even recognition ceremonies. Their appearances enhance the affair; in fact, crowds are willing to wait hours on anticipated arrivals. During elections, politicians make several brief appearances to cover lots of electoral ground. They visit churches, synagogues, civic centers, colleges, banquets, recreation centers, and parks, making them visible and accessible. Constituents appreciate their presence as a way to interact with politicians (face-to-face) and get out the vote. Before or after surgery, some doctors are found in wait-rooms consulting with family members. Their appearance is anticipated and informative. After his concert, Musiq (hip hop artist) made an appearance in the auditorium lobby to sign autographs and visit with fans, and famous authors appear at bookstores and conferences to discuss and sign their latest volume. Whatever the circumstances, making an appearance could have lasting effects on audiences.

Making an appearance is vital in making connections with, and appealing to others; it is an attempt to manage the impressions of others. But *making an appearance* gets at being in the immediate presence of others and sharing their space.[2] "Others" may now see, touch, and converse with "appearance maker"; individuals may appraise and evaluate. Conversing with others in close proximity implies a certain confidence, assuredness, and even trust; such closeness augments the appearance. Additionally, the length of appearance is critical, for staying too long could hamper the affect. A short and concise appearance seems most valuable; leaving an impact on the environment is the goal and viewers maintain a visual image of "appearance maker." Defining a "short" appearance is tricky; it ultimately depends on environment and what one is attempting to accomplish.

The current analysis of *making an appearance* investigates how individuals use this method to convince others of their explanation. *How does a willing appearance support an explanation?* It suggests that one is not hiding or dodging; thus, one willingly places him or herself on display for examination and further explanation. For example, as passengers were boarding the plane, storing luggage and getting settled in, an announcement came over P.A. system, "Captain is delayed in traffic. He should be here in about 15 minutes." Minutes later, the announcement repeats as passengers continue their boarding activities. When most are settled and aisles nearly vacant, the assistant captain briefly appears in the cabin. He walks through first class and about ten rows of coach, greeting, conversing, and acknowledging passengers. Soon, he approaches a female passenger who is seated; he smiles and jokingly asks, "Are you mad?" She returns his smile and nods in a no motion. The assistant captain then assures passengers that "the captain will arrive soon and we will depart." While his uniform gets passenger attention, his physical presence and demeanor dismisses any anxiety and doubt held over from the original announcement. Within minutes, the captain arrives, greeting passengers through the P.A. system. He continues by informing, "Good thing that there is a tailwind; a tailwind all across the nation, which should allow us to get there faster."

While passengers did not see his arrival, they heard the captain's voice. His voice and motion of the plane assures passengers of departure. Moreover, the original explanation along with the assistant captain's appearance and finally captain's arrival confirms all reasons for delay. Such delays can prove aggravating, for customers have no way of knowing whether explanations are true, and passengers have little control over when captain will arrive or departure of plane. Thus, methods to persuade passengers are invaluable for the company's reputation. And in an industry where delays are common and explanations questioned, this company was able to demonstrate credibility by leaving within a timely manner.

Theoretically, explanation strategies become relevant and most effective in their specific environments. The context and person implementing strategy has much to do with how explanations are received. In the case of *showing,* Rosa's gesturing and eye contact were ineffective; Anne needed more explanation, more evidence. Conversely, *making an appearance* by co-pilot was most relevant and convincing to passengers. The difficulty of showing passengers the pilot was obvious, but more natural to display the assistant captain, inhabiting the same space and communicating directly with passengers. *Eye contact* alone may not sell an explanation, but knowing how to use *eye contact* along with other gestures and words convinced Latoya and Isaiah of Angela's explanation. In short, eye contact was "topped off" with an explanation. Hence, the strategy is designed to fit the environment and situation, though forcing a strategy in an unusual setting proves limiting. There are times when collective explanations are appropriate (as in the case of pilot delay) in contrast to individual explanations, for example, "showing" at Sears. Clearly, collective explanations require that institutional representatives convince more people. But whether collective or individual, it is the context that determines how the explanation is given. Does one publicly shout an explanation to a group (so everyone receives the same reason) or does one address individual concerns? It follows that the goal of collective and individual explanations remains the same, for example, convey and convince customers of the wait-problem.

To what extent are explanation strategies rehearsed or spontaneous? It is difficult to determine—yet work experience is ordinarily a good indicator of how strategies are managed. Generally, seasoned employees know how to calm and satisfy customers. They have encountered problematic situations before, and thus acquired a stock of knowledge on managing explanations; they possess insight. Situationally, various circumstances will dictate whether spontaneous or planned strategies are used or a combination of both. Like actors, the advantage of rehearsal is fewer flaws and a more convincing performance. As well, actors and employees alike may encounter unsuspecting issues that were not written in script or employee manual. In such cases, employees may improvise, finding ways to sway customers, which may later become a rehearsed strategy.

In the cases discussed, strategically, the institutional representative recognized a possible delay and initiated an explanation. This is not to say that customers were not thinking about delay; for instance, when entering a crowded hospital wait-room or standing in a long line, the question of delay is generally apparent. But in the cases presented—the institution and not the individual (or group) raised the question of delay. Why? Presumably, the institution wishes to ward off negative labels and maintain its clientele. In short, the institution wants to get in front of the problem. Still there are times when customers raise questions about delay to the institution, for example, what can be taking so long? Why did he get his meal/food before me? One possible reason is the institution has not provided reason for delay so the individual feels compelled to ask. It raises an important theoretical issue: how long is too long? The other possible reason is simply that the order of service was violated. For example, though Miguel ordered first, Shaka received his food before Miguel. Cognizant of the informal norm, "first come, first serve," Miguel initiates the topic of delay. He asked the clerk, "Why did he get his food before me?" This guides our understanding of *response conditions*. That is, under what conditions are proactive explanations given by institutional representatives? And under what conditions are reactive explanations requested by customers. The nature of the interaction generally determines *response conditions*.

Finally, while *showing, eye contact and making an appearance* have been examined, there are additional explanation strategies. For example, *repeated explanations* in that three separate officials provided similar wait explanations within one hour to the same group. Also, *written assurance* was used to explain problems and guarantee service. After waiting hours, several concertgoers wondered whether they would see the "sold out" show. Those near the front were given vouchers explaining problems and assured entrance; those without vouchers were disappointed and left. Another explanation strategy and certainly the most common was *telling*, that is, simply informing customers of the situation and encouraging them to wait. Explanation strategies guide us through the maze of clarification types, for example *showing, eye contact, making an appearance, repeated explanations, written assurance, and telling*. What is the best approach to handling patrons, and explaining why they are waiting? The idea is not only to explain but also to convince and assure customers that one's explanation is valid, which in turn gives customers reason to wait and even return.

PRIVILEGE AND EXPLANATION

Privilege is another consideration in my analysis of waiting. Those in privilege positions may take advantage of their status, deciding whether to give an explanation or not. Under what conditions does one intentionally arrive late, lie and/or give no reason for his/her tardiness? How does privilege and social status impact the persons waiting to receive an explanation? What are the expectations of those waiting?

Social Status and Wait Explanations

There are cases, however, when persons in authority believe it unnecessary to provide explanations. As when judges arrive to court late and when teachers arrive to class tardy. Their audiences are waiting and wondering whether judge or teacher will show, and eventually they arrive with no explanation. Such authority figures are not required to provide wait-explanations to clients and may proceed with business as usual. If tardiness is atypical of judge and teacher, then audiences are likely to understand and display little concern. But if lateness is habitual, talk among audiences may ensue, permitting negative labels of authority figures to emerge, which could in part damage reputations and social positions. Wait explanations may or may not emerge with habitual lateness, and such tardiness may affect audience promptness and attentiveness.

Subordinates appear more likely and more obligated than super-ordinates to provide wait-explanations. The student who keeps his professor waiting; the employee who keeps her boss waiting; the lawyer who keeps the judge waiting; the teenager who keeps his father waiting; the parishioner who keeps his pastor waiting; and the client who keeps her social worker waiting may all potentially experience sanction when explanations are not provided. By the nature of their relationship, subordinates have more to lose. On the one hand, it shows a type of disrespect for authority; on the other hand, and before business actually begins, authority figures are expecting explanations and apologies. Failure to provide them, explanations and apologies, could clearly strain relationships and lead to sanctions. And for these reasons, explanations are almost automatic. Conversely, professors are not obligated to provide explanation to students who are waiting outside his office for their appointments. Arriving late for a scheduled appointment does not necessarily hamper their relationship; in fact, students are expected to stay, considering the busy schedules of professors. Failure to wait signals a lack of interest, rigor, and focus on academic pursuits, leading professors to question whether the student should remain in the program.

This is not to say that authority figures do not provide wait-explanations. It is to say that such explanations are not necessarily expected and/or required in same way they are by subordinates. Social worker, Sharon Simpson, whose caseload is overwhelming, consults and counsels several clients weekly. Clients typically sign in and wait for a receptionist to call them. Sharon says that if she runs into problems, like a client needing more time, or an emergency call or an unexpected abuse case, "I'll tell the secretary that they have to reschedule due to unforeseen emergencies, or that it may take me a little more time to resolve Keisha's problem—so be patient, I'll get to you." Similarly, Sabrina Sampson, a college EOPS counselor, is another authority figure who has little problem providing explanations. "Taxiing" her daughter from school to home to extracurricular activities means that Sabrina routinely leaves campus and returns to resume work. While she is popular among students and shares her children's activities, it is not uncommon for Sabrina to call ahead informing secretary of her late return, "but tell Nailah (student) to wait." Upon seeing students, Sabrina may acknowledge student waiting, "Thanks for waiting—I wanted to see whether my daughter's team would win."

Again, while waiting explanations by authority figures are not required, out of courtesy, some feel compelled to give them; yet others do not. Stratification among super-ordinates and subordinates helps us understand the basis of this contradiction; a contradiction that subordinates learn to cope with and adjust to. Super-ordinates use privileges not accorded to subordinates, taking advantage of their position at the expense of lower-status groups. Alienation is little concern for some superiors in that high-status individuals are freed up when subordinates fail to wait; super-ordinates also concede that it is the subordinate seeking attention. Subordinate groups rely on and value privileged groups for services, and yet recognize that extended waits are annoying. It follows that wait explanations among unequal entities have a preexisting meaning before they occur. Generally, such groups conform to their expected roles and statuses.

Still, various intriguing questions remain about the likelihood of receiving such explanations. For example, are women more likely than men to provide wait-explanations? Are Blacks more likely than whites? Are Asians, Arabs, Armenians, and Latinos more likely than whites? Are homosexuals more likely than heterosexuals? Are lower socioeconomic groups more likely than higher socioeconomic groups? And, are immigrants more likely than non-immigrants to provide wait-explanations? Given the social structure of the United States, seemingly status, stemming from sex, race, sexual orientation, and class influence whether one provides an explanation.

Lies as Explanation

To what extent is receiving a *lie* better than the truth or no explanation? Stretching the truth, a little white lie and cutting corners are linked by their attempts to deceive. One phrase may sound better than the other but the end result is falsification. Using such phrases helps us avoid the negative label "liar" and thus further deceiving ourselves and others. These phrases, in part, reflect our perception of self and our attempts to manage the impression of others. Still a "watered-down lie" is just that—a lie, and while some persons have difficulty "stretching the truth," others possess a natural gift of deception. Lying then has become an ordinary occurrence in society; it is observed within institutions and individuals alike; it varies from situation to situation and in order to *save face* lies are tolerated by most (see Barker and Carter, 1990). Strangely, lies possess an interesting dichotomy, that is, lies have the power to help or hurt; they can bring individuals together or set them ablaze.

Determining their intent gets at the context of the situation and therefore how to manage lies.

In his analysis of "Secrets and Lies" (2007), Richard Kent conveyed the following: "A patient is admitted for investigations and the results show he or she has an advanced terminal condition. The relatives are informed and ask that the information be withheld from the patient." Why? "The family decided that their relative 'would not be able to handle the news.'" So, at what point does the patient learn about their condition? And what are the repercussions of temporarily withholding the terminal condition from the patient? Similarly, patients lie about taking medications consistently, and "physicians' prescriptions often fail to comply with practice guidelines" (Powsner and Spitzer, 2003). Why? The situations and motives are different. Relatives may wish to stall a crisis, patients may wish to please doctors and prevent their scolding/scorn and finally, the physicians may wish to satisfy patients. Whether noble, self-serving, or pleasing to others, each person rationalizes his or her lying.[3] Lies compromise the truth; lies may ease stress and conflict by telling people what they want to hear.

Untrue wait-explanations serve the same purpose by tickling the client's ear and thus avoiding quarrel. Placing a positive spin on customer delay suggests concern and sympathy to those waiting. Yet, there are some customers who are difficult to deceive; they recognize that one's explanation is nothing more than a lie. For instance, Yoo-jin disclosed, "When I am waiting at the doctor's office or at a restaurant, I often get explanations such as 'the doctor is with a patient' or 'it is backed up in the kitchen right now with orders.'" Yoo-jin critically thinks through each situation and continues:

> I know for a plain fact that these are lies because I was a receptionist and a server myself. The truth is that the doctor is late because he can be (due to his status among society)—whether he is in a meeting, sleeping in for the afternoon, or *fine* dining at lunch. As a server, many times it is true that there are a lot of customers, but several times it is because they forgot to call in the order. And currently as a secretary, I often give "explanations" that the lawyer is in a meeting with the client. Because I have experience myself, I am no longer fooled with these "explanations," but it's easier for me to be patient because I understand their purpose of giving these "explanations."

Given her work experience, Yoo-jin understands how "explanations" and "excuses" work. She recognizes that employees are hired for service as well as protecting the company with excuses. And most employees are likely to comply with company expectations. Telling the truth may only lead to greater frustration, and possibly sacrificing or losing customers. So, lies become as ordinary as apple pie, as routine as breathing. Similarly, when husbands lie to their wives, and wives lie to their husbands, are they attempting to avert clashes that could derail their relationship? In these situations, the "choice" is obvious. Truth-telling could lead to strain and may pose severe costs to employees and couples.[4] Experience becomes a clear issue, that is, at what point and in what situations does one explain-away reality?

Explaining-away reality or lying has additional unintended consequences in that it may display a certain respect for customers. Armen believes that "an explanation accompanied with an apology is far better than just an apology, even if the explanation is a lie." He explains:

> By giving an explanation with an apology, I am given the impression that there was some unforeseen or unavoidable circumstance that created and therefore justified my wait. Even if the explanation was a lie, I believe that the individual giving the false explanation felt guilty enough about my waiting that they needed to lie to ease my irritations. This would give me the impression that the apology was truly meant.

The extent to which the apology is "truly meant" is debatable. The apology is often standard with no true affection, no true guilt—it is simply part of the job, a routine, a habit. A job which requires employees to lie and then apologize for waiting or lying or both? Still the lie is meant to appease, to make Armen and others feel better about their waiting—that they are not waiting in vain, but clearly service will soon materialize. Conversely, if the apology is "truly meant," why is it necessary to lie? Seemingly, a true apology is accompanied by a true explanation. Finally, and given the current scenario, sincere apologies are in fact possible by employees. That is, companies require that employees provide a standard explanation or excuse to customers. This however does not mean that apologies are disingenuous; they may be very meaningful. As a consequence, employees may so tire of deception or standard explanations that they eventually quit.

No Explanation

There are times when explanations never emerge from wait-situations, and yet some persons continue to wait. Given our socialization, individuals recognize that waiting is simply part of life's experiences, and so waiting additional time may be harmless. Still, under what circumstances are wait explanations not issued? How often do we wait without a reason? Is it normal or bothersome to wait without a reason? Why do we wait without a reason? And how is the lack of explanation managed by client and customer service representative? Lisa, for example, recalled that "they [the restaurant] didn't give me any excuse. They just kept telling me to wait 15 more minutes. And

I did. I enjoyed my waiting time by talking on the phone with my friend." Having an interesting conversation is likely to keep one's mind off of waiting, and acknowledging one's presence takes away the worry. That is, Lisa conveys that "they just kept telling me to wait 15 more minutes," suggesting that she was approached more than once. Moreover, the fact that she was approached acknowledges her existence in that "they" have not forgotten about Lisa. While Lisa was not bothered by her delay and "explanationlessness," Christopher became impatient and irritated. Consider his experience:

> Last month I went to get a smog check. The guy said it would take thirty minutes. While I waited, I walked over to the grocery store about a block away to pass time. I read some magazines and bought candy. I headed back over exactly thirty minutes when he told me. When I arrived, no one was there to greet me or tell me about my car. This made me impatient because the guy said it would take thirty minutes, and so why isn't my car ready? I am myself a very punctual person, if someone says to me a time frame, they better stick to it or I become *impatient and irritated*. The smog check ended up taking about forty minutes, ten minutes more than what the guy said it would take. *The guy gave no excuse for the delay, nor did I ask for an explanation. I didn't want to confront him over ten minutes. Even though that was the longest ten minutes ever.*

Christopher wanted an explanation but believed that asking would escalate his irritation. He was not after a fight but simply wanted his car on time.[5] The fact that no one was there to greet him or inform him about his car heightens his frustration, sensing that no one cares. Then again, Christopher's wait might be further lengthened by the tech taking time to talk to him. It follows that Christopher's body language is firm and unsympathetic. Given that the mechanic did not keep his word, an explanation would have benefited all involve, consequently, it is not likely that Christopher will return.

Finally, there is Sean, who was so hungry that he was less concerned about a reason and more interested in eating. He shares, "When I ordered a pizza one time from Domino's, it took them close to an hour to finally deliver it to my house. I was so hungry that I did not even care to ask the delivery man what took him so long to deliver the pizza." Sean did not challenge him on the thirty-minute pizza delivery guarantee and thus insist on a free pizza; he was annoyed, hungry and simply wanted to eat. But the lack of explanation gets at a sort of insensitivity to customers and inconsideration for their disposition.

In each case, no one asked for a wait-explanation; individuals often assume that explanations are automatic and there is no need to inquire. But Christopher and Sean felt slighted when an explanation was not received. Seemingly, customers deserve *reason* given that they have entered a mutual agreement—they have agreed to do business. Providing an explanation displays one's

attentiveness to customers and therefore their value. Customers feel significant and not estranged. Requesting or demanding an explanation changes the
nature of the encounter. Now, one does not feel special or appreciated. One
must take his or her situation into their own hands by inquiring and observing.
Situationally then, no one asked because they felt visible (Lisa) or invisible
(Christopher and Sean); each circumstance and its characters are different,
but the common theme is *no explanation*; individuals are unclear as to why
they are waiting, and thus they make assumptions based on what they see,
hear, and feel; or they make assumptions based on what they don't see, what
they don't hear, and how they don't feel.

While our personal time clocks are different (Levine, 1997), one's interpretation of *waiting too long* varies. In the case of Sean, waiting too long
was connected to hunger; for Christopher, waiting too long was connected
to punctuality, and for Lisa, waiting too long was linked to boredom (not
talking on the phone) and invisibility (failure to acknowledge her waiting).
Theoretically, *waiting too long* depends on the situation, personal time clocks
and situational variables. Reactions to *waiting too long* also vary by situations, personal time clocks, and situational variables. That is, some persons
will wait given the situation, for example, Christopher and Sean, the flexibility of not waiting is clearly an option for Lisa.

Finally, there are wait scenarios that need no verbal explanation from
customer service representatives. That is, the wait situation explains itself.
For example, waiting to check out at Ralphs and the customer in front is
using food stamps and food vouchers. The clerk must scan and inspect each
voucher individually. This takes lots of time and most customers avoid wait
lines where customers are using food vouchers. Also, car traffic requires
no explanation when one can clearly see the accident ahead. And watching
customers struggle with wrong PIN number provides a clear reason as to
why one is delayed. In short there are some situations that require no verbal
explanation; observing the situation makes the explanation apparent.

EXPLANATIONS OFFERED BY ORDINARY
OTHERS AND INANIMATE OBJECTS

Wait-Explanations by Ordinary Others

In everyday life, waiting explanations seem quite common when inquiring
about one's extended delay. Many times, explanations evolve not from firms
or established organizations but from *ordinary others*, like friends, siblings,
spouses, co-workers, strangers, and those within our immediate space. It suggests that we live in a *culture of explanation*, for example, "there must be a

reason for your delay." In such a culture, explanations are not only required but expected; it is normal to provide reason and such reason enhances or sustains one's moral character, one's social position. Failure to explain is inconsiderate and may have consequences for future relationships, associations, and one's personal image. A *culture of explanation* gives reason for what we do, and why we are late—it is a part of our socialization, part of our social etiquette. Whether wait-explanations come from ordinary others, institutional representatives, professors to students, or clients to lawyers, explanations are anticipated and valued, helping us make sense of the situation. A culture of explanation is most pronounced within the court system. Not receiving an explanation raises questions and even suspicion, which further explains why explanations are part of our culture, our way of life.

When experiencing a lengthy wait for someone's arrival, individuals begin to wonder "what's taking so long?" In some cases, like late arriving dates, persons willingly and automatically provide an explanation, a reason. They believe one's lateness warrants a cause for tardiness, given that X-person has been waiting. Failure to provide explanation could hamper the encounter and even lead to conflict. So, in part, one function of waiting explanations is to maintain smooth, continuous relationships. When arriving late and upon seeing his date, James explains, "Hi Melissa, I'm sorry. I made a wrong turn and got lost. Hope you haven't been waiting too long?" Such an explanation, whether true or false, recognizes that one deserves reason for tardiness, and providing cause gets at a certain respect and empathy for the one waiting; this relationship is likely sustained, unless such behavior continues. Moreover, and given technology, one may call (or text) ahead, forewarning date of tardiness and providing reason along with approximate arrival time. It follows that even upon arrival and as a point of conversation, one is likely to apologize and somehow refer to and/or discuss tardiness.

Reasons and motives vary as to why *ordinary others* provide wait-explanations. Some may feel their self-image is misrepresented and seek to offer a more correct perception of self. When confronted by James, for example, Nancy explained, "I'm not cutting in line. I'm just standing over here to keep from getting wet." In this case, a line of three persons had formed outside the locked (closed) bank door; each arrived and stood behind the other. Then a middle-aged female arrived but did not wait at the end of the line. She walked to an awning near the line-front and waited. James who was talking on the phone suddenly shouted, "Excuse me ma'am but there's a line back here!" Somewhat startled, Nancy looks up in the direction of the shout; after recognizing the face and voice, she relaxes as they approach one another smiling; they embrace and exchange greetings. James resumes his cell phone conversation and Nancy returns to awning area. Those viewing encounter realize that James jokingly made this comment, yet Nancy feels compelled to explain why she is standing underneath the awning. Facing those waiting, Nancy declares, "I'm not cutting line. I'm just standing over here to keep from getting wet."

The extent to which an explanation was anticipated or warranted is unknown, though the fact that she provides reason displays consideration to those waiting and knowledge of unwritten wait-rules. In such a short line, those waiting are aware of who arrives first, second, third, and so forth. Standing to the left of the line and underneath an awning was not awkward. In fact, it was simply unique; Nancy did not conform and line up behind James. Moreover, patrons did not receive the impression that she was "cutting." Nancy's "cutting" clarification was sparked by James' initial comments. Waiting norms imply folkways about waiting behavior; about how one should wait and about waiting order. James' remark, "There's a line back here," is very real and significant. That is, persons expect those arriving after them to wait at lines-end and not in front; those who break this rule are often sanctioned, frowned on, stared at, or challenged in one way or another. *The back of the line is where individuals must start then work their way forward, hence cutting or somehow receiving an unfair advantage is rarely accepted, though it is clear that everyone does not begin at "lines-end."*

Nancy asserts that she was not cutting or cheating, but taking temporary cover. In part, she rejects James' definition of the situation and simultaneously redefines the situation and herself. That is, Nancy views herself as honest and open, intending only shelter. And while an explanation is not necessary, an explanation is given. For in a *culture of explanation* one often feels compelled to explain their actions, and by explaining one's behavior, he or she is also offering an *image of self*. Clearly then, such wait-explanations may stem from *ordinary others*. *Ordinary others* become an integral part of our institutional wait transactions; they are classmates, friends, relatives, co-workers, and carpool drivers who apologize for tardiness. They are teammates and sorority sisters who maintain bonds but realize that misfortune happens. It is the delay that must be explained, and next time, the same mishap is likely avoided.

Finally, there are times when *ordinary others* provide explanation in place of institutional representatives. For example, when professors are late, and students arrive after the official explanation was given—ask a fellow student, "Where's Professor Anderson?" Student explains that "Professor Anderson is in a meeting; he'll be about 10 minutes late." Similarly, when customers wait in a stalled line to purchase crafts, Pedro walks up inquiring, "Why aren't we moving?" "The clerk went to get change." The responses and interaction of *ordinary others* gets at their significance and how society relies on them for explanation and clarification. Pedro begins his wait—along with the others. Needless to say, wait-explanations from *ordinary others* is a common and informal occurrence in everyday life.

Inanimate Objects and Wait Explanations

Typically, individuals are accustomed to receiving wait-explanations from significant others, ordinary others, strangers, control officials, and institutional representatives, for example, humans. Explanations are performed in the immediate presence of others, allowing face-to-face dialogue and even social contact. Clarifying explanations is an important advantage of face-to-face interaction, and thus confusion is minimized through verbal and visual exchange. Yet, there are times when *inanimate objects* provide wait-explanations, and in most cases, they are intended to provide explanation when humans are absent. And it is impossible to ask questions or debate wait-explanations;[6] it is further difficult to read any type of body language, because inanimate objects do not move, nor do they have life; they simply exist within one's wait space and humans tend to accept and/ or receive wait-explanation. In short, individuals may "receive" explanation but not believe explanation. Yet, the value of inanimate wait-explanations is that they exist—when animate objects (humans) are scarce and unavailable, inanimate objects in fact provide reason for waiting. It follows that inanimate wait explanations may have little to do with human scarcity. It is driven by advanced technology and therefore a consequence of the culture of waiting. The most obvious examples are signs. Not only do signs offer instruction but many provide explanation. Audio recordings and videos are additional ways to receive inanimate explanations. Billboards, radios, cellphones, computers, TVs, freeway/subway signs, marquees, newspapers, and a host of other artifacts are intended to provide *inanimate wait explanations*. Clearly, this is a unique way of receiving reason but technology has driven society to become more impersonal, more deceptive, and more efficient.

There are lots of signs and symbols in hospitals that provide instruction, direction, and information. Given the nature of this institution, it is important that patients (young, old, and middle-aged) have clear instruction and direction. When one is suffering from a stroke, getting to the appropriate area is vital. Appropriate signage gets at hospital efficiency and accessibility. Additionally, hospitals attend to and address a variety of medical issues, such as surgery, ENT, optometry, blood work, dermatology, and so forth. Thus, the significance of signs in hospitals is unmistakable.

The X-ray department is one such area that contains signs as explanations; it is an area involving frequent use by patients, an area that is "in between stops." That is, determining a broken arm requires a doctor's exam, an X-ray, and a return to doctor's office for results. The X-ray lies between the exam and the results. Patients are directed to X-ray waiting area, where they submit paperwork, then wait their turn. Near the mail slot, patients observe the following sign: "Some patients may be X-rayed ahead of other patients because of the type and extent of injuries and/or medical status. We will make every effort to handle all requests as quickly as possible." Such a sign indicates that waiting for X-rays may not follow a "first come, first serve" procedure, but one's wait depends on "the type and extent of injuries and/or medical status." Thus, if Sophia entered before Maria though Maria was/is X-rayed before Sophia, it is understood, based on the sign, that Maria's medical status is worse and a cause for more immediate attention. Thus, there is no need to explain why Maria preceded Sophia. If questions are raised, the sign explains the issue. In part, signs are designed to assist the bureaucracy by eliminating verbal explanations. Compliance to sign explanation is often contingent upon reading sign verbiage; hence, failure to read sign explanation may ignite question and conflict; while those who read signs are not likely to challenge procedure.[7]

New York subways provide another example of *inanimate wait explanations*. Here, a voice or recording is heard over the intercom explaining delays; it is not uncommon to hear the following explanations: "Ladies and gentlemen, we are delayed because of trains ahead of us. Thank you for your patience." Or, "we are awaiting passengers from train number one." And finally, "the conductor has not allowed clearance." Such announcements may occur through the day and evening, while trains are motionless. Passengers sit or stand listening to announcements; sometimes they are emotionless and other times they are expressive. When passengers are emotionless, they simply continue behaving as they are; that is reading a book, or newspaper, or talking to friends, listening to I-pods, observing others, and even sleeping. Conversely, emotions are expressed by sighing, complaining aloud ("oh no" or "enough already!") and by slapping a newspaper against the rail. Either way, passengers recognize their powerlessness; they have little control and are reduced to waiting. The *inanimate wait explanation* provides important information with real consequences. Given the nature of inanimate objects, announcements are not emotional; they simply exist; they are heard and received in a radio-like, monotone voice.

Speaking of radios, the radio is not only an inanimate object but an important source of information as well. During emergencies, citizens are often instructed to tune in to certain radio stations for announcements and updates. Traffic delays, whether expected or not, also prompt us to tune in to news radio stations. One evening while traveling the 710 freeway, unexpected traffic began to form.[8] While the traffic did not bother Akeem initially, later, he would glance at his car clock realizing that he'd been in traffic for thirty minutes and had forty minutes before the scheduled Marcus Miller concert. Akeem became more alert, somewhat worried, and more aware as he watched and contemplated traffic moving slowly and cars changing lanes in an attempt to locate the most rapid, consistently moving lane. Some drivers tire of waiting and/or changing lanes thus elect to exit freeway; some may even know alternate routes. But as Akeem observed this, it occurred to him "turn to a news radio station to uncover the problem." Interestingly, a news radio station reported that a big-rig had wrecked, blocking the three right lanes on 710-freeway. The news station further suggested alternate routes and reported accident location; still there was no prediction regarding wait time, and by this time cars were stationary. So, the radio station became a valuable source of information and explanation, permitting Akeem to make more informed decisions about changing lanes, exiting the freeway or simply waiting it out. Given the "inanimation" of radio, announcers, however, can express emotion; that is, announcers may sympathize with drivers in traffic. But announcers use an inanimate object to report traffic and news; passengers and drivers cannot question announcers (typically, drivers do not call-in), they simply receive explanation.

Without question, cell phones are an important source of inanimate wait explanation. It is an important vehicle for obtaining information quickly. Whether traffic, traffic predictions or traffic redirection, our cellphones maintain the same information value as signs, computers, and radios. Phones then have become the most convenient and favorite tool within our culture. While inanimate explanations are generally voluntary, such a system gets at our (the public) need to know and thereby our ability to organize our lives. Persons may call ahead to inform loved-ones or superiors of their delay. Inanimate wait explanations further remove or reduce any worry and concern of the unknown. Again, the explanation is designed to give a reason in which individuals cannot negotiate. In short, the inanimate object becomes part of the *culture of explanation*; part of what humans expect in contemporary societies.

FUNCTION OF WAIT EXPLANATIONS-WE

Throughout this chapter, indirect attention has been given to the *functions* of wait-explanations. Clearly, there is no single function to wait-explanations but several, ranging from crowd control to enhancing one's ability to wait. The functions of wait explanations include, but are not limited to, *social control, reassurance, sustaining customer business, sympathize, cover-up, inform and image of self*. For example, *social control* (Price, 2005), most customer service representatives provide explanation to lessen confusion and prevent chaos. Here, one is concerned with customer complaints and becoming disruptive. The explanation prevents grievances and challenges before they arise, and thus keeping situations calm. Additionally, wait explanations are issued to offer *reassurance* that service is forthcoming, and one's wait will soon end. There is a sort of relief and comfort in knowing that waiting is temporary. Moreover, the fact that waiting is limited gets at the institution's respect for another's time, helping customers maintain schedules, and other appointments. *Sustaining customer business* is another function of wait explanations. Customers recognize that they have options and may patronize other establishments if service is not forthcoming. Here companies tend to employ several gimmicks. For example, after receiving an explanation, yet the wait remains long, companies are likely to offer food, drink, discounts, and even free service. The idea is to develop and retain a relationship and therefore trust in order to keep one's business. Customer service representatives are typically very apologetic and willing to do almost anything to satisfy customers. At times, explanations are designed to *sympathize* with customers. It allows employees to place themselves in the role of the other and thereby potentially feel what customers experience. It demonstrates respect for waiting parties and thus believing that they (waiting parties) are not taken for granted. Such explanations may well reflect the character of "explainer" or institution, who may offer regular updates to customers. Finally, explanations are offered to *cover up* errors by institutional employees. For example, Ms. Parson conveyed that "Last night, I flew in from Boston. After a two-hour delay and a six-hour plane ride, our bags came out thirty minutes late. They blamed it on 'technical difficulties.' But we later discovered that the grounds crew placed our bags on the wrong carousel." "Technical difficulties" is a typical excuse that is almost meaningless, and once discovered, real reasons may severely disturb customers. Thus, in the end, the *function of wait explanations, as it pertains to institutional representatives, is to provide stories that will temporarily satisfy and appease customers—in an effort to inform, control, and maintain business relationships.*

Regarding ordinary others and inanimate objects, the function of explanation is to *inform*. The ordinary other has little concern about losing customers given their relationship to the situation. If a clerk, for example, announces a wait-reason and all customers are not present, the ordinary other may repeat explanation to late arriving and inquiring customers. Hence when ordinary others provide an explanation about the store or post office opening late, it is simply to *inform*. The same is true with inanimate objects, that is, the sign, the radio, and the video screen are all designed to inform. We cannot respond to inanimate objects, yet we are empowered with knowledge so as to decide on a course of action. This gets at how technology is used to explain delay and how technology has become an important part of our *culture of explanation*. Additionally, in the cases of "Nancy-cutting in line" and keeping one's date waiting, ordinary others provide explanation not only to inform but also to offer an *image of self*. It is to clarify who they are, not what the circumstance has defined.

While there are more functions, the aforementioned purposes afford a working analysis of wait-explanations. It is important for employees to explain to customers the nature of their wait, for example, why they are waiting? Presumably, individuals have been programmed to wait, and clients expect and deserve explanations. Failure to offer reasons may cost an establishment the client's patronage. Each wait-situation is unique, allowing wait-explanations to emerge out of specific contexts; so, while the context is relevant to the explanation, the wait-explanation must make sense. That is, one assumes that "a shortage of cooks" pertains to restaurant wait explanations, and an inability to locate auto parts refers to an auto service explanation; thus, it goes without saying that auto mechanics are unlikely to explain their delays on "cook shortages." In short, any explanation will not do; it must fit the situation. Finally, there are some explanations that are generic to many institutions and circumstances. For example, understaffed and over-crowdedness may fit several situations of wait. Such explanations may explain delays in banks, restaurants, hospitals, grocery stores, retail stores, court proceedings, airport terminals, and a host of other situations. But it is clear that generic explanations must maintain a sense of integrity in that such explanations must be viewed as plausible. For these reasons, generic explanations are utilized, that is over-crowdedness and understaffed are real occurrences in which many have experienced. In fact, when people approach crowded lines and venues, they often think twice about remaining for service. Hence not only are such explanations given but over-crowdedness, and at times understaffing, is visually verified.

SUMMARY

Theoretically, to what extent is waiting more bearable when individuals sympathize with persons supplying explanations and recognizing that *messenger* has little control over delays? Much of this depends on how the explanation is delivered. Do *messengers* feel the pain of "waiters"? Or, are *messengers* impersonal and abrupt in their delivery? Do *messengers* attempt to provide comfort? Or, are *messengers* distant and detached? The extent to which waiting is made more bearable is situational, and how *messengers* affect such situations; consequently, there are times when each situation rings true. Having little control over delays is often no fault of *messengers,* yet *messengers* represent institutions and may receive indirect blame by insensitive explanation deliveries. *Messengers* become blameless and delays are viewed as "one of those things" when compassion is shown to others. The *messenger* then is the mediator, determining how explanations are received.

While the context of explanation is crucial, this chapter is guided by reasons that are specific to situations, and therefore how context may explain delays. This chapter examines the nature of wait-explanations and the importance of receiving one while waiting. Generally, wait-explanations explain why one is waiting, and in the U.S. society, individuals are accustomed to receiving explanation. An explanation has become as much a part of waiting as waiting itself; waiting without an explanation may prove counterproductive, for one is placed in limbo, a state of anomie. Consequently, how can situations have meaning without anticipations—without knowing how long? And for what reasons? Wait explanations are intended to answer these questions.

Approaches to wait-explanation vary by situation. There are times when verbal explanations don't work and thus *showing* customers relieves their worry and distrust. Put simply, *showing* helps clarify and verify wait-explanations. *Eye contact* is another method used to convince and validate wait-explanation. Sincere body gestures are invaluable techniques when used properly. *Making an appearance* was the final technique used to convince customers. Such strategy is significant for it allows "waiters" to have direct communication and contact with institutional officials. It is a way to quell mysterious explanations that seem unlikely.

Social status is central when determining whether an explanation is offered. Those in authority may deem it unnecessary to provide an explanation, while subordinates are not only likely to give an explanation but feel obligated. Stratification among super-ordinates and subordinates helps us understand the basis of this contradiction; a contradiction that subordinates learn to cope with and adjust to. Ironically, there are times when explanations never emerge (e.g., *no explanation*), yet individuals continue to wait. Such situations may cause frustration and anger, and such behavior comes more from institutions than ordinary others. Never receiving an explanation is odd, and at times, *offensive* given our cultural expectations and socialization.

As one might imagine, *lies* are also used as wait explanations. Lies have become as normal as waiting in that saving face and protecting one's company are important motives behind falsehood. Interestingly, lies possess the power to help or hurt and while one is interested in doing-good, truth may actually have negative consequences for terminally ill patients. Regarding industry, the truth may stigmatize companies and lead customers to patronize other establishments. So, lies are tricky and may pose moral dilemmas for those using lies as wait explanations. Finally, employees experiencing ethical difficulty in "stretching the truth" often reconsider their employment and may end up resigning.

Ordinary others provide explanation to friends, co-workers, siblings, spouses, club members, and strangers in everyday wait occurrences. For example, when Pastor Hilliard was late to Bible study, Dorothy informed

Mildred (Bible study members) that "he's making a long distance call to the Bishop. He'll be down soon." Additionally, expecting and receiving reasons for delays suggests that the U.S. society reflects a *culture of explanation.* Failure to receive explanation could lead to discord, anomie, and negative perceptions of others.

The analysis of *inanimate objects* conveys that wait-explanations are given by entities other than humans. That is a sign, billboard, radio or video recording may offer reasons for delay. Since inanimate objects are not human, face-to-face interaction and communication is unlikely, leaving explanations open to question and even confusion. Inanimate objects then get at society's ability to move forward technologically in that scientific advancements have allowed humans to create and display explanations without being present.

The *functions of wait explanations* are many, ranging from crowd control to enhancing one's ability to wait. Specific functions include *social control, reassurance, sustaining customer business, sympathy, cover-up, inform, and image of self.* These functions permit a meaningful *analysis* of wait-explanations, providing definition and conceptualization to wait-situations. Individuals expect and deserve a reason for waiting; in many cases, persons desire to know "how long is our wait"? The *analysis* then helps us understand why an explanation is given in the first place and the extent to which wait-explanations make sense. Noteworthy, the type of explanation often reflects the situation and the image certain institutions and individuals wish to convey.

Ladies and Gentlemen, we are still servicing the aircraft. Hopefully, we will be ready to board in 5-minutes. We apologize for the delay.

NOTES

1. This chapter does not analyze differences between explanations and excuses; such an analysis is valuable and much needed; this undertaking examines how explanations are used while waiting; it is clear then that some of my data may be viewed as excuses, not explanations. Still, as I interpret my data, explanations seem intended to convince the hearer while excuses appear to deceive the hearer. The end result is the same, for example, the hearer receives a reason for his or her wait—whether convincing or not.

2. See Elijah Anderson (2011) for an analysis of civil behavior in public spaces.

3. Also see Tukufu Zuberi's *Thicker than Blood: How Racial Statistics Lie*, 2001.

4. To what extent is truth-telling deviant? Theoretically, this question naturally emanates from our current discussion. In what situations does truth-telling make us uncomfortable? Truth-telling deviates from the norm of "let's just get along."

5. See Elijah Anderson (1999) for settling disputes.

6. Note: Cellphone and computer technology permit certain inanimate objects to talk back to us.

7. See Joel Charon's (2004:57–58) analysis of signs and symbols.

8. Patience and order become real assets in unexpected traffic. When one encounters unexpected traffic, not knowing traffic reasons or how long one is struck—such anomie could ignite impatience, nervous and stressful emotions. Emotionally, one is not prepared to wait, but wait nonetheless in order to arrive at his or her destination safely. Such emotions reflect the unpredictability of traffic, length of traffic wait and a possible late arrival. Still, it is amazing how order remains during unexpected occasions; that is, everyone slows, some even permit drivers to change lanes and drivers become extremely attentive yet careful when passing accident. Failure to slow and remain attentive to brake lights could result in more accidents, more traffic, higher insurance and longer, more stressful waits.

Chapter 6

Business of Waiting

Most companies are interested in minimizing customer delays as ways to maintain business and maximize efficiency. And where waiting is inevitable, competitive institutions exercise extensive and expensive maneuvers to distract customer waiting. Waiting line models are constructed and studied to determine whether additional channels (customer service stations) are needed or whether extra technology is required. Moreover, wait-line simulation studies are conducted to determine whether one remains in line too long (see Anderson et al., 2008). Remaining in line too long is problematic for business, leading some customers to leave. Discovering that customer waits are too long, competitive institutions are likely to make changes, that reduce wait time, reduce customer service, and/or improve customer service. For business, their concern with waiting is monetary; they resent unhappy customers and losing business.

The goal here is efficiency, that is, how might institutions minimize waits and rapidly serve customers? Anxious customers, who have short lunch breaks, are frequently eyeing their watches or the clock above the menu. One wishes to rush through bank lines, post office lines, fast food lines, supermarket lines, and juice bars in order to return to work. Arriving at the bank and seeing no-line reduces the anxiety of waiting and one's concern about returning late. For Ritzer (1996:35), efficiency gets at "choosing the optimum means to a given end," that is, finding and using "the *best possible*" means. Efficiency then is accomplished by streamlining the process. In other words, rather than waiting in line, call-in orders or deliveries are likely to shorten the process. In short, establishments must develop creative strategies to prevent long, uncomfortable waits and thus maintain one's business.

Minimizing customer delays to maintain business is one way of examining the business of waiting. It is a conventional strategy that focuses on satisfying and keeping one's client base. This chapter is not interested in the conventional model; I am more interested in expanding the business of waiting by examining waiting through different angles. For example, *waiting* is at the *center* of the *business of waiting*; here, one is not concerned with wait-reduction, one is more concerned with waiting as an enterprise ("how might I make money off these people waiting?"). The "business of waiting" focuses on *how* organizations or individual entrepreneurs' profit from those waiting. It is a unique market niche. As noted earlier, waiting is a necessary condition; we all must wait. And given this condition, organized establishments have set up vending machines, slot machines, snack bars, coffee shops, and news-stands near waiting areas. Such innovations are designed to take one's mind off of waiting, that is, distraction, and simultaneously make money.

The *business of waiting* is both formal and informal. The formal perspective is connected to "the institution"—as when waiting in the airport and one decides to purchase drink, ink (reading materials), or mink (clothing). Conversely, the informal framework is linked to the everyday—as when waiting at traffic signals and street entrepreneurs entice motorists to buy flowers. The significance of the informal framework gets at the creativity and brilliance of street entrepreneurs. How they recognize and exploit a market niche that is usually unmonitored though provides a minimal living. Like the formal perspective, street vendors locate themselves in areas where human volume is high, recognizing the importance of having one's product visible.

BUSINESS OF WAITING: FORMAL PERSPECTIVE

The business of waiting has a formal element that is connected to the company. The formal perspective recognizes that the business is legitimately sanctioned with formal permits, insurance, and fees. Such businesses maintain an obligation to clients by sustaining competent and resourceful customer service. The formal element recognizes the totality of customers in that customers may purchase merchandise, return merchandise, complain, sue, and suggest changes. It follows that official business may contract vendors who wish to sell merchandise within an organized company (as when vendors are contracted by college campuses and hospitals); or the merchandise may be owned and displayed by the existing company. Either way, the idea is to sell to those waiting. While wait-duration varies from short to long, location of one's product is crucial. That is, with little effort, customers must be able to see and browse merchandise.

One example of the formal perspective is routinely observed at supermarket checkout stations. The supermarket checkout register is conveniently set up to assist one's wait. Magazines are generally located near checkout aisles along with candy/gum of all types. For grocery stores and even hardware establishments, such waiting is good in that it allows customers to take their time in making candy, gum, soda, and magazine choices. When children are present, the candy option becomes magnified. The bright colors of candy wrappers grab their attention, while pleading and begging parents to make candy purchases. Yet, when there is "no waiting on check stand number 9," one's ability to review magazines and make candy choices is hampered. So, while the supermarket does not want customers to wait, magazine publishers and candy/soda producers do; minimizing one's wait often forms return customers; prolonging one's wait may lead one to purchase goods that one was enticed to. So, had the candy not "screamed" at you, you might have left it on the shelf? It follows that supermarket waiting becomes an economic gain, not only for markets, but also for candy, snack, and magazine entrepreneurs.

Another example focuses on intermission and early arrivals to concerts and theater productions. Typically, there is a bar setup near auditorium entrances, selling alcoholic and nonalcoholic beverages along with snacks, such as chips, cookies, popcorn, and an assortment of candies. As patrons wait for auditorium entrance, they frequently talk and laugh with companions, people watch, use restroom, and buy drinks and snacks from the bar. The bar is strategically located outside the entrance door and there seems an unusual delay before concertgoers or theater attendees are permitted auditorium entrance. Might such delays reflect the business of waiting? It is clear that before most concerts and plays, and during concert and/or theater intermission, drinks and snacks are sold. Not only is socializing important, but frequently, business is the order of the day. Such bars are rarely open at the conclusion of concerts and plays. Why? There's nothing to wait for—entertainment is no more; it's time to go!

The final example examines a vendor that is not associated with the organization. Dramatic Jewelry is not associated with Kaiser though they rent space near the surgical outpatient wait room. Submitting a formal rental space agreement, paying fees, adhering to vendor, and hospital guidelines are required. Dramatic Jewelry maintains a vending table tactically displayed outside waiting-room, that is, one must pass the vending tables before entering the wait-room. Often, surgery is time consuming, leading to many hours in the surgical wait-room. The entrepreneur is female and warmly greets all who enter. The velvet tablecloths and bright jewelry draw customers to her tables, and they typically admire and inquire of bracelets, earrings, rings, and necklaces. Many items were purchased. In the same area, there is a small Kaiser souvenir shop where guests visit and purchase candy, soda, flowers, plants, and cards. It follows that the vendor and souvenir shop are strategically located to interact with those waiting; in short, it becomes a business opportunity.

There are several other examples that illustrate the formal features of the business of waiting. Yet, waiting in line at supermarkets, purchasing drinks during intermission, and vending tables near surgical wait rooms are three significant illustrations. We learn that visibility, time of day, location, product type, and minimal competition are crucial. Often, entrepreneurs are drawn to formal organizations because there is little competition and heavy human traffic. Whether the product is associated with the organization, as in the supermarket example, or unrelated—as with jewelry vendors, it is clear that waiting is the motivation that sparks the entrepreneurial venture.

BUSINESS OF WAITING: INFORMAL FRAMEWORK

Conversely, there exists an informal component to the business of waiting, and the unofficial version negates most practices of conventional business. For example, the informal framework is not tied to mainstream business, nor does it possess 401c status; further, informal entrepreneurs may not possess business addresses, business cards, business licenses and without notice— move from location to location. Street vendors are unlikely to report informal earnings and the public cannot hold street vendors accountable for defective products; it is a risk incurred by customers. It goes without saying that rules, procedures, and restrictions applied to formal business are not maintained in the informal industry. This is what makes it informal, for example, one's ability to deregulate; its ability to fly under the radar. Still, many informal ventures were so successful that they eventually became formal organizations.

My concern here is *how* certain individuals benefit from those waiting. Again, such persons view those waiting as an economic resource. That is, while I wait, is it possible to turn a profit, to make money? Is it possible to make me a potential client? The informal component examines these questions by investigating situations involving *street vendors, beggars, pay to wait, business cards,* and *rewards for waiting.* All of which are interested in making money, and yet, some are illegal, leading to innovative entrepreneurial methods. The significance of informal business components is that it represents an alternative, an opportunity, and recognition. It provides an alternative to the standard business model, an opportunity to acquire resources and recognition that such a market and niche exist.

Unofficial Street Vendors

An unofficial street vendor is someone who does not have a permit or license to do business. Such vendors may sell openly or covertly. Flower, fruit, apparel, and jewelry vendors sell their goods openly on street corners and in various parking lots. They have become part of our environment, and recognizing or ignoring them is quite routine during everyday activities. Waiting at stoplights, flower and fruit vendors wave their goods to gather our attention; their prices are usually cheaper than formal florists, yet one does not have time to inspect the quality of street vendor goods. The street vendor recognizes that someone may wish to purchase and give flowers to mother, sister, spouse, daughter, girlfriend, friend, or partner. The street vendor is fulfilling a need (flowers for Mother's Day, Valentine's day, birthday, etc.) that was almost overlooked or forgotten by customers. The customer saves time and money, while vendors have provided a crucial service. If there is consensus among both parties, it is a win-win situation.

Conversely, there is the covert venture of informal street vending; the scheme in which one is hiding his/her goods from authorities but not from customers. For example, at MCJ[1], the visitor's line is often long and time-consuming; being first means arriving early because many visitors line up at least an hour before visitation begins. On weekends and some weekdays, the line is more than 125 yards long, extending well into the street. Depending on the number of persons visiting, one could remain in line for two hours. Those visiting loved-ones consist of women and their children, parents, spouses, friends, ministers, brothers, sisters, and former employers. While waiting, one is likely to observe the scenes and characters within this environment, e.g., people watch. For example, children-at-play draws much attention, as well as sheriffs in uniform who occasionally walk-the-line but usually remain near lines-front giving instructions. One is further likely to observe other persons in line, like their clothing, race, gender, hairstyles, conversations, and whether they possess gadgets like cell phones, newspapers, books, magazines, cigarettes, ear-pods, and iPods. In such a line, one is struck by unusually bright earrings, or colorful fingernails or exotic body art that captures your attention. It is variety and difference that maintains one's interest.

Other persons in line are more constructive and entrepreneurial in that Keisha was selling *Sees* candy bars. She casually walked between the two lines, hand-displaying *Sees* candy bars and asking, "Would you like to buy some candy?" Many purchased the one-dollar bar, eating it in line. Her boldness and resourcefulness were amazing. Certainly, she was fulfilling a snack desire, and appealed to the many children wanting sweets. Moving forward in line, those waiting proceed around a lady (Roberta) with a stroller. This segment of the line was temporarily stalled given the possible problems with baby in stroller. So, in Spanish, Viviana (who is behind Roberta) asked her whether there was a problem; Roberta said, "No," signaling the line to proceed around her. We walked around her without giving further thought to the baby or stroller. Yet, it was soon discovered that the stroller had no baby, but was covered with a blanket to appear as if a baby was inside. Given that many mothers with strollers are present, one would not think otherwise, that a baby is inside stroller. However, as she lifts the blanket, a store of wrapped candy, gum, popcorn, chips of all types and sodas of all types are stocked and concealed. Thus, Roberta, the "stroller entrepreneur," sells to those in her surrounding area. One observes the exchange of money for candy, chips, soda, and/or gum. Some customers approach her stroller, examine merchandise, inquire about cost, and then make purchases (items range from 25 cents to one dollar). Other customers signal Roberta to come in their direction for purchase, while children wanting candy often result in return customers. Finally, Roberta who is small and round walks between the lines carrying her jug of candy, inquiring in Spanish whether one wants candy. The candy is always an eye-catcher and attention getter among children; they often notice the bright and colorful candy jug before Roberta's inquiry, and thus begin nudging their parents, pointing to the sight of candy.

Roberta's goods are concealed for they are not permitted and Sheriff discovery would promptly remove her from premises. Moreover, customers are not likely to "drop dime" (snitch) given that their relationship with authorities is frequently strained, but more importantly, customers recognize that vending, legitimately or illegitimately, is what she does. It is her hustle. It is her business. And like any other entrepreneur, Roberta has competitors, namely, Keisha who is selling *Sees* candy and vending machines, which are inside of the visitor wait room. While Keisha's stock is minimal compared to Roberta's, Keisha provides an option in this small marketplace. Finally, Keisha and Roberta are exemplary representations of the informal component of "*the business of waiting.*" They recognized a need (snacks) and market (Men's Central Jail waiting line), and without fuss, creatively fill consumer desires. Those who have visited loved-ones previously are more likely to purchase from Roberta and Keisha, for the vending machines inside are pricey.

Beggars

Beggars are often an overlooked and forgotten group when studying the *business of waiting*. Their methods are central to the business of waiting in that their approach and tact has consequences as to whether one receives resources. Their job is literally to beg for money. Yet, *how* do beggars approach their craft? How do they get the most out of begging? Some beggars take advantage of motorists waiting at certain traffic signals, usually near freeways; others "park" in front of various store entrances holding a cup filled with coin change or a frail animal by his side, and still others wait near churches to appeal to the moral conscience of parishioners. And finally, some female beggars show up with infants while awaiting and approaching gas station customers. Wherever they set up shop, strategies are often considered to maximize their efforts.

Certain freeway exits provide more customer diversity and more opportunity to beg. During key traffic points, like morning, evening, and holidays, beggars stand on center islands, and/or on left side of street (where traffic is stopped) to beg for food and money; some even offer to wash windows. For beggars, a *sign* may read, "homeless—please help," or "Vietnam vet: willing to work for food. God Bless You" or "Homeless—Hungry, Need Work, Please Help," or "Happy Holidays: A little means a lot. Thank You." The idea is to acquire money from motorists; and the sign represents a nonverbal appeal to motorists. The motorist is waiting for the red light to turn green, and as they wait, beggars solicit them for money. Many motorists are indifferent to beggars, refusing eye contact and stopping several feet from stop signal to avoid an unfortunate encounter. Others are amused by *signs* indicating how money will be spent, for example, "I'm not going to lie; I need money for beer." Still other motorists, hold out a dollar while passing or simply give coin change while stopped. Like salespersons who frequently face rejection, homeless beggars seem unbothered by disappointment, and pleased by those who give coin change, acknowledging "clients" with a "thank you" (or "God Bless You") and a smile. Here, there is no tie, no connection, and no obligation because the money comes with no strings attached. They are strangers, and they are not likely to have recurring encounters. In such cases, beggars are taking advantage of a waiting opportunity that could bring resources.

While some beggars maintain *signs*, others don't. The sign is relevant for their location, that is, near freeway exit or stop signal, and the sign could indicate an unwillingness to communicate personally; in short, their encounter remains estranged and nonverbal. Conversely, those without signs are forced to communicate their desire (although standing in front of a busy hotel with cup-in-hand could suggest one's desire).[2] Somehow the *sign-less groups* must get our attention, and this is done covertly and overtly. For example, Woody routinely stands in front of Starbucks making soft clicking sounds as strangers pass. Woody may even verbalize a soft "hi" —to get one's attention. But once you look in his direction, you know he is talking to you. "Any loose change," he asks? Many ignore him as they look, and then look away. Yet, he remains persistent "addressing" those in his space. His persistence often pays off in that some give loose coin change. Woody is about sixty years and always thanks his "clients" after receiving monies; he nods and speaks simultaneously. After giving coin changed, I asked, "How long do you stay out here?" "About five hours. I'm here around 5 in the morning and leave at 10." Woody further explained that he is on disability and receives a check each month but the disability check is not enough to pay his motel expenses.

At a gas station, Gilberto approached me desiring to wash my car windows. I declined given my windows were clean. I asked, "How long do you stay out here?"

Gilberto was unclear of my question and asked, "What do you mean?"

I replied, "How much time do you spend here attempting to wash windows for money?"

He says, "Oh, about an hour or two; you know, long enough to make enough money to eat."

It follows that Gilberto and Woody were pleasant, willing to converse, and appreciative whether they received gifts or not. But all is not well with *sign-less beggars*. On one occasion I was scolded for not giving loose change. "The hell with you!" Jack uttered as I casually refused his request. It follows that one is uncertain how *sign-less beggars* will respond to rejection or to others, but it is clear that their requests must be made verbally otherwise their purpose for standing in front of the store or near the gas pump is blurred. Moreover, the lack of signage alters the course of the interaction, permitting more options within the encounter and more opportunities to hear and question their stories verbally.[3]

The nature of any business recognizes the importance of location. One's location determines the amount of foot traffic and therefore the amount of business. Businesses pay dearly for specific locations, recognizing that location reflects return. Moreover, time of day or night is crucial for business in that one must maintain enough stock and service representatives to service customers. Certain beggars are no different in their understanding of time and location; they too are attempting to maximize return. For example, positioned right outside the front door exit of "Whole Saints Church," a *bag lady* waits for service to end. Responding to the name Becky, the *bag lady* sat on a brick wall in 98-degree weather. She wore several layers of clothing and was surrounded by several bags, some labeled "99 cent store."

Becky appeared tired yet determined as she asked two by-passers, "Is church over yet?"

"I'm not sure," "I don't know" were their responses.

Still, she waited in the heat, for this was her window of opportunity. And sure enough, as parishioners exited the sanctuary, several gave coin change, church pamphlets, and one member encouraged her to attend "homeless ministries every Wednesday night."

Whether *sign-less* Becky attended homeless ministries is unknown, but she did receive smiling faces, money, and church information. Her *orchestration of self* and location was remarkable. That is, Becky constructed herself as a poor homeless female, waiting for "worship completion," and then asking churchgoers for help, either money or food. Given the liberal nature of "Whole Saints," and Christian principles in general, homeless Becky was counting on positive donations. What better place and time to wait; a place where persons will soon exit; a church, a place clearly identified by homeless and a place where a return is likely. Their faith is being tested: whether one truly believes in helping the less fortunate, as Jesus did.

Pay to Wait

Holding a space in line is a courtesy extended to those who leave temporarily. James needs to use restroom and Martha left her coupons on the dashboard. In each case, both ask the person behind to hold their space and their positions were held. While the above instances are quite normal, it is less routine to pay someone to wait, and even more unusual to intentionally wait in line with the aim of selling your spot. Such was the case with Seth, who realized that many were interested in acquiring the long awaited and much-anticipated iPhone. His wait began a full day before iPhones went on sale. Near the front, Seth causally informed those around him and those passing that his space was for sale. Many ignored him and others thought his behavior strange, but an hour before the Apple Store opened "I sold my spot for $200 to a guy in a wheelchair." Seth is not so strange now and possibly envied by those who originally thought him peculiar. The outcome changes their perspective, giving waiting a whole new dimension. So, without question this is an innovative venture, requiring "informal street hustlers" to know the logistics of certain merchandise and demands of potential customers. Whether for iPhone, iPad, video games, or play-off tickets waiting has created diversified approaches to the market.

In another case, Brad was offered pay for *line cuts*. That is, according to Brad, "This guy said he would pay me if I let him cut in front of me." I said "No-way, all of these people would get mad at me." Standing next to Brad, Raymond agreed, "No-way man. You'd just be asking for trouble." Trouble is quite likely given the long hours of waiting by customers, and the pay would not be shared with others. But "this guy's" offer speaks to the value of waiting, a phenomenon that instructs our behavior and environment. Some, for example, may have difficulty waiting and can afford *not* to wait; they can afford to pay others and thus would rather pay than wait. Others have little choice and little income—therefore they must wait. They become part of the crowd and/or make a job of waiting. Herein lies the similarity in that both cases recognize the unique value of waiting, yet differences are also apparent. On the one hand, Seth is willing to release his spot for pay, on the other hand Brad envisions conflict for cutting, and consequently less willing to give up his position. Were he to give up his place in line conflict may lessen.

Business Cards

Business cards are used throughout industry to identify individuals and the companies they represent. The business card is designed to identify one's status, that is, bereavement coordinator, therapist, professor, engineer, attorney, and contractor. Additionally, personal information appears on business cards, like license number, phone number, e-mail address, business address, and even symbols, such as cars, scissors, books, or flowers that represent person or business. The idea is not only to identify the individual but also to locate and maintain contact with potential clients or associates. Given the card design and information included, the business card becomes a representation of one's self. It may determine whether one receives and maintains contact.

Business cards are often distributed and exchanged in social, recreational, and business settings. Such environments are ideal for making and maintaining contacts. In business, one is expected to possess cards to exchange, though the lack of cards may cost various entrepreneurs important relationships. There are times, however, when strangers are awaiting restaurant seating and strike up conversations about swimming or children. While the conversation begins as small talk, it may lead to more specifics, like schools for children and occupations of strangers. Your table is ready, yet you wish to explore the conversation more or follow up on various issues discussed. Politely you ask, "Do you have a card?" "Yes." Cards are exchanged and pleasantries are extended. One then proceeds to table and the possibility of further communication is established. The assumption is contact will be made and a business relationship, or some other relationship, is possible. The card exchange may now provide more information about strangers, so one may intelligently decide whether to maintain or forgo association.[4]

The business of waiting recognizes the importance of business cards. Good entrepreneurs understand their environments and take advantage of the suitable opportunities to distribute business cards. For example, while waiting in an unusually long line to enter the courthouse, two members of the "legal council" began distributing their cards. The line moved in orderly fashion as court-goers exercised patience. Various persons in line began raising questions, like "why is the line so long?" "Are you a juror?" "Is this your first day here?" Carmen, a female security guard responded to the "long line" question, *explaining,* "The line is so long because we are short of staff. Three sheriffs got promoted and we are using temporary staff." In the meantime, "legal council" sieges the opportunity by distributing business cards to anyone who would take. They distributed cards on the sidewalk, right before persons entered courtroom lines. The card solicited business to become one's criminal attorney, specializing in "drug cases." Many in line politely accepted the card, though when the line disappeared, many red business cards were observed on the sidewalk.

In another instance, Fred expressed that he too distributed business cards while waiting to purchase an *iPhone*. A community often develops during long waits, especially with *iPhones, iPads*, and *Harry Potter*. Waiting over ten hours to purchase the newly advertised *iPhone*, Fred took advantage of the wait-opportunity to establish friendships and network with others. He reveals, "I have my own business, so I've passed out my card." Some may use the card to stay in touch or get their computer repaired, but the opportunity was not squandered. Thus, Fred and "legal council" have utilized waiting to advertise, promote, and make business contacts with others.

Giving a card is like handing an invitation to someone; one is inviting "the other" to attend and participate. Specifically, to participate in an event sponsored by card-giver, an invitation to explore an event, relationship, or situation. Sometimes, the card-giving invitation is impersonal, as when one walks into a bank, beauty salon, barbershop, art gallery, laundromat or contractor's office and a series of business cards are placed on a table or business counter. Cards are neatly displayed with a nonverbal invitation to "take one." "Taking one" depends on whether a *need* or *desire* exists. So, the possibility of ignoring the card or letting it remain on the counter is real. Conversely, the personal invitation always carries the advantage of clarification and persuading participation and contact. One is less likely to refuse the card or ignore the card-giver, as in the case of Fred and "legal council." Nonetheless, the business card communicates to us by sending a variety of messages that attempt to gain our attention and participation.

Rewards for Waiting: External Compensation

Rewards for waiting examines *how* institutions compensate customers for their willingness and the inconvenience of waiting. Usually, *the wait* is no fault of customers or the normal waiting procedure, but *the wait* is more of a problem within a specific company. For example, unusual flight delays and lingering car repairs. Additionally, *the wait* may naturally involve a long process, so certain companies provide tangible rewards as a way to acknowledge *the wait* and show customer appreciation. The function of compensation is to sympathize with customers and therefore retain their business. Showing sensitivity to customers by giving rewards implies that businesses are aware of customer plight, and that customers are not taken-for-granted. This type of reward involves a sort of *external compensation* where customers receive a tangible product. The product is not given in exchange for money, and is not sold to the customer; but external compensation is given in exchange for *the wait*. The customer is made to feel that he or she received something free.

During recessions, customers look for bargains; whether in supermarkets or retail stores, a good bargain grabs our attention. Seeing or hearing a good deal, a person might think, "How can I take advantage of that deal?" The same is true for waiting; that is, how can waiting be commoditized? Is there a bargain to be gained by waiting? Those bargains that are available are frequently taken seriously by customers. The airline industry, for example, is likely to offer additional plane tickets for their mistakes as customer service agents politely announce and persuade passengers. "We overbooked," the clerk announces as passengers prepare and ready to board a United Airlines plane. "Is there anyone who would like to give up their seat in return for a *round trip ticket*!? We will put you up overnight—and you may take a flight out in the morning." For some, this is an irresistible deal, as two passengers immediately accepted, citing, "I have no pressing business at this time." The two passengers may experience slight "inconveniences" by giving up their seats but the reward is far greater in that they receive a pleasant night in a nearby hotel and a "free" round trip ticket to any place in the United States, including Hawaii! United Airlines also benefits in that it maintains their solid customer service reputation by leaving on time and accommodating all customers.

In another case, free food was offered in exchange for one's delay. Sisters Ashley and Lindsey conveyed that they went to Jack-N-the-Box drive-through, ordering curly fries, a chicken sandwich, tacos, a shake, and pitas. When they approached the pick-up window, the clerk informed them that their food was not ready and instructed them to park and servers would bring food when ready. Ashley and Lindsey waited in their car for about seven minutes, talking and listening to radio. Realizing that their time in the car was longer than expected, the eldest, Ashley, marched in restaurant inquiring about food. "The manager and employees recognized me immediately. It was like my entrance reminded them of our food. They were very apologetic, saying, 'Oh, we're sorry; we're so sorry you had to wait.' They handed me our order and included a piece of chocolate cake. Then she said, 'Sorry, hope you enjoy the cake.'"

Reviewing the scenario in her mind, Ashley thought aloud, "They probably forgot about us." It follows that Ashley was not expecting anything; she simply wanted her food, and thus receiving chocolate cake came as a pleasant surprise, a generous way of saying, "We're sorry, please come again." Perhaps, businesses are truly sorry and gifts become a symbol of their regret, atonement, and acknowledgment. However, such gifts may be pseudo gestures to cover one's mistake. Whether true or false, a gift was given and an unexpected bonus lightens one's stress, making *the wait* more bearable and more forgivable.

Finally, external compensation may take the form of "first in line." If I arrive first, I should receive service first; but if I have waited unnecessarily at the expense of the company, should I receive compensation? The L.A. Criminal Courts building is known for its long waits; in fact, waiting is built into most criminal court systems, and for these reasons, potential jurors, defendants, and loved-ones in support of defendants often bring something to do while waiting. However, when an inconvenience is caused by *the court* (judges/lawyers/sheriffs), the court tends to apologize and adjust wait-experiences of clients. In one case, an attorney called-in sick and no other public defenders was available to take his case. The defendant waited over two hours before informed by the D.A. After receiving the explanation, the D.A. apologized to the judge and defendant. In turn, the judge apologized and promised to "take the case first thing in the morning." The judge believed that defendant deserves compensation, honoring defendant with a first-case privilege.

It follows that *waiting* at the expense of the company is frequently compensated. The compensation has less to do with obligation and more to do with perception. That is, how others perceive your company, the situation and those involved. Additional plane tickets, chocolate cake, and first-case privileges are clearly symbolic but offering rewards for waiting reflects an image of institutions, and such perceptions hold consequences for future interactions and customer relations. Institutions are not required to compensate no-fault wait customers, but they do and customers appreciate such consideration. Noteworthy concerning customer appreciation was Target's gift to customers. A "goodie bag" was the gift for customers who waited on a cold Black Friday morning. Receiving a "goodie bag" made the wait seem shorter. Also, inspecting and examining the contents of goodie bag gave customers something to do and talk about while waiting. Additionally, the mood of the crowd changed. Shoppers now appeared perked and joyous. Receiving a free and unexpected gift often puts people in a festive mood. Customers were smiling more, laughing, and talking aloud as they examined the contents of the bag. There was a crowd chatter which did not exist before. One corporate employee mentioned that "giving away 'goodie bags' was Target's way of thanking its customers." She mentioned, "It was a worthwhile promotion." And indeed, it was a worthwhile promotion by altering one's morning mood and perceiving Target as a sensitive company.

"WORTH THE WAIT": INTERNAL GRATIFICATION AND SELF-IMPOSED WAITS

Internal gratification and self-imposed waits introduce a new twist on the business of waiting. That is, is what I'm waiting for *worth my wait*? Worth my wait emotionally and/or materially? Is it worth my time? My investment? And, my eventual goals? Ultimately, what will I receive as a result of waiting? Here, one may not necessarily receive money; though money is possible in the form of savings and/or receiving a specific job. "Worth the wait" is experienced in a type of pride and pleasure of assisting someone or being proud of oneself for intentionally waiting and accomplishing a goal; in short, the wait or sacrifice paid-off by receiving a new car, a new job, or losing weight. The common theme is that it was *worth it*; it was worth it because I accomplished what I set out to do. And gratification is tangible and/or intangible. As with business then, there is planning in order to achieve self-imposed waits, and generally, certain outcomes are anticipated.

There is another type of reward received by individuals that is not related to money or material goods. Such a reward is not linked to a company nor does it have marketable value. *Internal gratification* is connected to anticipation and hope of a positive outcome. Those who receive it experience *internal gratification*, that is, a type of internal happiness resulting from wait-outcome. Negative outcomes are less likely to spark satisfaction and could lead to regret. But pleasant results, and therefore *internal gratification*, can lift spirits, justify *the wait*, and rationalize why the wait made sense. Positive outcomes may produce optimism and have consequences for future waits. *Self-imposed waits* are linked to self-discipline in that individuals willingly wait for specific material items or social positions. *Self-imposed waits* are planned, requiring specific steps along the way. *Self-imposed waits* are often longer, as in becoming chief surgeon, and yet they could be short, as in achieving straight A's during fall semester. *Self-imposed waits* might be viewed as long-term goals; such goals require planning, working, and waiting. The plan requires a strategic method of accomplishing goals. And yet why does one set goals? Why is one willing to wait? Reasons vary from lack of resources to lack of experience to self-improvement, but at the completion of the *self-imposed wait* there is a reward that justifies one's wait (see Grushin, 2010).

Internal Gratification

As mentioned before, *internal gratification* is connected to anticipation and hope of a positive outcome. There is no material benefit as in receiving a new iPhone or chocolate cake, but the reward is intrinsic bringing an internal joy, enlightenment, and/or happiness. An internal joy that is stress-free, wanting to celebrate "the other's" accomplishment, like graduation or election to office. David experienced such an emotion when transporting his son to Coca Cola for a required physical before being cleared to work. David recalls, "My son is getting a job at Coca Cola and I had to take him to get a physical. I thought it would be about an hour, but it ended up being five hours! Man, what do you do? But when it was all said and done, he got the job, so it was worth the wait." In another case, Jeremiah paid $10 and waited 3 hours and 45 minutes to see and hear Minister Farrakhan. According to Jeremiah, the doors opened at 5 p.m. and Minister Farrakhan was scheduled to speak at 7:00 p.m., but he did not arrive and speak until 8:45 p.m. "I could not leave because I've heard so much about Minister Farrakhan that my curiosity had to be met; it was worth it because there was a rush of excitement and anticipation when he came on stage, and I learned so much."

Waiting for family members is seemingly obligatory, and thus receiving good news makes waiting tolerable. Specifically, children obtaining a good job is significant news to parents; it means that children are more financially independent and parents are required to provide less. Employment then brings honor to parents, so that fathers may proudly announce, "My son works for Coca Cola Company." The joy and honor of making such a report indicates the insignificance of *waiting*, especially with positive monetary outcomes. Suppose David's son was unsuccessful; joy then is less likely, yet hope and encouragement are probable. Similarly, waiting for celebrities brings about much anticipation, looking forward to what he will say, what she will do, audience reactions to him, unanticipated occurrences, and even the possibility of meeting her. The *waiting place* or environment is also important given that all are there to see the same person. The celebrity may reflect various demographics of crowds. In the case of Minister Farrakhan, the crowd was predominantly African American, and according to Jeremiah, "I was surrounded by *conscious people*, where arguments of denying racism and white exploitation of Blacks do not exist." Waiting for celebrities may also produce the "Wow-effect" in that one is truly awed upon their appearance. The crowd stands and cheers in appreciation of their superstar; some even stand on chairs or climb trees to get a better gaze. The environment itself influences the entire audience.

The mother who sits in court awaiting the judge's decision experiences a rash of emotions. She is interested in whether her son will receive jail time or probation. Carmen cried tears of joy when Judge Connelly sentenced Petro to two years of probation. She could hardly contain her tears hugging everyone in her party. She, like David, believed that the judge's decision was "worth the wait."

Elaine Bartlett is another who found joy in her prison release and reunion with family members. Gonnerman (2004) writes:

> Once she passed through the front gate, she headed straight for a young man (her son, Apache) in a gray parka . . . Elaine placed her hands on his cheeks, kissed his lips, then raised herself on her tiptoes and hugged him once more, this time

wrapping her arms around his neck. He held her tightly, too, as if to ensure they would never be separated again. Neither of them wanted to rush the reunion. After all, they had been *waiting* for this moment for sixteen years, two months, two weeks and four days . . . One reporter asked Elaine, "What's the first thing you're going to do when you get home?" "I'm going to *enjoy* my family and hold them and just show them how much love I've carried all these years and let them know that without them, I couldn't have made it."

While one does not want to wait sixteen years, with little control over judge and Governor decisions, Elaine endured and matured as a person and mother. Unexpected and coerced separations led to pain and the disappointment of separation and letting down loved-ones. One is unsure of next steps and length of split, but the delight of hugging children and starting anew is overwhelming.

A common theme among David, Jeremiah, Carmen, and Elaine is *worthiness* after a lengthy wait; there was an internal sense of bliss that justifies their wait. While positive results rationalize our patience, certain persons and loved-ones do so as well. For instance, at Harold's funeral, the Duarte Mayor expressed, "He was late a lot, but he was worth waiting for." The mayor indicates that there is value to waiting; the value is exemplified in support of loved-ones and anticipation of positive results. "Worth the wait" suggests that *this situation* is worth my time and my investment; it is a personal decision whereby one accepts the consequences, recognizing the clear possibility of *waiting in vain*. While *waiting in vain* is likely to produce the opposite emotion, one frequently finds a silver lining or lesson when waiting-results are painful.

Waiting then is associated with hope, the prospect of optimistic outcomes. There is nothing worse than a child waiting for his parent—who fails to arrive. It has a lasting and emotional effect that creates distrust and skepticism. The child likely learns defense mechanisms to avoid such pain. Kevin, a bank manager, shared that "My worse waiting experience was waiting for my mother. I used to sit by the window all day long waiting for my mother and she never showed up. See, I used to be in foster care and my mother said she was coming to pick me up—but she never showed up. I'm still waiting on my mother, not because I need her to come by, but to fill a void in my life." Waiting "all day" would have been worthwhile had Kevin's mother arrived, though failing to show up left a void, an emptiness. The hope and anticipation of something to come is indescribable, and the image of an innocent child peering through a window is unforgettable. Like David, Kevin was willing to wait for his mother *all day*; and had she showed, clearly it would have been "worth the wait," for a child could want nothing more than to spend time with mom. Yet, it is clear that certain wait-*situations*, waiting for mother, are more significant than other wait-*situations*, for example, waiting for furniture to arrive. But at the end of the day, whether mother arrives or deliveries are stalled, it is the wait-outcome that influences our emotions and how we proceed.

Self-Imposed Waits

Self-imposed waits reflect a type of deferred gratification. Individuals who experience *self-imposed waits* are cognizant of their goal and motive. While waiting, plans are refined but intentions remain the same. Many persons have experienced *self-imposed waits*; it is a routine part of our existence in that most have goals they wish to achieve. That is, individuals wait to buy and own their dream home, dream instrument, dream yacht, dream stock, dream diamond, obtain a dream job, or acquire admission into their dream university. A motorist has a license plate holder attached to her car; it reads, "I waited 14 years—look what I'm driving now." She was driving a blue BMW Sedan; her dream car seemed well kept with shinning rims, sealed paint, and tinted windows. It was an eye-catcher, and the license plate holder expressed her sacrifice and patience. The owner of the BMW reveals an important characteristic of *self-imposed waits*, and that is, individuals are likely to care for, maintain, and even treasure the item in which they waited. The item may possess a certain symbolic meaning, ranging from sacrifice to status. Those who impose self-compelled waits may or may not wish to communicate their experience to others, but it is evident to the owner—that the car or social position was absolutely *earned*, possessing a deeper meaning than if it was simply given.

Perhaps the best example of *self-imposed waits* is experienced by various parents who sacrifice for their children. Some parents naturally deny themselves so children receive benefits. It is not uncommon that parents forgo vacations, new cars, house repair, and even new clothing so Keisha could purchase drill team attire and/or pay Jamal's high school/college tuition. Many parents expect to sacrifice for their children; they believe "it goes with the territory." Parents reason that sacrifice allows children to participate and compete, and even expose them to new and challenging environments. If children show promise and/or dedication to certain activities, such as swimming, piano, violin, ice-skating, etc., parents are likely to assist in cultivating the child's activity with physical, psychological, and financial support. Who knows, youngsters may be child protégés? And thus, the parent is obligated to find out. At their own expense, certain parents are willing to yield so children may move forward. Witnessing childhood success makes parental sacrifices worthwhile; it is an investment that most parents readily accept.

Wanting a well-defined body could lead to sacrificing fast foods; moreover, desiring better health and weight loss may also alter one's diet. It follows that practical sacrifice and discipline are involved in losing weight; many try to shed pounds though rarely successful. Those who are successful take pleasure in their weight reduction and comments received concerning their new image. One's self-perception and self-esteem is raised while new opportunities emerge. One respondent confessed that "the greatest self-imposed wait I have done is losing weight." She explains, "It required me to monitor the food I was eating as well as the amount of physical activity I had each day. This process caused me to set realistic goals and wait long periods of time in order to witness results. This process required me to plan, work, and wait in order to become healthier and more fit. This self-imposed wait took 6 months, and the results are a 75-pound lighter me!" *Self-imposed waits* of any type require discipline, and often leading to impressive outcomes, for example, "good things come to those who wait."

Of the 311 survey respondents, most are willing to sacrifice for practical matters, like school, weight loss, and family. School was most evident in that a common theme was forgoing social events to achieve academic goals; somehow "the party of the year" was less important than accomplishing an "A" on the final or scoring high on standardized exams. The data also revealed that respondents are willing to sacrifice for material articles, like cars, guitars and vacations, but in the end, these material pleasures served important functions for respondents, such as getting to work on time and avoiding late buses.

While *self-imposed waits* are usually advantageous, they may also have negative consequences, like missing out on opportunities. One does not expect to shun opportunities, yet caution and delay could have unanticipated costs. For example, investing in stocks may cause brokers to pause. That is, wondering whether "the stock" will continue to fall is risky. Given market unpredictability, "the stock" could rise or fall at any given time. Waiting may result in higher market prices, leading to missed opportunities. Waiting to accept a full-time job offer is also tricky given the circumstances of the market and the needs of the institution. And passing up on a record deal could result in lost possibilities. Bob recalls that his band passed up a valuable opportunity because they thought that they were too young; He writes, "Two years ago, I was a part of this band that played local L.A. gigs. After a couple of months, we started getting a larger fan base and started to get recognition from the music industry. We had begun playing shows at places like 'The Troubadour.' Almost a year ago we were offered a record deal. We decided that we were too young and not ready to do tours yet, and that another opportunity would come along. Since then, our band broke-up." Seemingly, self-imposed waits have positive and negative effects, and negative costs are difficult to retrieve. Failed experiences may lead to regret, though if similar opportunities recur, one's wait strategy or one's assessment appears more informed.

SUMMARY

This chapter has introduced and provided unique perspectives on the *business of waiting*. Unlike conventional models of waiting, this alternate perspective places *waiting* at the *center* of the *business of waiting*. My view is more concerned with waiting as an enterprise, that is, "*how* might I make money off persons waiting?" In short, the *business of waiting* focuses on how organizations or individual entrepreneurs' profit from those waiting. In this sense, waiting becomes very functional for persons doing business in that a human market emerges to test, advertise, or sell one's product.

The business of waiting examines formal and informal business ventures that take advantage of those waiting. The formal element is connected to the established business, which maintains city permits, insurance, company policies, and fees; in short, it is an established and recognized business. Customers are important and participate by purchasing products, returning merchandise, complaining, and evaluating company performance. The official business may sponsor vendors who wish to sell merchandise within an organized company, or the merchandise may be owned and displayed by the established company. Examples of the formal element of business include supermarket checkout stands, snack bars at concerts, and Dramatic Jewelry who paid for vending space at Kaiser Hospital. The informal component of the *business of waiting* examines unofficial business and relationships among clients and entrepreneur. There are no contracts or binding agreements; returning merchandise is unlikely and bargains are appealing. "Clients" are attracted to informal entrepreneurs because they fill a temporary need or desire and often they are in the right place at the right time; the informal vendor has studied the market, placing him or herself in proper locations. Our concern here was *how* street entrepreneurs maximize their efforts by those waiting. How and why is this market attractive to them? For one, the bureaucracy of establishing and maintaining a legitimate business is unnecessary; paying dues, taxes, and license fees do not exist. Unofficial businesses are clearly unregulated. Such deregulation is attractive and risky for unofficial business ventures. Our study examines four such cases of the informal component of doing business, for example, *street vendors, beggars, pay to wait, and business cards*. All of which represent their own challenge, which gets at the fascination and innovation of unofficial business.

Worth the wait explores an interesting twist on the business of waiting, analyzing two important categories that examine the benefits of waiting. Such categories include *internal gratification* and *self-imposed waits*. *Internal gratification* is linked to anticipation and hope of a positive outcome. This reward is intangible and those who receive it experience a sort of internal joy resulting from wait-outcome. Expressions like "worth the wait" were a common sentiment in this category. The final wait category was *self-imposed waits*. This category recognized that waiting was a clear choice; a choice, however, with a specific goal in mind. Whether long term or short, *self-imposed waits* require planning, working toward one's goal, and waiting.

Generally speaking, the "business of waiting" is an interesting phenomenon. It explores an untapped area of sociology that isolates interaction between unofficial street vendors and street beggars with ordinary citizens. For many, begging and street vending is what they do; it is their job and a key feature is their willingness to wait. *That is, wait-for people to occupy and share their space.* The sophisticated beggar knows well how to size up his/her client. For example, when "clients" leave store or when "clients" arrive. Which persons to approach, and which to let go? *How* to approach clients and *how* to avoid others? Consequently, using the appropriate demeanor and script are critical to success. Good beggars then are careful not to startle or intimidate clients, for this is detrimental to giving. Good beggars are skilled at seeing their clients before clients see them. In fact, beggars are clever with impression management, appealing to our politics, religions, and sensibilities. As with politicians and clergy, all beggars are not the same; unsophisticated beggars outnumber and lack the skills of mature beggars. Some beggars are threatening and may lead customers to complain. Yet, while most beggars look similar to the general public, good beggars make sophisticated distinctions among everyday people.

NOTES

1. MCJ represents Men's Central Jail.
2. Note that a *cup-in-hand* is often viewed as a sign. The cup may signal that money is requested. Still, in the cases of Woody, Gilberto, and Becky, they had no sign or cup. They verbalized their requests.
3. *Smooth* is another homeless person who was begging without a sign. With his head bowed between his legs and sitting on the concrete surface, *Smooth* asked for change as customers entered El Pollo Loco restaurant. Such positioning (sitting on the concrete surface and head lowered) is significant in that he does not wish to intimidate. *Smooth*'s hair was well groomed. It was short and "processed" (Haley, 1965) backward. He wore sunglasses, earrings, and his face was clean-shaven. His face jerked and appeared somewhat reserved as he asked for money. After asking for

money, *Smooth* would lower his head, as if to bow his head and then held out his hand to receive possible coins. I gave coins, he thanked me and I proceeded to ask about beggars and territorial rights. That is, "would another homeless person beg in your immediate area? You know, in this very spot? Or would you invade someone else's area?" *Smooth*, barely raising his head and no eye contact, responded, "No, I would not go and ask for money if another person was there. I would respect their space—and usually, they don't invade my space." Interestingly, *Smooth* appeared somewhat reserved as I showed interest in his lifestyle. That is, his head was bowed and he looked away as he responded. I felt that he was uncomfortable talking with me and wanted me to rush along; seemingly, he did not wish to engage.

4. Another area of exploration is conversation termination, for example, offering a business card to end communication. Put another way, how are business cards used to terminate conversations? Offering a business card does not always mean, "please call me later." It may be used as a polite way to end interaction, and having no intention of reestablishing contact. After all, how many times have we exchanged business cards and contact is never made?

Chapter 7

Waiting with Strangers

Variation and diversity among strangers make them extremely interesting and complex. Some strangers are "normal" in that they are harmless, and asking questions will yield predictable answers. Other strangers appear "unusual" for they are often seen *talking to themselves* in ways that question their sanity. Finally, some strangers are viewed as "scary," insisting on unwanted stares, glares, and making others uncomfortable. The common theme among *normal, unusual,* and *scary strangers* is that *they are persons we do not know*; therefore, our space is somewhat guarded in the presence of strangers, and our interactions are temporary.

Waiting in line presents opportunities for individuals to entertain themselves by watching and evaluating strangers. In fact, persons become linked to strangers in various wait-situations. For instance, waiting at the bus stop, waiting for the train, and waiting in financial institutions are situations where individuals are surrounded by strangers; several of our experiences exist around people we do not know. The bus stop, the train station, and financial institutions are familiar situations where strangers abound. Given our many trips to the bank or ATM, individuals are not uncomfortable—for this situation is familiar, and yet strange (see Peter Berger, 1963). Order and organization are present in that strangers adhere to conventional norms for specific settings. Such situations only become uncomfortable when "unusual" and "scary" strangers are present and inconsiderate. It is clear then that one's *linkage to strangers* occurs in everyday situations.

It is indeed possible for *stranger linkage* to occur by church membership, gym affiliation, and even waiting in line for theater entrance. Waiting in line for theater entrance is clearly a most interim experience, though it presents opportunities to become less strange and more acquainted. Church and gym memberships are more enduring, yet one may remain a stranger to others within these environments. In short, individuals exercise options to remain unfamiliar or develop friendly acquaintances. Wherever waiting, that is, taking classes or sitting next to foreigners on airplanes, one's linkage to strangers is varied and our choice to maintain distance depends on many variables.

While we are *linked to strangers* in different ways, there is little, if any, obligation to them. Persons feel more compelled to greet and speak to family members, friends, associates, and acquaintances rather than strangers. At times though, we greet strangers—for it is courteous; it is polite. Grocery shopping is often performed among strangers; generally, individuals search for products and compare brands without thinking, "Who is watching me"? Moreover, interaction among "normal strangers" may lead to conversations about "best brands" and specific products. But suddenly, the shopper's attention is diverted from the brands in question to movement down the aisle. The male shopper raises his head, gazes down the aisle, and notices a female acquaintance, Jane; an acquaintance that male shopper (Paine) does not wish to acknowledge and converse. In this situation, Paine is more willing to converse with strangers than a familiar person. Why? If female acquaintance detects him, Paine may appear occupied. Suddenly, Paine feels no longer anonymous but very visible, becoming more cognizant of his behavior. His sudden visibility makes him uncomfortable, for Paine does not desire social contact and wishes to avoid Jane by walking the other way. Has Jane become a different type of stranger to Paine, for example, someone he knows but chooses not to acknowledge at this time? Does Paine's behavior make him a permanent stranger to Jane? Here, it is important to realize that we have hatched the *complexity of strangers.* That is, who is a stranger? How are we linked? And how do we distinguish among various types of strangers? *It is important to maintain the idea that strangers are persons we do not know,* but also strangers are those we choose not to know, not to acknowledge. At what point does someone become a stranger? When an acquaintance behaves oddly in public, causing embarrassment? When one is shocked to see an acquaintance at a strip joint? When friendship dissipates?

In his analysis of "talking with strangers," Fred Busch (2006) examines strangers and their willingness to converse with others. That is, what signs, objects, and gestures do strangers provide to inform others of their communication or noncommunicative interest? A variety of symbols are used to convey interaction intent. Sleeping, reading, and peering through a window suggest different messages to others. Our interpretation (or misinterpretation) of these symbols determines the extent to which conversations are generated. While taking the train from L.A. to San Diego, your compartment companion looks interesting. He is middle aged, well dressed, wears glasses, and carries a trumpet case. His face is mature and his hat is brown and classy. You want to converse but you also wish to respect his privacy and space, for such a trip may be his time to rest and enjoy some sights. Though his trumpet-case rests on the seat beside him, two initials (M.D.) appear on the side of his case. There are no signs of earphones, computers, or tablets, so you take a chance and introduce yourself. His responses and gestures to your initial comments and questions will indicate whether M.D. is interested in conversing or resting. Eye contact is made and introductions begin.

Waving his hand, Zach says "Hi, I'm Zach."

M.D. nods with a slight smile, speaking softly, "How ya' doin', young buck, I'm Miles. Keep your eye on my trumpet while I get some rest."

Zach has critically assessed M.D. as someone who is older, tired, well dressed, trusting, and possibly a musician. Zach's interest in conversing with Miles is not mutual, thus he settles for "keeping an eye on my trumpet." M.D. also assesses Zach by referring to him as young and trusting enough to guard his instrument. Individuals evaluate and assess strangers in seconds, leading to appraisals that guide their behavior. Though strangers are near, there remains distance. Strangers are usually in our immediate presence, our immediate space; a far-off stranger remains a stranger but the likelihood of "interaction" is diminished. The possibility of interaction is more probable when strangers are nearby. Clearly, individuals assess nearby strangers and, to some degree, remain distant. For "immediate strangers" can do most harm or inspire fascination and interest. Our distance between strangers is not so much physical as it is mental, cultural, and social. We do not know each other, and it is the situation of shopping, traveling, or banking that brought us together. So, conversing with strangers implies an unavoidable proximity.

Recognizing that stranger-assessments are reciprocal, as in the case of M.D. and Zach, it is important to realize that stranger-assessments are not always verbal. Various stranger-evaluations are mental, gestural, and sensual, for example, nonverbal. For example, as Jessica and Venus watched a popular movie in a crowded theater, Jessica began to smell a horrible scent. She looked in several directions to determine the nature of the scent, and on closer observation, she realized that the smell came from a guy sitting one seat away. "His breath was so bad and so strong that for most of the movie, I leaned towards Venus and covered my nose with a napkin . . . It was awful! But the movie was so crowded, there was nowhere else to move." Such nonverbal stranger-assessments are often more common than verbal in that, on average, we are less likely to speak with strangers but make mental, sensual, and gestural appraisals, keeping such assessments to ourselves or sharing with significant others.

Though there is social and mental distance among strangers, Harvey (1962) found that people react more positively to strangers than friends— when each is designated as the person who evaluates them positively. Other studies (Stevenson et al., 1963) show that strangers have more impact on the behavior of young children than parents. Such studies reveal our politeness and kindness toward strangers. While we have nothing to prove, we are often concerned with managing the impressions of others. Consequently, we have little reason for hostility or unfriendliness among "normal strangers," in fact there are times when we show unusual acts of kindness. For example, when the customer ahead of you is short 50 or 25 cents, often one is happy to cover the cost, and at times, customer service representatives may forgo the remainder of the balance. When poor families can't afford funeral services or a cap-and-gown for graduation, strangers are more than willing to help by contributing to their "go-fund-me" request. Seemingly, individuals are moved to aid those in need, and possibly, such actions have little to do with "the stranger" and more to do with someone needing assistance. It goes without saying that our reactions to strangers are mixed, depending on the situation and type of stranger. Conversely, individuals routinely "dump-on" friends and family who they have known for years. Loved-ones know our problems and hang-ups—so it is not necessary to manage impressions . . . as much. It is more common to "be real" and straightforward, in order to prevent confusion and provide constructive criticism. The studies of Harvey and Stevenson reflect a type of consistency in one's behavior and treatment toward strangers.

COMMUNICATING *WITH* STRANGERS

On one level or another, individuals tend to communicate *with* strangers while waiting. Disposition reflects how or whether one desires an exchange of ideas. It is clear that props, signs, and rails guide individual and collective wait-patterns, yet there is an expectation among strangers that one will not only respect wait-norms but that strangers will honor the privacy of others, or will not cut in line or harass others. Still individuals protect themselves by keeping a certain spatial distance, awareness of one's immediate environment and securing personal belongings. *Breaking wait rules may lead to longer waits, confrontations, and/or sanctions.* In short, *much of our waiting is among persons we do not know.* This does not mean that getting to know strangers is impossible, but it is surely rare and it could be risky or rewarding. While strangers may express few passing words or a conversation while waiting, it is unlikely that such interactions continue.

The guiding question of this section examines the conditions and situations under which strangers are likely to converse. Put another way, *under what conditions are strangers likely to converse while waiting?* There are several conditions and some include: utilitarian communication, proximity, waiting consistency, unusual events, accidents, confronting strangers, and revelations to strangers. Each condition is analyzed within its specific context of waiting, and often, the circumstance influences whether communication occurs. The condition itself may emerge naturally as when one's place in line needs saving, or conditions could prove formal as when ordering a meal or requesting a pillow from flight attendants. Either way, our concern is communication and how it occurs among strangers while waiting.

Utilitarian Communication

Utilitarian communication is a type of talk that is practical and informative; it is functional in that it provides necessary information such as direction, instruction, and facts. It is often an essential interaction because a stranger is in one's immediate presence, and the stranger is used as an information resource. *Utilitarian communication* is typically short, yet there are times when utilitarian conversations are prolonged. The idea is to obtain "the information" and move on; it is assumed that "the stranger" has more knowledge than "the novice" about the environment and may therefore prove useful. So, such questions, and hopefully answers, will assist persons in understanding and navigating their current environment.

"Excuse me! Excuse me!? Where is Cherry Street?" "Oh, take Euclid for about a mile; turn right on Glenn Ave., and look for Cherry Street about two blocks down." "Thanks. Sorry for the trouble." "No Problem." This encounter illustrates how *utilitarian communication* works. James is anxiously waiting at a stop light; he has driven around for several minutes. Seeing Arnold in the adjacent car, James yells through his window, "Excuse me! Excuse me!? . . ." Without question, James is seeking information that will potentially assist his travel. Such incidents are common when one is lost, individuals routinely ask unfamiliar others for direction. Strangers involved in utilitarian conversation may encounter a wide variety of questions, some of which include: "Where's the restroom?" "My earring seems to have disappeared. Did you see a stray earring?" "Where's the drinking fountain?" "How much?" "Are you in line?" "Are you next?" And, "what time is it?" Utilitarian questions often pertain to current situations, requiring immediate or near immediate attention. And all are meant to inform in some fashion.

At the laundromat, there is little talk among strangers; conversation is primarily among those who arrived together and appear acquainted. Still, those present are cognizant of their environment. They are visually aware of current patrons and their locations within laundromat. When strangers interact, typical questions involve, "Are you using this machine?" "Are you using that dryer?" "Do you have change?" And, "How long does it take to complete a washing cycle?" On one occasion, Celcia noticed that Andrew was standing near a faulty machine; he placed his clothes basket in front of washer and began to load quarters. Before Andrew could push in his coins, Celcia warned, "Don't use that machine, it doesn't work too well." Andrew thanked Celcia and moved on to another machine. Similarly, while waiting at a bus stop Anita asked Wanda for bus directions, for example, "Which bus should I take to go to Leimert Park?" "Oh, take this next bus, the 734 South. That should get you there." "O.K. Thanks." Again, there conversations are short, sometimes spontaneous and information oriented. In most cases, strangers are not seeking acquaintanceship or friendship, but practical responses to their inquiries.

At times, *utilitarian communication* may extend its temporary flavor and yet the goal remains the same, for example, obtain information. The wait-environment may contribute to a lengthier conversation. For instance, waiting in line at MCJ[1] is an eye-opening experience for the novice. For one, the novice is struck by how many women and children are waiting; moreover, the sheriffs possess attitudes that reflect "us against them," and finally, the commitment of those waiting to see and visit with loved-ones. On weekdays, visitations start at 10:00 a.m., and the line begins to form at 9:00 a.m. Unfamiliar with visitation procedures, Jeff spots a sheriff and inquiries about the visitation process. Jeff locates the wait-line and seems surprised to see approximately seventy persons waiting. A temperature of about 75°, Jeff begins his uncomfortable wait by standing behind two Latinas. Shortly, there appear an additional thirty-five persons behind Jeff. Keisha stood directly behind Jeff talking on her cell phone. Apparently, Keisha was talking to a friend. In their conversation, Keisha seemed shocked when her friend mentioned, "The line is usually out to the street."

After completing her conversation, Jeff asked, "How long does it take to get through the line?"

Keisha, "I don't know."

Over hearing Jeff's question, Pedro inserts, "It depends. I've been here times when it took two hours and 45 minutes; I've been here other times when it took me 8 minutes. That time—I was shocked! Sometimes, you can wait for a long time, and not get in!"

In disbelief, Keisha exclaimed, "What?!"

"But when that happens," Pedro explains, "they give you a pass."

Jeff seems confused, "But what does that mean?"

Pedro, "Next time you come, you are one of the first to get in. Nowadays, the pass-line is starting to take long. But after you get to the front of the line, you go inside and wait again, that could take a long time too."

Jeff, "Do they search you?"

Pedro, "No, but they take your name and run a check. So, make sure you don't have any warrants."

Jeff, "Yeah, Okay. How long can you visit?"

Pedro: "Fifteen minutes."

Jeff, "That's it? For the amount of time we wait, 15 minutes is not long."

Pedro, "Yeah, they try to get you in-and-out of there."

The nature of the situation gets at the type of *utilitarian conversation* that ensues. The questions are very information specific, that is information pertaining to MCJ visitations, and to the novices (Jeff and Keisha) such knowledge is very valuable. As strangers, their exchange does not include personal information, like "Who are you here to visit?" or "Why was your brother arrested?" The sole purpose of utilitarian communication is to obtain practical information. However, it is the length of wait-time and proximity that drives their conversation. Such *proximity* then overlaps into the next category.

Proximity

As noted earlier, our critical question focuses on the conditions under which strangers are likely to converse while waiting. It has become increasingly clear that proximity influences whether conversation emerges while waiting. Persons are more likely to speak when sitting or standing near to one another; yet, it is more difficult to converse when sitting or standing several feet away. Crowded situations, such as jury assembly rooms, emergency rooms, trains, planes, bus stations, lines for entrance, etc., offer examples of stranger closeness. In these situations, there is no empty chair or space between strangers, and if standing, less than 6 inches separates them while they constantly adjust themselves to keep from bumping one another. It is clear, however, that proximity does not guarantee conversation; in fact, it may deter conversation because of personal space considerations.

Jury assembly rooms are formalized wait-situations in that jurors are summoned and required to wear official badges while serving. Jury assembly rooms are most crowded during morning sessions as orientation is provided. After a lengthy orientation, the final words to emerge from the administrative clerk's mouth are, "Your main function is to sit in this room to see if your name will be called." Interestingly, if jurors are not selected for a panel, they could remain in the juror assembly room, or wait room, all day. The juror assembly room is the size of a medium auditorium, and within its confines, potential jurors are seated next to the other and many jurors are standing. A wall and computer terminals separate the assembly room, preventing some jurors from seeing the administrative clerk, so they watch orientation by monitor. Still, throughout the day and recognizing juror space conditions, a variety of conversations and exchanges occur. Consider the following observations:

Leroy (age 60), Angelica (age 60) and Matt (age 20) seemed to enjoy their conversation as they sat next to one another during jury orientation and beyond.

Leroy sat on the end-aisle seat; Angelica sat in the middle between Leroy and Matt. Leroy and Angelica initiated conversation and eventually Matt joined their discussion. As they talked, Angelica produced a picture from her purse. Angelica smiled as she handed it to Leroy and then showed it to Matt; both Leroy and Matt nodded as Angelica shared the picture's contents. This group began talking at 9:40am and continued through 11:45am. They seemed to like one another—for as Leroy, Angelica and Matt conversed, they also smiled, laughed, shared pictures, excused themselves when leaving and generally appeared engaged with one another. Angelica got up twice, once when she was called by juror services and once for a restroom break. Each time she returned, they resumed conversing. While gone, Leroy and Matt maintained conversation.

Within the jury assembly room, it is not uncommon to observe others, their behavior, and to overhear conversations. Jane, who is an elderly white lady, looked over Bridget's shoulder while reading a novel.

Jane politely asked, "What are you reading?"

Somewhat surprised, Bridget, who is also white, turned and said, "*With No-One, No Witness.* It's by Elizabeth George; I really like her books."

This was the start of a short conversation; and in short order, they discussed books, authors, and some of Elizabeth George's upcoming projects. They smiled while talking and apparently shared a reading/author interest. At one point, Jane expressed to Bridget that "We are ferocious readers at my house." Enjoying the book more than the conversation, Bridget excused herself and continued reading.

Additionally, there are times when conversations are intermittent. That is persons in one general area will engage in small talk, read a newspaper article, or go to the restroom then resume their conversation. *Intermittent conversations* are not constant; they are interrupted by cell phone conversations, restroom breaks, reading breaks, and vending machine breaks. While individuals remain in the same general "place," each recognizes and accepts the other as their conversation piece. Consider the following observation:

Apparently, once a communication bond is established, it is typically interrupted by panel assignments, lunch breaks or movements of some sort. At times, one may feel comfortable re-establishing conversation after it has temporarily ceased, i.e., by someone going to restroom or snack room and returning to original "place." Manuel and Rudy (two males, one 34 and the other 62, respectively) did not talk constantly as did Leroy, Angelica, and Matt; they talked intermittently. Between comments and conversations, Manuel and Rudy read, stared at others, went to vending machine and restroom. Still, they remained comfortable engaging and talking with one another. At one point, Manuel got up to stretch and walk to vending machine. When he returned, Manuel's seat was taken by

Alex Tong. Manuel promptly stood nearby until Mr. Tong left—then reclaimed "his" seat, allowing Rudy and Manuel to resume their *intermittent conversation*. Apparently, they created a temporary bond that lasted throughout the day. Manuel was willing to wait for Tong's departure so he could reclaim his "place" and interaction with his newly acquired friend. Mr. Tong, on the other hand, had no idea that Manual was waiting.

Again, it is important to note that conversations and interactions usually emerge among those who are in close proximity. The above cases are exemplar in showing how communication among strangers emerges within structured wait-areas. Still, in these same places, individuals may not hold utilitarian communication or intermittent conversations. Somehow, persons manage to display and convey *communication disinterest*. *Communication disinterest* is often conveyed by reading, that is, engrossing oneself in a novel, newspaper, or magazine; talking on cell phones; putting markers[2] between seats, like purses, computers, books, snacks, backpacks, etc.; sleeping, computing, wearing, and listening through earphones. Communication disinterest signals to others that talking to strangers is undesirable and even burdensome. In fact, persons may sit next to one another and yet be miles apart. Talking on cell phones may serve as substitutes for talking and interacting with strangers. For instance, the juror may wish to talk but does not wish to pry or impose. Going through the trouble to introduce oneself could take more effort than not. Phoning a friend requires no "getting acquainted effort" in that one calls and conversation ensues. Clearly some jurors talk on cell phones because they are not interested in "getting to know" the other; they wish to remain estranged. In some cases, jurors talk to non-strangers (friends, family) on cell phones to keep them company while waiting. They catch up on gossip, weekend activities, and reacquaint themselves. But the phone serves as a companion in the same way that on-hand strangers do while waiting; such conversations allow time to pass faster, particularly for the unprepared jurors, who bring nothing to keep them occupied.

Again, talking on cell phones is further indication that certain jurors are not interested in mingling or conversing with strangers. One lady (Marla) was heard to say, "All these people sitting here—bored out of their minds." Such a comment suggests that waiting in the jury assembly room is tedious, not only for the subject but also for the other jurors; and that talking (to strangers or friends on phone) could enhance one's wait. It is clear, however, that persons make and receive multiple cell phone calls that keep one's mind off waiting and thereby giving her something to do.

Conversely, *communication interest* is an appeal to correspond with others. This is done by engaging in small talk, by sharing a picture or part of one's newspaper, by offering food, responding to questions, and various other communication strategies. One is not restricted by earphones, DVD, or video viewing. Though when one is found knitting or drawing, the nature of such activity could lead to conversation. Conversations that begin with "what are you knitting?" or "that sweater reminds me of my grandmother's shawl." And later, express comments and conversations about certain occurrences within the jury assembly room, like jury panels, orientation, and/or persons talking too loud on cell phones. It is the art, the knitting, the photo, a decorated purse or reaction to a private comment that becomes the initial conversation piece. Finally, a willingness to take part in social exchange; it must be mutual. Someone who is asleep or engaged in serious calculations seems far more reluctant.

As a way to invite conversation, persons usually display their best behavior. Manners are polished and diction is clear; assisting others and standing for pregnant women displays a special kind of courtesy. Best behavior means awareness, sacrifice, and consideration—all of which are designed to manage impressions and invite conversation. And who would not talk with such a person? In fact, many would desire to sit near such "jewels," getting to know him or her. Still, the invitation to converse is almost natural; it is not forced nor is it imposed; parties sense security, that it is okay to converse; that she is safe or he is harmless. One may relax and share. After all, jurors have been screened and required to wear name tags. The closeness then of our beings has spawned a conversation that would have otherwise not occurred.

Waiting Consistency

Waiting consistency refers to regular patterns of wait-behavior; it is a practice that occurs daily, weekly, and even monthly, whereby individuals develop routine waiting patterns. Individuals, who wait for the same bus at the same time during the week, have developed a type of wait-consistency. The likelihood of facial recognition and eventual conversation is real. The same is true with parents who taxi their child to ice-skating practice every day, watching and waiting in the same spot. While bus riders and fellow ice-skating parents begin as strangers, such consistency makes them less strange. Overtime, and as faces and environments become more familiar, strangers will gradually interact.

Allen Ballet Studio presents a case in point as to how conversation and interaction among strangers emerge and manifest. Typically, parents bring small children to a one-hour ballet class and wait in the areas provided; the lobby is where most parents wait, sitting in patio-chairs which are bolted to the floor making chair movement impossible or difficult at best. The chairs are bolted side by side, so when one sits, one is in close proximity to the other. Usually, there are not enough chairs for parents, their children, and the advance ballet class that arrives early to stretch and socialize on the floor. Consequently, many persons sit on the carpet floor, stand, or stand-and-watch their children's ballet class through an open door or window. If several parents are watching class, often comments are made about dancers, dance instructors, or upcoming programs, usually *Nutcracker.*

Ballet classes are ongoing in that children may begin at age five and progress through more advance dance levels; many dancers continue through high school, where ballet becomes extremely technical. Parents and children often start as strangers but end up befriending fellow ballet parents and children. As class progresses and parents wait, faces become familiar presenting opportunities to converse. In due course, many strangers have become friends, and while waiting, they eventually engage the other in conversation. It is quite possible to see parents caring for their infant children, knitting, reading books, assisting children with homework, watching ballet classes, and daydreaming. Given that children befriend each other faster than adults, it is no surprise when children invite ballet classmates to upcoming birthday parties; such parties allow strangers to become more acquainted. Additionally, parental volunteer requirements present opportunities for strangers to become more familiar.

As ballet classes develop into a routine, regular parents become accustomed to waiting in certain seats or certain areas; in short, one becomes accustomed to a *waiting place.* One's familiarity with a waiting place along with recognition of recurring faces increases the likelihood of conversing with others while waiting, and it decreases the stranger syndrome. In time, one can better anticipate the other's behavior so decisions to converse are less challenging. Moreover, such waiting arrangements and routines do not apply to other waiting areas such as hospitals, airports, train stations, and post offices. In short, there is higher *waiting consistency* among "ballet-waiters" than "other waiters" (e.g., hospitals, airports, post offices, etc.), allowing familiarity to evolve among "ballet waiters."

Ballet waiting, which can become *social waiting,* is experienced in other situations where parents or others wait consistently for children. For example, club activities, like soccer, swimming, gymnastics, basketball, hockey, ice skating, volleyball, and so forth have similar wait-routines by parents. In many such venues parents are required to participate in club activities (fundraisers, swim meets, snack bars, etc.). This reduces stranger syndrome and heightens awareness and recognition that many participants in club activities have similar values and lifestyles. It goes without saying that the social circumstances of waiting and contact with strangers are heightened by specific wait-environments.

This phenomenon is also apparent at community coffee shops or any venue where waiting is routine. It begins as foreign and develops into the familiar.

Habitual wait-situations allow one to break down and overcome alien environments and individuals. Here, it is assumed that one is seeing and routinely interacting with the same persons. The environment is what drew strangers to such location and the atmosphere is made friendlier (or otherwise) as time lapses. What was invisible initially—later becomes detectable and recognizable.

Unusual Events, Accidents, and Confronting Strangers

An *unusual event* is another situation that leads strangers to communicate. Such events catch our attention because these incidents are unexpected and even odd. Some examples of *unusual events* include loud ringing cell phones while waiting in bank lines; sudden public arguments among spouses; children violently crying as a way to draw attention; and police arresting and carting off a shoplifter as customers observe and wait for service. Not only do such events lure ones' focus, but frequently unsolicited and spontaneous comments are blurted and exchanged.

Regarding cell phones, one respondent wrote that she was shocked to hear the piercing of a customer's cell phone. His phone rang as he was being serviced by the bank teller. "The ring was so loud, so deafening that I covered my ears and said to the girl in front of me, 'My, that's a loud ring!!' She turned in my direction agreeing, 'Yeah, it's veeerrrry loud!!'" Had the phone not rung, it is debatable whether these strangers would have communicated; would have expressed their surprise at the phone volume. Consequently, the unusual and loud sound invaded and grabbed their attention. Such events and in many cases, one's response is knee-jerk and unpredictable. But such an event generates small talk and gestures that are designed to verify that this situation was in fact *unusual*.

Similarly, car *accidents* and emergencies cause strangers to gather and converse. A car accident is sudden and action oriented; seeing the accident may lead one to stop, view, and even offer assistance. It is clear though that *something* must be done. The colliding cars and sirens from emergency vehicles lure one's attention and people begin to gather (see Price, 2005). Many wish to know, "What happened?" and/or "How can I help?" Stories of the crash emerge from eyewitnesses allowing spectators to receive a sense of the accident, for example, "the Porsche ran the red light." Spectators gather for different reasons. Some will assist and others will simply observe. If celebrities are involved, our curiosity is heightened and the time we spend at the scene is extended. Stories of the accident are modified as they are retold. Calls are made; pictures maybe taken. But, it is the accident that drew these strangers together and the scene along with participants that produced a basis for commentary. No accident is the same, but we have all seen and heard of accidents; a harmless gathering is generally expected, and the gathering itself becomes familiar for there is little to do except watch.

While most are unwilling to *confront strangers*, there are times when it is necessary. Our fear of *confronting strangers* has much to do with the unknown. We have no idea of what to expect or what will happen; so rather than confront strangers, individuals ignore or remove themselves from the situation. To be sure, one will not confront strangers who are perceived as intimidating or physically threatening, though individuals are likely to size up strangers and use appropriate tactics. For example, the juror assembly room maintains a moderate noise level and several individuals are able to work in this environment. Persons are reading, writing, and computing amid the moderate assembly room noise. It appears that jurors learn to tune out various conversations, sounds, and other noises. Interestingly though, Janet was disturbed by Alicia's pen-tapping. Alicia was tapping her pen on the arm of her chair. As Janet is reading and writing, she hears the annoying sound; she raises her head to track down the culprit. Janet traces the pen-tapping by looking across the aisle, locating and watching the pen's movement—then making eye contact with Alicia. Janet's eye contact is combined with a blank facial expression but not a smile. Realizing that she is disturbing others, Alicia ceases her pen-tapping as Janet resumes reading and writing. It appears that certain noises disturbed Janet and other jurors, for others also looked in the general direction of the tap.

While Alicia's pen-tapping was gentle, it was bothersome. Words were unnecessary and seemingly glaring sent a clear message. Interaction with strangers must be cautious and delicate because reactions are uncertain and etiquette may reflect response. In assembly rooms where medium nose is constant, Alicia could have ignored Janet's eye contact and tapped her boredom away. Changing "places" for Janet was difficult given the morning juror crowd. Realizing juror constraints and being considerate of others, Alicia ceased her behavior.

Revelations to Strangers

While persons are waiting and something interesting or unusual happens, it may jar our memory, leading one to confess or reveal to strangers what he would never reveal to family or friends. In a survey conducted among college students, participants were asked to respond to the following statement: "We are sometimes guilty of revealing more to strangers than friends and family. Do you believe this to be true? Thoroughly explain, why or why not?" The results of table 7.1 indicate that the majority of individuals, 79 percent, are likely to reveal more to strangers than friends and family. It is equally interesting to review their explanations.

Table 7.1   **Disclosures to Strangers**

	Yes	No	Partial	Don't Know	Total
# of respondents	82	10	10	2	N = 104
% of surveys	79	9	9	2	99

By the author.

Situations in which one divulges to strangers vary and yet include bars, vacations, inpatients talking with nurses and visitors talking while waiting to see inmates. Carina explained:

> Some time ago when I was younger, my then husband was incarcerated and I had gone to visit him there. I met an older lady that was there visiting her husband as well. We got to talking while we were waiting for our husbands to be brought out. We shared our struggles and frustrations. I told her how I was unhappy and tired of the lifestyle my husband was living; so, she gave me some advice and told me her story. One thing she said was not to stay with him because of the children—that eventually the kids grow up and start a life of their own and get into trouble like their father; she used herself as an example. Because she was older, I sort of trusted and believed her and eventually left my husband. I felt comfortable talking because the possibility of never seeing her again—made it easier.

Dae is another who feels strongly about revelations to strangers, and given one's environment, it is not uncommon to hear strangers share. Certain environments, like bars and strip joints, seem more conducive for exposing one's self. Dae Chan explained:

> I was a bartender and when I was working, I met many people that would be passing by and getting a drink. Some were regulars and some were not. In that time, I noticed that they would share some intimate feelings and thoughts, like cheating and returning to the straight world after being homosexual; things that they would probably not share with other people around them. I would kindly listen and refrain from passing judgment for a few reasons: 1) they trusted that I would not judge them. 2) I felt that they could talk openly about their thoughts and never have to see me again, so I wouldn't argue with them. 3) It's interesting to hear how other people view the world. It often was a way for me to learn.

And finally, the internet has become a place to share with the unknown. Rather than the everyday, mundane entries, some persons reveal hidden thoughts and desires for the world to read. Shant believes that Vlogers (Video & Blogs) on YouTube is a case in point:

> I am very fascinated by the amount of information that people are willing to share to an unknown crowd. My reasoning behind this is that they are willing to hear what a stranger thinks about them because they are less likely to get hurt. As for family and friends—who we get a major part of our *self* from, they could not understand the other parts of us. We think of it being difficult for them to see us in any other light but the one they know.

And Chien adds:

> I know that Youtube is very popular and that anyone can upload a video of anything. One thing that sticks in my mind is that thing where someone tags five people and they have to tell five random facts about themselves. Many of them oblige even though they don't really have to.[3]

Generally, individuals disclose to strangers for several reasons, some of which include embarrassment, judgment, and invisibility. Some persons are embarrassed to tell friends and family about their hidden secrets in that it may cause shame and ridicule. Such revelations may further strain close relationships, causing individuals to become self-conscious. Additionally, individuals divulge secrets to strangers rather than loved-ones because of judgment. The fear of judgment by family members is anticipated, so talking with strangers reduces judgmental evaluations. In fact, strangers are more likely to be unbiased when hearing and receiving various revelations. Strangers might offer unbiased support and advice because they do not know this person; strangers have no history and are not tied emotionally to this person. And finally, the invisible nature of strangers, the fact that "I will never see you again," reduces one's hesitancy, and ensures that their secrets are safe. Individuals are less interested in trusting strangers and more concerned about dumping, revealing, venting, and/or confessing information that one no longer wants to retain. It is quite possible that revealing information to strangers allows that person to talk about an issue that they are not ready to discuss with friends and family. In fact, this may be practice for the real encounter.

Consequently, one major advantage of talking with strangers is its therapeutic value. Is talking to strangers therapeutic? Individuals often talk with psychiatrist in confidence; likewise talking to strangers may have similar effects in that one's issues remain private and persons feel better, for they are no longer holding onto their personal and/or troubling secrets. Similarly, this may mirror confession in the Catholic Church. For example, at times, one confesses his/her sins to an unknown person, who does not really see him/her, does not know him/her, yet one obtains absolution. Ashley experienced release and comfort when sharing with a family who was visiting loved-ones; she felt the need to share as a way to help. Consider her revelation:

I volunteer at a hospital and came across a family visiting their loved-one in my ward. The daughter, age 17, asked me for ice, and when I brought it to her, I asked her if she needed anything else. She divulged to me that not only was her brother sick, but she found out that her mother was diagnosed with breast cancer. My mother had breast cancer and I sympathized with this young girl and how terrified she was. I told her about my mother, and how scared I was, but how I concentrated on making my mother's life happier and easier. I empathized with her and said that I would say a prayer for her family, to stay strong and no matter what—stay positive. I would have *never* told that girl, or anyone else for that matter about my mother, but I felt a personal connection, an outreach for help. It made her feel better, but strangely enough, I felt better too. I typically do not talk about that period of my life and it felt good to address it, to share it.

There are certain benefits to disclosing to strangers and remaining anonymous. Reputation, self-image, venting, and an unbiased evaluation are significant advantages when sharing with strangers. And while one talks frankly and anonymously, in part, the deep secret remains secret, securing a feeling of release and relief. Because they are strangers, one does not know who they are, and who they know. Thus, a clear disadvantage is that strangers may know part of one's social circle, that is, it's a small world. Presumably, this could wreak havoc on the aforementioned advantages. And God forbid, after divulging to strangers, the stranger decides to stalk you and use such information as leverage. It is for these reasons that 10 percent of the sample would not share with strangers.

SPACE *BETWEEN* STRANGERS

Seating arrangements in public waiting areas are often imposed because individuals have little control over seat-positioning. One enters the room, examines the environment, locates, and carefully selects a seat. Where possible, persons attempt to maintain space between and among strangers. Individuals place coats, newspapers, computers, book bags, and/or purses in the space, or seat, next to them, preventing close contact with strangers. It is only when wait-rooms are crowded that one sits next to the other, and within such crowded areas, seating is a commodity for it takes on new meaning; that is, the seat becomes more relevant than the stranger. Still given a choice and appropriate space accommodations, it is not likely that strangers will sit side by side.[4]

The freedom to make a choice is liberating and comforting; one's wait appears more bearable and doable. Options may further positively influence our perception of wait-situations. For instance, when boarding an airplane and passengers settle in their assigned seats, the stewardess announced, "There are many open seats, feel free to relocate and space out." Passengers appeared somewhat relieved, as one customer shouted "cool" and decided to move and find an open seat. Not only did passengers relocate, several sat in rows with no other traveler. Consequently, after reaching cruising level, many passengers laid out and/or spread out their work materials. Seemingly, those passengers remaining together were couples of some sort or parents traveling with children. Another interesting relocation occurred within the movie theater among two middle-aged ladies (Mildred and Lena) and a younger gentleman, Alonzo. Alonzo sat three seats into his row as he leaned back, ate popcorn, and watched the trailers. Suddenly, in the darkened theater, Mildred and Lena spot two seats and flop down as they adjust their garments and condiments. Realizing that he is being invaded, Alonzo gets up and moves to the next seat, leaving a *space between strangers*. Mildred, who is closest to Alonzo, looks in his direction but says nothing. The theater is somewhat full but not so crowded that one cannot find an open space, and apparently, Alonzo desires distance.

The above examples get at choices strangers are likely to make when given the opportunity. And there are some institutions where individuals have such options to sit side by side or space out. If loosely populated, laundromats, dental offices, buses and car repair wait rooms offer space choices. Yet, there are situations where space choice is not available and strangers must sit side by side. For example, buying tickets to watch the L.A. Dodgers or Russian Ballet places one in close proximity with strangers. While it is difficult to determine one's "seat neighbor," it is nonetheless interesting how individuals are on their best behavior (see Elijah Anderson, 2011). If one accidentally bumps the other, she is likely to excuse herself; and when sneezing, one covers his mouth and then says, "Excuse me." In turn, the stranger replies, "Bless you," "Thanks." Even if one believes that he will acquire flu symptoms, his movement is limited, for he is contained by the situational nature of formal ticketing and formal seating. So, the lack of choice is disheartening; while we can choose our seats, we cannot choose our seat associates—seat neighbors are random.[5]

One issue that strikes a major chord is the *impersonality of waiting* with strangers. While waiting, one can sense the impersonal distance among "waiters." Through utilitarian communication, persons are not speaking *with* one another as much as they are speaking *to* one another. Strangers then rarely talk or make eye contact but simply scan the wait-environment as a way to see who is present and where one might place himself. Further, distance is crucial because strangers do not wish to sit or stand too close to the other, and when close proximity is necessary, individuals are often uncomfortable and guarded. It follows then that the very nature of *stranger* implies an impersonal relationship and therefore impersonal behavior. If anything, one's relationship with strangers is secondary and not primary (see Cooley, 1964). Individuals are unlikely to give birthday cards to strangers or visit them in hospitals. Persons are more likely to avoid them by keeping distance and declining invitations to interact.

In part, impersonal distance among unfamiliar individuals is due to the stranger syndrome, for example, "we do not know one another, so why should we converse?" The stranger syndrome refers to intentionally ignoring and avoiding those that one does not know. There is no desire to connect. As a result, such impersonal distance reflects a preoccupation with safety and security. More so than other type waiters, *bus waiters and subway waiters* are frequently on-guard by watching their bags, searching for their bus/train, being alert to their environment, and keeping a safe distance from others. This group clearly wants to protect themselves, guarding against any danger. One consequence of the stranger syndrome is removing oneself from harm's way. For example, at a bus stop in Alhambra, a short conversation occurred between Yin-Yu and Elroy Jenkins. Jenkins was sitting under the covered bench prior to Yin-Yu arriving; when she arrived, Yin-Yu stood about two meters away and to the rear of Jenkins. Engaging in utilitarian conversation, Jenkins turned and asked, "Does the bus come on time?" Shocked by the question and responding as though she does not wish to converse, Yin-Yu replies, "I don't know." After their brief verbal exchange, Yin-Yu eased further and further away from Jenkins. She backed away—behind a large sign-placard where they could not see each other; and now there is barrier between them, where Yin-Yu appears more guarded. She seemed concerned with her safety and security, and not wishing to talk with or have anything to do with Elroy Jenkins.

Similarly, the safety issue is apparent at the Crenshaw-Stocker bus stop. For instance, two males stared down two females while they walked pass the bus stop; as they proceeded forward, one male continued turning his head and staring at the two young ladies. These ladies never acknowledged their stares and glares; they simply ignored them. Their stares were not amusing but intimidating and even threatening. Such "looks and faces" may explain why impersonal distance exists among strangers at bus stops. Ultimately, safety is a major concern among certain strangers at specific wait-areas; one does not know the other and the potential harm that may ensue.

The major theme that travels through impersonality of waiting and space between strangers is caution. Impersonality and space could reduce injury.

Though surveillance cameras exist, one is more cautious at bus stops and subway stops than at airport boarding areas. In part, it is because airport boarding areas are far more restricted and controlled than bus stops or subway trains; there are more security personnel at airports. Social class may also influence these venues in that it is cheaper to ride trains or buses, while reservations are necessary for air travel. Homeless persons and rival gangs occasionally appear at bus and train stops leading to more caution by others. While one is never sure of possible dangers at airport boarding areas and even medical waiting rooms, such customers appear far more relaxed. Environments are clearly different allowing for variation in precautions.

SUMMARY

Waiting with strangers has a familiar and unfamiliar reality; one is not familiar with a customer standing next to him/her in the bank. Yet, one is familiar with his/her environment, the bank, and what is expected of customers and employees. Societal socialization permits individuals to become institutionally aware, and such institutions guide our behavior. While we are not familiar with strangers, culturally, we learn to anticipate their behaviors within specified settings. A stranger then is a person we do not know, yet individuals are frequently surrounded by strangers, recognizing that the closer we are to them, interaction appears probable.

Communicating with strangers raises an important theoretical question: *under what conditions are strangers likely to converse while waiting?* The question implies that communication is likely, though situations are influenced not only by communication, but by various forms of communication and interaction as well. Such conditions include utilitarian communication, wait consistency, proximity, unusual events, accidents, confronting strangers, and revelations to strangers. Utilitarian communication is a talk that is practical and informative. It functions to provide information, such as direction, instruction, and facts. Such interactions are typically short and polite. Wait consistency refers to patterns of waiting that occur daily, weekly, and monthly. Individuals who wait for the same bus, in the same place, at the same time, daily have developed consistency in waiting. Consequently, faces become familiar and gradual interaction is likely. Whether or not one desires communication, close proximity leads to conversation. Logically, one recognizes that it is impossible to socially interact with someone in another room. And revelations to strangers may prove therapeutic in that venting, complaining, and confessing to strangers could lift emotional and social pains. An added benefit is that one's deep secrets remain private given the anonymous nature of strangers. Talking to strangers then is like writing in one's diary;

ideally, one's thoughts and desires are vented, they remain unexposed—while receiving a certain release and satisfaction.

Space between strangers examines individual desire for distance among others. The cases of Alonzo and passenger seating provide stellar examples of one's need for space; but persons recognize that such desires are not universal. In other countries (France), it is common to observe strangers sitting side by side even though vacant spaces are available. It follows that seating arrangements are often imposed by institutions, leaving customers little choice in structural design and seating choice. Generally, institutions are interested in capacity while individuals are concerned with space and comfort. For example, when given a choice, persons are likely to leave a space between the other; when space and therefore choice is limited, individuals conform to institutional seat arrangements. But to further illustrate individual interest in space and comfort, there are times when customers rearrange chairs that don't accommodate its environment and audience. Which in part gets at the *impersonality of waiting* with strangers and how waiting with unfamiliar others can prove aloof and inhospitable. Waiting for the doctor to return from lunch, one observes that patients rarely talk or make eye contact. They deliberately look off or sneak gazes as not to acknowledge the other.

In the United States, one's preference for space is real, and it reflects an overall desire for safety. Take public arenas for example, we have no knowledge of the motives of strangers; moreover, we are taught to keep safe distance, and children are ordered, "Do not talk to strangers!" While we are waiting, we exist among each other, but we do not know one another. We are more familiar with the environment than the stranger sitting next to us, and yet the stranger is part of the environment. Making plans to attend the Russian Ballet, we take pains in selecting the best seat (aisle seats are popular); still, we cannot choose our "seat neighbor." This person is clearly a stranger. I do not know him. He is imposed on us by institutional and formal seating arrangements. However, are they really strangers—given that most people who attend New York's Ballet are white, middle to upper class, suburbanites and Protestant? They are strangers with familiar characteristics, and thus their concern with cautions is somewhat reduced. Overall then our socialization is to maintain space between strangers.

NOTES

1. MCJ: Men's Central Jail.
2. As well, markers may facilitate conversation.
3. Facebook and other social medias have similar chain conversations.
4. This idea reflects mainstream U.S. culture.
5. And then there is the arm rest.

Chapter 8

Alternatives to Waiting

Want it Faster? Go Prime on Amazon

A key and consistent feature in the advancement of society is technology (see Grint and Woolgar, 1997). It permits us to live longer, work faster, and travel farther. We are faced with more choices, more information, and faster reception of data. Through technology, our communications have advanced and our ability to hide is reduced, all in all, technology has brought on unparalleled progress and advancement: *advancement* that changes the structure of interaction and our cultural perceptions of waiting. That is, members of industrial societies move at faster speeds; members are socialized to receive information faster; individuals become accustom to driving faster, arriving faster, producing and preparing faster goods and services. In part, this is market driven and one cannot discount the importance of efficiency. Additionally, technological innovations provide more choices, allowing one to take advantage of options produced by technology. Consequently, waiting becomes less and less rigid; it is not fixed but quite flexible. Technology has spilled over into wait-structures providing flexibility and alternatives to waiting. Our fast pace, quick-fix-society has ushered in wait-options that are utilized by many. *Alternatives to Waiting* then examines *how* societal institutions and individuals reduce waiting and thus attempt to obtain services sooner.

Technology assists us in *wait-management though not wait-elimination. Complete eradication of waiting is impossible.* We frequently wait for loved-ones to arrive, election results, and the birth of newborns. But the arrival of loved-ones, election results, and children are made easier with technology; that is, one is likely to arrive faster by car than bike, likewise, birthing complications are more manageable through technology. While technology aids us in wait-management, individuals develop management strategies that assist persons in coping with and adjusting to delays imposed upon them by bureaucracies. So, waiting is inevitable, and the more we wait, the more alternatives we uncover.

STRATEGIES USED TO AVOID
OR MINIMIZE WAITING

George Ritzer's (1993) *McDonaldization of Society* is a classic case of society's search for faster, more efficient service. His major principles (efficiency, calculation, predictability, control) offer a new bureaucratic paradigm to institutions in the market. In part, a McDonaldized society gets at our resistance, and at times, our inability to wait, wanting more options and faster alternatives. American society is one that stresses individuality, innovation, and choice. It seems primitive to offer one type or one brand. Consequently, restaurant customers are accustomed to viewing menus and making food choices; seasoned shoppers expect to examine many garments before selecting the "right" one. Children are made cognizant of choices by the options offered by parents, for example, "Do you want *Captain Crunch* or *Cheerios*?" Sometimes our choices are so vast and so varied that it is difficult to make a choice. Yet, the difficulty of making choices is not the issue; it is having the ability, having the option to make choices. Such is the case with waiting. Individuals expect wait-options; that is, rather than stand in line at the bank, ATMs and online banking have evolved as worthy alternatives. Soon, few will have had the experience of waiting in a bank.

My investigation uncovered the following techniques to minimize waiting, for example, call-waiting, callbacks by institutions, online concert ticket purchases, computer technology, and scheduling medical appointments. Certainly, there are more strategies that seek to eliminate and/or minimize waiting, yet our focus will address the aforementioned issues. As I investigate these techniques, a common theme of *alternative* emerges. *Alternatives* represent the American value of choice, and how variety is reflected in our society. This is no small matter given the amount of time spent trying to simplify our lives, in order to maximize our pleasure, leisure, and essential life requirements.

Technology, for example, provides communication options that radically reduce waiting. When they work, texting, e-mailing, cell phones, land phones, skyping, call-waiting, and call forwarding assist us with diversified communication. Consider Jason's use of communication technology, "Jason, this is Tyler. Did I wake you?" "Nooo. I'm talking to my son; let me get him off the line. Hold on." This brief conversation represents how *call-waiting* technology can reduce one's wait and obtain information faster. Rather than receiving a busy signal, Jason hears a beep indicating that another party is on the line. For Jason and Tyler, call-waiting is an alternative to waiting; that is, Tyler is not required to call back and Jason may respond to the beeping signal. Additional benefits to call-waiting include the immediacy of information, answering important calls, receiving emergency calls, and choice. With call-waiting and caller ID, one can make informed decisions about answering. Jason then is in complete control of managing his alternatives.

Conversely, Roger, an elderly respondent, opposes this innovative technology. He believes that call-waiting is intrusive on his conversation, believing that if the line is busy, then one must wait. While call-waiting is viewed as an alternative to waiting, others perceive it as a rude interruption. Does Jason's son view it as an interruption? And must he wait to continue his conversation? Or does Jason Jr. understand and conform to the conditions of call-waiting? Does call-waiting depend on status or the importance of the call? Without question, our conversations and interaction are modified, yet how many Jason Jr.'s feel snubbed by intrusion and not ready to hang up? Alternatively, how many Jason Jr.'s are thrilled by intrusion and glad to disconnect? Roger is one who resents phone invasion and thus, his opposition suggests a certain "slowing down of life's pace," and traditional conversation etiquette that he is not prepared to relinquish.[1]

Another, less intrusive alternative is *callback by institutions*. This wait takes clear advantage of technology by returning customer calls, and thus displaying a certain value and respect to customers. For example, when calling Westjet, Kaiser Hospital appointments, or Spectrum, a message prompts the customer indicating the amount of wait-time (ten minutes) and provides the customer with options. The customers may wait ten minutes or press #2 to leave callback information, for example, name and number. The message further promises that customers will not lose their place in line and provides an estimated callback time. This option is considerate and convenient to customers who opt to do other tasks while waiting.

You can buy your ticket on-line
or you can wait in that long ass line at ticket-master!

Waiting in line to purchase KEM (R & B artist) tickets, the line begins to form fifty minutes before box office opens. There are twenty persons in line when business begins, yet two customer service agents thoroughly assist customers prolonging the wait of others. As customers wait in line and observe how employees are handling customers, various people complain, "Why is it taking so long for him to choose his seat?" Others wonder aloud, "What seating areas did she show him? What area is she showing him?" These questions are raised because concertgoers want good seats, and the longer one waits, the worse his seat selection. Thus, there is a certain anxiety and impatience when waiting in line for tickets.

Radio Host and Comedian Steve Harvey recognize that waiting in line is time consuming and may cost concertgoers quality seats. Of course, the issue is "why wait when you can buy on line?" This then presents an alternative to waiting. "Waiting in a long ass line" suggests that your ticket, that is your seat, will not be as good as someone who *buys on-line*, and worse, the concert might be sold out (if you wait in line). In part, this is a marketing ploy to buy (and sale) tickets ASAP. Still, the interested consumer is likely to consider such options, that is, whether to buy online or wait in line. And depending on concert importance and one's busy schedule, consumers may select the fastest option, for example, the online alternative. Which begs the question: to what extent do alternatives lead to disuse and/or modification? That is, will box offices become extinct or used differently? While *buying concert tickets online* presents a certain efficiency, it also represents a different type of waiting. For example, one cannot buy his/her ticket until the online box office opens at 10:00 a.m. Here, the would-be concertgoers are anxiously waiting in front of their devices until the bell sounds. After which, there is the rush to select seats and pay with your credit card; and God forbid any technical difficulties or errors in credit card data entry.

The rapid pace of *computer technology* provides yet another alternative. "What are you waiting for?" About ten years ago, Verizon raised this question in an advertisement displayed on a bus stop bench. The advertisement further reads, "Verizon Online DSL, twice as fast as before?" "As before?" How fast was it "before"? Before one's previous DSL or phone line connection? DSL became the alternative to phone line network connections. Phone line connections are being phased out and soon individuals will search for even faster internet connections, for example, high speed or lightning fast. But the advertisement implies that no one should be waiting for internet downloads or website navigations. According to the advertisement, one is to assume that downloads and navigations can happen faster than before, really fast, albeit twice as fast! While Verizon's advertisement does not clarify DSL speed, internet technology consistently moves forward—in an attempt to send and receive information instantaneously, for example, *instant gratification*.

Generally, if there is service stoppage, for some unknown reason, certain patrons are likely to ask, "What's the problem?" or "What are you waiting for?" These are familiar questions to most, and Verizon uses the latter in their advertisement. The implication is clear, "What is the problem?" Respectfully, this question is raised to identify the problem, in an effort to solve and move forward. Moreover, "What are you waiting for" implies that "it is *your* turn." "Please take your turn so I can take mine." The person raising the question is usually next, and possibly impatient. But when an advertisement raises this question, one ponders whether the intelligence of readers is being questioned. Seemingly, it is an indirect and impersonal insult on readers who have not switched to DSL, that is, the alternative.

More recently, the fastest network connection may range from 100 megabits per second (Mbps) to 100,000 Mbps. At home, for example, network speeds can range from 100 Mbps to 1,000 Mbps; for colleges and large firms, some of their connections might be up to 100,000 Mbps—and many organizations maintain multiple connections to support their clients. And let's not forget our precious cellphones. For U.S. cellphone users, 4G (fourth generation) is the most common high-speed mobile network, with peak speeds over 200 Mbps. In the next few months, 5G will replace 4G promising speeds twenty times faster.[2] Wow! A society that prides itself on innovation, shortcuts, and progress is shocked and even dismayed when users are not using the latest, most convenient technology. In fact, new technology may limit or eliminate outdated technologies, like phone line internet connections and analog broadcasts.

Another strategy to avoid waiting gets at *scheduling medical appointments.* How do some patients schedule medical appointments? Many patients select the first medical appointment available, anticipating the likelihood of minimal wait time. Our attempts to avoid waiting may not always materialize. Let me explain. The doctor may be late for some reason, for example, stuck in traffic, prolonged meeting, car accident, equipment malfunction, miscommunication, and so forth. The same is true when cars change lanes to avoid stoppage and delays of eighteen-wheeler trucks. Unfortunately, and given eighteen-wheeler obstruction, there are times when changing lanes leads to unforeseen delays, for example, car accidents, pedestrian crossing, stalled cars, and so forth. *The real point is that one is cognizant of waiting, and thus makes a conscious and active attempt to avoid or minimize her wait. Attempts to avoid waiting echoes alternatives to waiting.* It turns out that remaining behind the truck or making a mid-morning appointment may prevent unexpected delays.

Clearly, postindustrial societies offer alternatives to waiting; such options are interwoven into the fabric of our society. For example, rather than waiting in line at Jack-in-the-Box, customers may use the drive-thru or delivery options. Additionally, carpool lanes, kiosk technology, self-service, phone orders, fifteen items or less lines, instant foods, restaurant bar seating, scan and go, baggage carry-on, ATMs, and so forth represent alternatives to waiting. Choice has emerged as a significant part of our existence, ranging from the brands we choose to occupations we encounter, to the politicians we elect. We are lost without choice. When alternatives are unavailable, individuals tend to create choices, recognizing that alternatives emerge from human desire, human complaint, human need or simply human convenience. In short, alternatives emerge from the natural course of evolution.

One consequence of the industrial revolution is rationalization, that is, while efficiency is important, the rate of efficiency is also valued. Hence the above (drive-thru windows, scan and go, carpool lanes, online services, high-speed internet, etc.) represents strategies used to avoid or minimize waiting. It follows that creative strategies often emerge from market research, institutions, and/or individuals.

MENTAL HEALTH AND WAITING

I had to wait an hour at DMV³ to take the test.
Taking tests are already stressful.
But after waiting an hour, I was more stressed.

Another significant feature to alternatives to waiting is sustainability of *mental health*. Given one's personality, waiting could prove challenging and problematic. One respondent admitted, "In everything I do, I try to figure out how I can avoid waiting; because I can't wait. *It drives me crazy!*" So how does one avoid waiting? How does one remain sane while waiting? What innovative strategies are used to avoid waiting? In this case, if Hanna waits, she is likely to go "crazy"—though going crazy seems more problematic than waiting. If there is no alternative, one may remove himself/herself from situations of wait or wait-environments. Hanna continued, "There are some instances where you have to wait, like immigration. Here, there is nothing you can do. I go and I prepare myself to wait an hour; once that hour is up, I start climbing the walls. I start looking around trying to figure out the problem. *Waiting, stresses me out!*"⁴ It follows that "figuring out the problem" could limit one's wait, it could help one understand the delay. But, understanding the delay is not the issue. One's inability to wait is the problem. As discovered in previous chapters, certain individuals are willing to pay others to wait; the value of waiting has emerged as a significant feature as a way to avoid stress, crowds, and a range of wait-environments. Paying someone to wait is a viable option, and while Carmen contends that waiting is "very frustrating," she too is willing to "pay the extra dollar so I don't have to wait."

The above comments by Hanna and Carmen draw our attention to the sociology of mental health, which explores social environments and mental health. Aneshensel (2005:223) places emphasis on the *social consequence model* which "is concerned with the mental health consequences of specific social arrangements." Such arrangements could have detrimental and dysfunctional consequences on individuals (see Pearlin, 1989). In short, a negative reaction, for example, stress, anger, frustration, to wait-structures could signal a dysfunction in the system. That is, alternatives to waiting either do not exist or those that exist are inadequate. Moreover, Aneshensel (2005:224) recognizes that "the very structures and processes that make social life possible for most people create circumstances that are intolerable for some persons." This is a classic situation of a bureaucratized and organic society; recognizing our inability to please everyone, and realistically, everyone must wait. Although various wait-situations are intolerable for some, most systems-of-wait generally work, calling for constant assessment and refinement.

The idea of *waiting-structures* expands our mental health analysis, going beyond differential statuses resulting from stratification by socioeconomic status, race, gender, and age (Schwartz, 2002). Presumably, Schwartz's (2005) emphasis on "expanding the range of issues" would include waiting, market reforms, and even urban/rural arrangements. For example, in their most recent study of "Market Reform and Psychological Distress in Urban Beijing," Lai and Lee (2006) found that urban Beijing residents have experienced greater life stress and a rise in depressive symptoms. Here one may assume a regional cultural difference, in that rural residents become accustom to a slower pace where congestion is rare and waiting is tolerable. Conversely, urban areas are mixed with crowds, diversity, long lines, insufficient service and bureaucracy, leading to longer waits and greater life stress. "Expanding the range of issues" broadens our analysis and improves our understanding of matters related to mental health.

An everyday analysis of mental health and waiting reveals how ordinary structures could lead to stress and frustration; and yet, the stress and frustration may have very little to do with wait-structures and more to do with one's personal mood. For example, waiting is most difficult when one is in a hurry. Situationally, being in hurry seems to initiate stress and could even alter one's personality. Consider Megan's experience:

While waiting in line at Safeway, I noticed a line that possibly would take less time than the one I was standing in. So, I moved, and after a few seconds became increasingly frustrated because, in my hurried state, I thought the line should be moving faster. You see, there was only one person in line, and the line I left had three people in front of me. So, I left. But the line that I left moved progressively faster than the line I moved to. Part of my frustration was watching people in "the other line" check out before me, yet some arrived in line after me. I wanted to move back to the other line, but thought that as soon as I moved, the immigrant lady would complete her transaction and I would wait even longer. So, I stayed and *anxiously waited*. The immigrant lady was unclear on how to swipe her credit card and how to operate the credit machine at the register. Though given instructions by clerk, she frequently asked the clerk for his assistance. I believe she wanted him to do it; but this soooo held-up the line, and I wanted to scream!

Peter Berger's classic statement is relevant here, "Things are not what they seem." Generally, one receives service faster in short lines as opposed to long lines. This is the assumption made by Megan and many others, but such assumptions do not always hold true. In fact, regarding alternatives, all of the mechanisms were in place to speed the process along. There was more than one line open and debit machines were used. But one cannot always account for unforeseen variables. For instance, it is difficult to anticipate the problems of the "immigrant lady," but such problems lead to a more stressful situation for Megan. In everyday life one never knows the stress that awaits him, and our construction of wait-environments is designed to reduce wait time and/ or make waiting more bearable, for example, watching TV advertisements as one waits in the check-out line of supermarkets. But stress and frustration are real and our ability to manage and manipulate these environments has consequences for our mental and physical health.

While alternatives to waiting could reduce mental health problems, it could further lessen conflict, invasion of privacy, and crowding. There are varying situations where waiting could lead to conflict, as in waiting in line at gas stations, in bank lines, subway boarding, emergency rooms, and during traffic. Yet, the causes of conflict vary as much as these situations. Alternatives to waiting lessens crowd anxiety in that *choice* allows individuals to escape crowds, and either conduct other business or enjoy various social activities. For example, at Disneyland and Magic Mountain (California theme parks), a system called "fast pass" and "flash pass" has emerged to avert the tension of crowd waiting. The customer purchases a "fast pass" or "flash pass," giving him access to faster service; customers may then download the mobile app or use a kiosk machine to obtain ride and ticket information (kiosk machine: a ticket from a small computer terminal for his or her specific ride). The ticket or text informs customers of approximate time to report to ride. In the meantime, customers may ride other rides, eat, shop, rest, and even watch shows while waiting for time to lapse and thus avoid the traditional wait-experience. In the end, those who have *wait-difficulty* may utilize institutional options or create their own alternative. Barring both, the individual is not likely to wait.

Finally, while alternatives provide choices, to what extent are the choices efficient? Does *this choice* really address customer needs? Do our rationalized systems provide efficient service? Ritzer (1993) cautions that what is marketed as efficient may be inefficient. McDonalds and Jack-in-the-Box drive-throughs are often subject to long lines, incorrect orders, and impersonal service; waiting at ATMs could prove longer than waiting inside of banks; efficiency is further problematic when ATMs don't work. Or, how efficient is a self-service restaurant, like Souplantation or Hometown Buffet, when customers sneeze near food and taste with their fingers? The offering of rational alternatives may not be as efficient as assumed. *In fact, it may be inefficient and dangerous to one's physical and mental health.* Ritzer (1993:124) raises the classic question: "Efficient for whom?" For Ritzer, it may be more efficient for the organization than customers, and within the organization, it is most efficient for those "near the bottom of the system" as a way to control subordinates. So, *alternatives to waiting* is saddled with its own set of problems and uncertainties.[5]

CUTTING IN LINE: POSSIBLE RESPONSES

Cutting in line is viewed as a clear violation of wait-norms. It is a violation that may or may not be tolerated because seniors, women with children, and pregnant women are often granted permission to cut while teenagers are frowned on and even scolded for their attempts to cut. Still, *cutting in line* is an alternative to waiting given that one is attempting to circumvent the waiting process. Yet, the difference between cutting and other "creative alternatives" is that cutting is forbidden; it is a rude infraction on society's normative system and an intrusion that could disrupt the structure of waiting. Cutting is like cheating in that society frowns upon dishonesty, though respects those who show diligent patience in achieving their goals. We value those who study for exams and do well, yet we sanction those caught cheating and further devalue those who are known deceivers but not caught. In the same way the cheater receives grades and resources he did not earn, the cutter receives an unfair advantage. So, cutting is often problematic and in the long run, it could lead to conflict. Our guiding issue is tolerance. Under what conditions is cutting tolerated? Is all cutting similar? Or does toleration depend on the situation?

The scenario of someone cutting in line after waiting for thirty minutes was presented to a group of high school seniors. While I recognize that students are influenced by others, still, I wanted to know who would confront a violator while waiting in line to ride the rollercoaster. By a show of hands, five of thirty students reported that they *would* confront the individual; the others did not raise their hands, and one such student said, "I probably *would not* say anything." A discussion ensued about the "unfairness" and "rudeness" of cutting but most pondered whether a "hassle was worth it." In this situation, the class concluded that most would not confront the individual but most were likely to gesture and grumble. Probing further, students were asked whether they would support an individual who confronted the cutter?

And, whether they would reveal the truth if the manager inquired about the violation? Ninety percent (27 of 30) indicated support, while three students simply refused to get involved. One's response to cutting is situational, yet the dynamics of support (one's response) seems altered when someone takes the lead.

Waiting in line is often routine and ordinary. Typically, one walks up to an ATM machine, witnesses a line, and begins to wait. Those waiting appear mindful of distances between person at machine and next person in line to use machine. The distance between "next person to use machine" and "machine user" is greater than the distance of those behind the next person in line; and such a distance (between machine user and next person in line) reflects a respect for privacy and safety. Cutting in line *here* may signal a red flag of theft in that one must guards against robbery. But while waiting, there is little talk because most are strangers, and individuals are rummaging through wallets and purses to find ATM cards. ATM patrons appear cognizant of persons in front, behind, and to the side of them; they sense the "specific others" in their environment. At ATMs, patrons are so aware of their surrounding that an outsider cutting line would draw attention and a possible reaction. Generally, patrons appear patient and orderly while waiting; that is, no one is rushing the other or brushing against individuals in front or behind. Those persons experiencing a time-crunch often leave and return later. In short, patrons waiting in line are usually patient, recognizing that such a wait is relatively brief.

Cutting in line at the ATM is different than cutting in line to ride the rollercoaster. The worries and concerns are different; safety and security are concerns at ATMs, but losing one's place or waiting longer becomes the issue at amusement parks; waiting longer is less threatening than being robbed. So, *where* individuals decide to cut-in-line is clearly consequential.

While waiting for service inside a bank, customers appear to observe other customers standing in line, processing transactions at teller window, and completing deposit/withdrawal forms. One is waiting for the next available teller. Cutting then seems difficult to conceal given the environment. Customers look for signs as to whether the "cutter" is connected to someone waiting, for example, family member, friend, etc. And if the "cutter" is linked to friends or family, is this cutting? Certainly, customers will decide by their actions and reactions. Robert recalls that on one occasion, the line was long, about ten customers, and customer service was slow. "One individual noticed that his friend entered the bank and invited him to stand beside him in line; this disturbed me and the lady in front of me because we had been impatiently waiting; and here is a *person*—comes in the bank, notices a friend, and begins to wait near the front of the line." According to Robert, the two talked in line and when it was "their" turn for financial transaction, they went to the teller together; the teller handled each transaction separately. While no one confronted them, "we stared and discussed our dismay during the whole transaction."

It is possible that the structure of banks, including security guards, cameras, employees, and customers, discouraged overt confrontations. And under different circumstances, might a challenge ensue? It is clear that "Robert and the lady" were disturbed; they felt snubbed because "the friend" did not wait; the person in line was used as the alternative, and they considered no one behind them.

Yet, to what extent does the dynamic of cutting and one's toleration change with age and location? For instance, while waiting in line at Wang's Donut House, Mr. Dudley noticed a young adolescent, Trey. Trey rode his bike to the front door of Wang's Donut House; he laid it down and walked inside. Trey entered and waited at the end of the line momentarily. Then, he walked past those waiting—straight to the front, where he could clearly view the colorful donuts. According to Mr. Dudley, Trey possessed a five-dollar bill, which he waved in full view as he attempted to get the attention of Donut House employees. Those waiting in line and various employees were aware that Trey had cut. The employees tried to ignore Trey as he swung his five-dollar bill in their direction to receive their attention. Moreover, while Trey was swinging his money, one gentleman who was aware of Trey's cutting, aggressively stepped forward, to place his order. The gentleman was easily acknowledged by employees, for Wang employees appeared to intentionally look away from Trey, giving their full attention to their in-progress customers. As one male employee, Ernesto, finished servicing a customer, he began looking for someone else to help. Now, Trey was not only waving his money, but shouting, "here, here, here," so that any employee would acknowledge him, take his money, and service him. Such was the case with Ernesto who earlier ignored Trey but now ended up serving him. Others in line said and did nothing as they watched Trey disregard the informal rule of "wait your turn." *Doing nothing* means avoiding conflict yet permitting someone to take advantage and violate informal norms. Keep in mind that such rules are real only when acknowledged and acted on by others. Though Trey was initially discouraged from cutting, he was eventually serviced, cutting several persons who were in line before him. Questions: Did the lack of guidance (*doing nothing*) help or hurt Trey? Did customers and employees ignore a teachable moment? Were customers being entertained, wanting to see the results?

One situation that will rarely draw dispute is pregnant women who have a need to go. Such women usually receive empathy when cutting line to use restrooms. Often, the line to use a women's restroom is longer than that of men, and one's ability to hold urine is challenged by pregnancy. Some women may even offer pregnant women "line cuts." For instance, one respondent shared, "Last Saturday, I joined a group of fifteen women wait-ing in the line for the restroom. A few of them eyed my tummy and instantly offered a cut in line." The "offer" acknowledges sensitivity to a pregnant situation. It is not regarded as cutting but consideration. Other pregnant women do not await acknowledgment, some simply take advantage of the unwritten privilege and waddled straight to lines-front, saying, "I'm really sorry but I have two babies kicking my bladder and I can't wait." The likeli-hood of refusing a pregnant woman cutting privileges is slim; in fact, women are more likely to hold distain for *refusers* rather than cutting pregnant ladies. Recognizing the medical needs of pregnant ladies presents an important con-dition for breaking line.

Doing something may invite troubles or challenges, yet the reality of "first come, first service" materializes and support is probable. Thus, our situ-ational environment and individual *self*—determines how one will respond. Take Matt, for example, who entered a donut shop while five customers were waiting for service. Rather than waiting at lines-end, Matt gathers the group's attention by moving toward the front of the line and showing several dollars. While walking toward the front, Matt asked, "Everyone is in line for donuts, right?" Some nodded, others replied "donuts and coffee." Presumably, the implication of his question and behavior is "if you're buying donuts, and I'm simply buying coffee, then I'll move to the front and quickly pour coffee." This method would not prolong one's wait but allow Matt a faster exit and literally no wait. His seeking permission to cut was objected to by Shaneeka who was standing in line and immediately announced, "You still have to wait!" Shaneeka was not willing to risk a longer wait, in fact, she invokes the "first come, first serve" rule. By seeking permission, Matt also acknowledges the norm, and without debate or protest, he proceeds to the rear and waits. By moving to lines-end, Matt displays a certain respect for rules, order and the people in line; and thus "first come, first serve" is made real by Matt's initial behavior, question and reaction from others.

Cutting in line is an interesting and situational alternative to waiting. While some cuts are straightforward, others are not. Some cuts require more sift-ing, for example, was that really a cut? And why is the person cutting in the first place? Does the *cutter* consider others, for example, seek permission? Or does the cutter take advantage of an alternative? The cut maybe viewed as complicated, as well as the reaction to the cut. At what point and in what situations are persons likely to confront or ignore the cut? What is considered when ignoring or confronting cutters? For certain cutters (pregnant women), their situation is viewed as a necessary privilege; for other cutters (Matt), their attempts are viewed as violations. In both cases, the idea of alternative is front and center, that is obtaining entrance and/or receiving service before others who have waited prior to your arrival. Still, where alternative exists, we are likely to take advantage; and where they don't exist, some are likely to create alternatives, for example, cutting.

WAITING AND CONFLICT

Under what conditions and in what situations is conflict a consequence of waiting? There is some conflict that seeks to change that nature of institutions, other conflict is simply designed to confront, fight, or blow off steam. In Birmingham, 1962–1963, King was accused of being "in too great of a religious hurry." He realized that Birmingham needed a *push* for systemic change, and left to their own devices, the Birmingham establishment may never change. For these reasons, King and others could not wait (see King, 1963, *Why We Can't Wait*). Conversely, road rage or fighting over "who's next" does not address systemic change. While it could, such situations are individual manifestations that emerge from congested wait-environments. In fact, one significant feature of *conflict and waiting* is congestion; many people and often their cars are frequently nestled together where wait-time, crowdedness, or perceived abuse may lead to dispute. Someone feels violated and a confrontation ensues.

Waiting in crowded gas stations is a case-in-point, for there is little order in that persons are unclear as to "who is next" and whether the "next person" will actually follow. For example, Magic conveyed that he noticed Keisha in the car next to him. "I thought we were waiting for the same pump; but I soon learned she was waiting for the pump across the way. I had no idea she was waiting for that pump." Magic further conveys that when a car "across the way" left, Keisha rushed to the pump. Seemingly, another customer was more centrally located and preparing to move into the vacant space, but Keisha rushed into "pump position." Grady, the gentleman who was also waiting, drove up next to Keisha exclaiming, "I was next!" Turning off her car and pointing to the area where she was waiting, Keisha defends, "No, I was waiting over there for that car to leave." Keisha then exits her car, walking toward the Arco entrance door and all the while—Grady stares.

Many service stations possess no clear-cut entrance or exit procedures. Drivers proceed to open pumps regardless of who is waiting; moreover, some drivers must wait additional time because they are blocked by recently arriving customers who begin to pump their gas. Such confusion caused one customer to say "this is a mess!!!" recognizing that such a "system" pays little respect and consideration for those waiting and those pumping gas. The lack of guidelines is ripe for trouble. Unlike hospitals, banks, and fast food restaurants, gas stations have no waiting props—no signs or arrows to indicate entrance, exit, and most importantly, "who's next." In a society where members have grown accustomed to wait-structure and wait-order, the lack of wait-guidance is often problematic. Still, it is surprising that few problems occur, and astonishing to witness the patience exercised by customers. Solving the problem is easily managed by implementing wait procedures.

Similar confrontations are witnessed among those waiting for parking spaces. Crowded parking lots often bring out the worst in shoppers; such situations may lead to accidents, verbal arguments, fights, and sheer inconsideration. For instance, during a busy shopping season, like Christmas or Thanksgiving, parking spaces in malls, mini-malls, and supermarkets are rare and become significant commodities. As Mrs. Ortiz circled the parking lot in search of "anywhere to park," she detected brake lights of an SUV. Rushing toward the SUV, Mrs. Ortiz signaled as to indicate next occupant of parking space. Apparently, as the SUV backed out, a Honda Civic approaching from opposite direction swerved into "her" space. Her vision was obstructed by the SUV, and suddenly, the Honda was parked and two teenagers emerged from the vehicle, walking and pulling up their pants. In anger, Mrs. Ortiz protested, "I was waiting for that space! Move your car!" The teenagers said, "fuck you lady" and kept walking. Mrs. Ortiz responded in kind—though angrily resumed her search. There are times, however, when those who mistakenly pull into parking spaces recognize that someone had been waiting and back out. They apologize and continue their parking search. This was not the case with Mrs. Ortiz and the teenagers, for according to Mrs. Ortiz, "Those guys didn't care! I felt violated, victimized, and disrespected by those young thugs. Plus, I had to spend more time looking for another parking space."

One wonders whether conflict is inevitable during crowded situations, or is it the perceived unfairness and/or confusion that leads to conflict? The conflict itself is one way of expressing his or her disapproval of the situation or system; in part, the conflict functions to highlight and expose problems within the system, for example, one's inability to compromise or one's impatience. In one newscast,[6] NBC aired a story entitled "Im-patient?" The incident occurred at a clinic in Spokane, Washington, and announcers introduced the story by saying, "We show you how one impatient patient expressed his exasperation with his car." "A man waiting in a doctor's office is accused of impatience. Witnesses say the forty-three-year-old 'got frustrated about the wait to see a doctor' at a clinic in Spokane, Washington. He apparently stormed out of the room, jumped into his truck, and tried to blow off steam; but instead he lost control, and the trucked landed on top of two parked cars; he was cited for reckless driving." Electronic media is often criticized for incomplete stories, that is, NBC did not reveal why "the 43-year-old" had to wait or whether the clinic was experiencing problems or whether he criticized clinic personnel. NBC simply reports that the patient became frustrated and acted out. Presumably, the patient's behavior resulted from his perception of a flawed wait system.

While the forty-three-year-old lost control of his vehicle, road rage and Katrina situations are other instances where one is likely to lose control and act out. On the one hand, certain drivers are impatient with traffic and how one's car is cut off by another. This often results in angry honks, screams, inappropriate hand signals, shootings, and accidents. On the other hand, Katrina victims were given the run-around by receiving misinformation, disrespected by national guardsmen and instructed to wait in endless lines for food, transportation, medical attention, and other resources (see Dyson, 2006). The inefficiency of the rescue system caused Katrina victims to fight and argue over "who was first in line," "who's next," and "who will get the last loaf of bread," for example, scarce resources. *Conflict and waiting* are real and may reach boiling points if systems and individuals don't take measures (for crowd control) to handle crowded wait-situations.

Conflict emerges out of these situations; it is the type of conflict that expresses frustration toward individuals not systems. We often confront those in our immediate environment and lose sight of the system that caused pain and disorder. Though we face these crowded situations frequently, for example, gas stations, congested freeways and parking lots, individuals either develop patience or construct creative ways of managing congestion. So, congestion remains, becoming a routine part of our lives; and like any other confrontation, it grabs our curious attention and entertains us while we wait.

REFUSING TO WAIT

Refusing to Wait is situational and varies from individual to individual; further, the basis for refusal is best explored and explained by one's immediate circumstance. While some refuse to wait because of medical or biological (pregnancy) reasons, others encounter important meetings, deadlines, or emotions that prevent them from waiting. It is clear, however, that refusing to wait is tied to the cost and consequences of waiting. One ponders whether waiting is possible; hence, refusing suggests that the cost is too high and waiting is devalued; devalued in time, money, mental health, etc. At one time or another, we have all faced "*wait-refusal*," in that the timing for delay is inconvenient; yet, our refusal is less linked to protest and more connected to expediency. Denise Wells provides a case by using the men's restroom at a Houston country-western concert. She refused to wait for the women's restroom because the line was too long. Instead, Wells testified, "I waited a while, but it was unbearable. I saw a gentleman escorting a girl into the men's room, where there was no line, and I just followed them in." While Wells did not encounter a biological accident, her refusal cost her concert removal and a $200 ticket. After deliberations, Ms. Wells was acquitted—for her actions were not intended to cause a disturbance and she simply had no alternative. One juror, Frieda Felton told reporters, "I think women's needs have been ignored for too long. It's time we go back to public buildings and provide adequate facilities for women" (Smith, 1990).[7]

In part, Ms. Wells' refusal raises important questions about gender equity and consideration. Who designs and constructs restrooms for men and women? If wait-lines for women restrooms are consistently longer than men's, how might such lines be shortened? Architects must consider the personal needs of women and men, and that women frequently assist children in restrooms. Additional toilets in women restrooms begin to address the problem and reduce the wait. But in public restrooms where toilet disparity remains and crowds persist, women may continue to consider the men's room as a likely alternative.

What then is the difference between *refusing to wait* and *alternatives to waiting*? *Refusing to wait* suggests that one will not wait; he or she literally leaves the area or situation of wait. Here, time, circumstance, and/or stress are primary concerns. Individuals may not have *time* to wait and thereby simply cannot wait. In other cases, waiting may cause undue stress, so one refuses to wait to prevent anxiety. As discussed earlier, *alternatives to waiting* suggests that there is another method to waiting—that there is a faster way to accomplish one's wait; the amount of wait-time is reduced—in short, one has successfully minimized his or her wait. Yet, one observation records a combination of both. For example, it is after 8:00 a.m. and the post office has not opened. The line has not only formed but begins to extend; there is about fifteen people waiting. As customers wait, a male customer near the front shouts, "Have their hours changed?" A female customer at lines-front responds, as she reads the post office hours on door-window, "No! It says it opens at 8 o'clock." The male customer continues his anxious squirming. Soon, *two women also become anxious by looking at their watches then stepping out of line. One female, Doris, left the line and post office altogether without mailing; Doris walked swiftly to her car, got in and drove away. She left with letters in hand. The other lady, Helen, elected to use self-service shipping. Helen completed her transaction yet the post office had not opened.*

A combination of *refusing* and *alternative* is evident in the above scenario. The example highlights crucial differences and customer options emerge from differences. Some customers wait while others refuse to wait, and still others find alternatives. Such options depend on one's immediate circumstance and best ways to proceed. Refusing to wait may mean that one chooses to conduct business at another time. For instance, while waiting in line, one respondent disclosed, "I was in here yesterday and the line was out the door. I thought, 'I'm not waiting in that line!' So, I came back today, and this (line) is not bad." In short, the line is much shorter today than yesterday, thus waiting is tolerable. Conversely, when "the line is out the door," one must decide whether to wait. Does wait-refusal clash with perceptions of wait-time when going to work, returning to work, going to class or maintaining an appointment? One then weighs the cost of wait-time to scheduled engagements or commitments and acts accordingly. Theoretically, refusing to wait may imply some type of strain within oneself or one's obligations. In *refusing to wait*, one does not wait; there is a personal or situational dilemma; conversely, *alternatives* focus on reducing wait time by using different wait-methods.

Walking the streets of Manhattan, one notes that pedestrians rarely wait at stop signals. Pedestrians typically walk through street crossing (or cross walks) during red lights. It seems that red lights only pertain to cars, trucks, and (sometimes) taxis; frequently, cars, trucks, and taxis honk at pedestrians to alert them to oncoming traffic. Pedestrians who wait at stop lights are left behind as others proceed forward. One respondent, Wade, remarked, "You can always notice tourists and visitors; they always wait at the red lights." "Why don't people wait at stop lights?" Wade, "Why wait when you have places to go!?"

For Manhattan, New York, refusing to wait has become normal for members of that community while waiting is seemingly abnormal; and those who are new to Manhattan, even temporarily, soon adapt. Interestingly, police officers do not confront or ticket anyone for refusing to wait at street crossings or red lights. Such waiting behavior is clearly regional, for in downtown Portland, residents are more likely to wait at crosswalks when the light is red. *Empty intersections*, that is intersections without cars, may be the site of pedestrians waiting for signals to turn green. There are some cases where teenagers and college students cross during "empty intersections," but typically most pedestrians wait, especially the elderly. Again, this is not the case in New York-Manhattan; once residents believe that they have a clear crossing path, though the signal is red, most will cross. Culturally, Portland residents maintain a casual lifestyle; they do not appear hurried and/or impatient, as do New Yorkers (see Lai and Lee, 2006).

Regional and cultural differences can explain one's refusal to wait. The difference is simply fascinating, not right or wrong; it simply fits their community. One is socialized to wait while another learns to "make-tracks," for example, go. Congestion such as subway crowds, elevator crowds, and expressway traffic may lead to wait refusal at traffic signals. And the lack of such constant congestion may give reason for pause and admire one's surroundings. But refusing to wait is a part of our society and those who exercise this option—do so for a variety of reasons.

SUMMARY

Strategies used to avoid or minimize waiting recognizes the importance of technology in advanced, industrialized societies. Without question, such technologies assist in our alternatives and wait-choices. Advanced societies offer choices in garments, foods, automobiles, banks, houses, music, schools, and presidential candidates, so why not provide choice in waiting. Some strategies are innovative while others are institutionalized; market research has led to viable options. Such options become a necessary condition for competition and sustenance. Still as society advances so does wait-options. Various forms of communication, online purchases, Mbps, drive-throughs, instant foods, self-service, and medical appointment techniques represent alternatives to waiting. That is, alternatives to conventional ways of obtaining services. Ideally, the alternative provides a faster and sometimes more efficient option.

Mental health and waiting considers anxiety that is triggered by waiting; some persons literally have difficulty waiting, and stress is the result. One respondent admits, "I can't wait. It drives me crazy!" So, the likely alternative is to create mechanisms to avoid or limit waiting. This may include cutting, paying someone to wait or using institutional mechanisms like "quick pass." Given institutional structures, Aneshensel (2005) draws our attention to the *social consequence model,* which is concerned with the mental health consequences of specific social arrangements. It is clear that certain procedures and wait-environments could have dysfunctional consequences. While at the same time, one's hurried state could further contribute to one's tension while waiting. In short, rushing may create more anxiety than otherwise—and calmness, in Megan's scenario, might encourage her to assist the "immigrant lady."

Cutting in line is an interesting phenomenon and one is not all together sure how others will respond. It clearly depends on the situation but women who are pregnant are typically permitted "cutting courtesy" (cutting due to medical or biological reasons). Barring pregnant women, seniors and medical emergencies, cutting in line is viewed as unfair, placing an unnecessary burden on those waiting and taking advantage of others. Yet, our high school survey along with interviews and observations reveals that most persons are not likely to challenge or confront cutters. Many will wait the extra time to avoid the "hassle" of confrontation; others will confront cutters and insist that cutters wait their turn. At stake is the "first come, first serve" norm. Most observe this informal rule, as they enter establishments and stand behind those currently waiting. Here, conformity is one way this folkway becomes real. But attempts to violate the rule also give credence to this principle, as in the case of Matt and Shaneeka. Support of those who confront cutters is likely and further provides evidence that cutting is offensive.

Waiting and Conflict is another issue that helps us understand alternatives to waiting. In the case of crowded gas stations and parking lots, some customers are forced to find alternatives when they are slighted by someone else. Additionally, in the case of the forty-three-year-old whose truck landed on top of two parked cars, it is possible that his rage would have remained subdued had there been an alternative. Given the aforementioned cases, everyday conflict reflects confrontations with others as ways to blow off steam. Among those involved, the conflict is not designed to change the system; it is a temporary means to express one's disapproval and frustration. Marx and Engels (1848/1988) would contend that the object of frustration (the other customer) is misguided. Instead, the focus should address the system or institution that masks their flaws and fails to consider human needs.

Refusing to Wait gets at one's unwillingness to wait; refusal is less linked to protest and more connected to expediency. The Wells' case illustrates that there was no mal-intent but a severe need to go (to the restroom). *Refusing to Wait* also examines the cost and benefits of waiting. For instance, is waiting worth it given my time, given my schedule? Needless to say, wait-refusal varies from person to person, case to case, and region to region. New Yorkers are far less likely to wait than the residents of downtown Portland. Whether to wait becomes a cultural phenomenon, which is learned through behavioral experiences. And regional differences are exciting to note, for they are not right or wrong, good or bad; they are simply different; and the difference fits their environment.

Finally, refusing to wait is also associated with crisis. When a crisis occurs, one is not likely to follow the etiquette of waiting; one cannot wait because the crisis may worsen and potentially affect others. For instance, when Daisy lost her purse, she became frantic and shopping turned secondary. Looking in her shopping cart and realizing that her purse was missing, she reacts, "Oh my God! Where's my purse!" (reactions are similar with phones and keys). Such a snap was loud enough for others to hear. Daisy acts immediately by frantically searching her cart. She suddenly became anxious doing away with any wait-etiquette. She rushed to the line-front of photography, and though customers were in-line, Daisy asked clerk, "Did I leave my purse!!?" Martha, the clerk, quickly scanned her area, looks Daisy in the face, and frightfully answers, "No." Leaving her shopping cart, Daisy runs out of the store to search for her purse. Daisy's cutting was so abrupt, customers simply watched with little reaction and no verbiage. Clearly, it is difficult to wait during perceived crises; individuals are concerned with resolution, not etiquette.

Refusing to wait takes on several twists and turns. Crises, however, are significant reasons not to wait, and emergency vehicles rarely wait when transporting heart attack or shooting victims to hospitals; police rarely wait when pursuing bank robbers. Refusing to wait then is both individual and institutional; it is situated in the moment, calling for action and refusing delay. Institutional refusal affects both the individual and groups, while individual refusal usually affects the individual. Again, institutional refusal is best exemplified during crisis as emergency personnel rescue hurricane, flood, earthquake, car accident, and airplane crash victims. And, while emergency vehicles refuse to wait, their wait-refusal during emergencies has become institutionalized; their behavior is normalized. A reversal has emerged. Passenger vehicles and spectators are socialized to wait for emergency vehicles.

While we rush to curtail our "waits," there are some "waits" that we simply cannot abridge; or, is it possible that such "waits" are permanent? For example, L.A. traffic, airport lines, and popular restaurants. Carpool lanes, no-check baggage lines, and calling ahead result in "just" another wait. Why are these "waits" so difficult to penetrate and diminish?

NOTES

1. Are those who oppose "call-waiting" against other forms of wait-options?

2. Matthew Kiaman, Director of Technical Services at Pasadena City College, provided this valuable information on network connections.

3. This comment was made by a sixteen-year-old high school student, who was applying for a drivers' license and experience the Department of Motor Vehicles (DMV) for her first time. The DMV is very confusing. That is, when one enters, persons must figure out "what to do"? Which forms are necessary? How to complete forms? Where to obtain forms? And, in which line(s) to wait? This initial confusion contributes to one's anxiety.

At the Pasadena DMV, there are two lines with overhead posted signs. In huge bold/block letters one sign reads "Start Here: Appointment Only"; another sign, in the same vicinity reads, "Start Here: Non-Appointment." These are the lines in which customers begin their wait. While DMV contains signs, rails, and ropes to direct waiting and human traffic, it remains necessary to seek and ask for assistance. Why? Before waiting in long lines, one must ensure that she or he is waiting in the *right* line. Questions are often directed to security personnel, who are dressed in blue uniforms and posted by entrance and exit doors, and roam the DMV interior. One would think that an information booth would be set up, but such is not the case.

After waiting in the "Start Here" line for fifteen minutes and being processed at the window, one is directed to one of two wait areas. One wait area is open for all to see. On the west side of Pasadena DMV, chairs are set up in auditorium style. Entering DMV from the west entrance door, this area is immediately visible. Customers are seated and looking up at a TV monitor. They are waiting for their number to appear; the number received when processed. When your number appears, it indicates the window in which the customer should seek service. The other wait area is somewhat concealed and enclosed; it is bigger, containing more chairs and the TV monitor becomes the focal point; again, customers are awaiting their number to post.

The number appears on the monitor and customers go to the prescribed window for further processing; one waits in the waiting area for about twenty minutes. Further processing includes paying fees, vision exam, verifying information, and signing documents; then, there is another line and wait for picture taking; after picture, one gets into another line for driver test and after passing test, one waits in another line to process drivers permit or drivers' license. *All in all, one waits in 5 different lines.*

Most persons dread DMV. Why? It is crowded, impersonal customer service and time consuming. It is most congested before and after exams—when preparing to submit paperwork for passing exam. Here, there is a small, narrow hallway where there are lines on either side of hallway and customers travel between these lines bumping other customers who are stationary and waiting. At times, one hears "excuse me," or "I'm sorry," and at other times, one is simply bumped. Additionally, the public dreads DMV because customer service is often poor and rude; workers appear alienated and intolerant. Finally, various customers contribute to employee estrangement by being rude and disrespectful to employees. For instance, when one customer failed a written test, he yelled and scolded an employee, indicating that it was her fault that he failed. In short, one may encounter hostility and disorganization at DMV.

4. Hanna is a German immigrant.

5. Should fast food restaurants, that offer drive-through options, be required to post drive-through time estimates? To what extent would such a requirement facilitate waiting by allowing customers to make decisions about waiting?

6. "Impatient" was story aired on L.A.'s NBC (Channel 4) T.V. station, March 20, 2005.

7. Also see People Staff (1990, August 6) *When Denise Wells Sought Relief in the Men's Room, Houston Police Said She Stepped Way Out of Line.* https://people.com /archive/when-denise-wells-sought-relief-in-the-mens-room-houston-police-said-she -stepped-way-out-of-line-vol-34-no-5/

Chapter 9

Emotions and Waiting

Waiting to Die

Waiting is often an emotional experience, and yet waiting for a loved one to die triggers several sentiments. Needless to say, death involves a range of emotions that assist persons in getting through a difficult circumstance. It is precisely *this wait* that permits emotions to emerge and manifest themselves. What type of emotions is experienced during "dying and death"? How are emotions managed when loved ones are near death? How is waiting used to comfort loved ones and significant others? Here, *I am interested in how individuals wait for loved-ones to die. And during that process, how they manage their emotions?*

While death is near, the remainder of one's (the person dying) life is tentative, and thus waiting is tied to emotional uncertainties. Emotional management is no easy task especially when one's encounters are varied and regular. That is, one must hold himself or herself together at home, work, church, school, community events, concerts, shopping, gym and while dining in restaurants. In short, the environment has implications for which emotion to be expressed and how. There are times when masking emotions are functional in that one may prefer to express happiness as a way to show support and encouragement for the person dying. One's emotional state may transfer to *the dying*, and though dying is imminent, one's positive emotional state could provide temporary but much needed strength. The individual who is losing the loved one must continue to participate in life outside his or her immediate loss. The professor who cares for and resides with his mother must lecture and interact with faculty and students. While work distractions are necessary, somehow professors and others must hold themselves together; and yet in professional atmospheres, individuals are more self-conscious about exhibiting certain emotions (see Tracy et al., 2007). There are some environments where significant others can simply let their emotions go, for example, private places, though other settings require more restraint. And still, regardless of location, certain emotions are so overwhelming that they simply spill out, emotional containment is impossible.

According to Lyon (1996:20), emotion has a role in the *organization of action*. "Emotions move us, but they do so by virtue of the social situation in which we find ourselves, or imagine ourselves to be." This gets at the broad spectrum of emotions, recognizing that emotions are not simply passive but action oriented. Images of police brutality often lead to protest and demands for justice. Inequality in bus seating may lead to anger, directing one's feelings into the organization of a bus boycott. Child abuse could lead to depression and self-doubt among victims. Learning of sexual abuse to his daughter, Ron Book became enraged and lobbied for legislation that would keep sexual predators about 2,500 feet away from places where children gather, e.g., "The Lauren Book Protection Act" (see Skipp and Campo-Flores, 2009). And finally, public officials who cheat on their wives may raise doubt among voters and feminists' groups to reconsider whether governors or mayors are fit to lead. Clearly, emotions have the ability to channel and guide our wrath, our action. They can result in positive outcomes for rational social movements. Social movements take time, energy, planning, and consistency; change is not instant. So often, when emotions are tied to waiting, our decisions are more thought-through and thereby more tactical.

This then is the rational side of emotion; but the powerful and even mesmerizing effect of emotions may lead to irrational behavior, like governors who cheat, victims who seek revenge, crimes of passion, and gambling away the mortgage in one night. This is to show that emotions are not always rational; at times, individuals simply react and possible sanctions are overlooked. *Road rage* can easily lead to death, accidents, or both. But at the time, one simply reacts. After the reactionary performance, one may reevaluate his behavior, contemplating the cost of his decision. Irrational behavior could lead to ostracism, labeling and worst, institutionalization. In short, while one fails to consider sanctions, irrational behavior often has real consequences.

So, exactly what is emotion? Emotion is an appraisal of a change in feeling (see Kagan, 2007), which involves physiological arousal and a label (Aronson, 1999:32). George Mandler (1975) provides a similar definition, arguing that emotion is the interpretation of change in the level of arousal. Emotion recognizes that our feelings change based on stimuli. The cognitive content of emotions gets at the interplay between the body and our social world. Thus, sociologically, the social construction of emotions is evident in our daily lives. Varying situations cause emotions to emerge, and the interpretation or appraisal of emotion is dependent not only on circumstances but also on individuals. For example, while young girls might scream at the sight of spiders, adolescent boys may show restraint, excitement, and interests;

such groups define the same stimuli differently, making emotions very social. Perception of gender roles is an important consideration in the above example. Additionally, an interpretation of self and/or group is being constructed. When one expresses certain emotions, what image and message is he or she attempting to convey? Girls may wish to communicate fear and innocence; conversely, boys may wish to convey strength and toughness. And to what extent do we construct those images in the appropriate setting, for example, funeral, wedding, and graduation? What about environments that are more neutral, like seeing a spider crawl under Megan's classroom desk or cheering at a basketball game? We are permitted to express a variety of emotions in neutral settings, and most are tolerated. But limited emotions are accepted in predisposed environments like funerals and courtrooms. Given our ability to manipulate emotions, they then become socially constructed.

The extent to which one will mask emotions is a very real option. Still the emotion remains constructed given the situation and the motive behind the mask. What is one's intent through expressing "real" emotions or masking others? In the case of death, real emotions may serve to express sympathies, and while in the company of others, there is consensus on certain relevant emotions. Masking happiness or sadness maybe one's way of getting through a tough and possibly awkward situation. To prevent embarrassment and discomfort, one conforms to appropriate emotions but may feel differently. So, our environment is a key feature in how emotions are constructed and expressed.

The following cases examine the emotions of those *waiting for loved-ones to die*. How do emotions emerge and change during the course of death? How are emotions used to rationalize situations? And what is their (emotion) value in sorting out imminent situations? The first case involves a professor who awaits his mother's death; second, I analyze a professor who waits for her husband to die, and finally a most popular case is analyzed as Armanda Agrelo awaits her son's death, Benito Agrelo. Benito Agrelo's story is true and was the subject of an HBO special, "Someone had to be Benny." In all such cases, a mixture of emotions take place but waiting and patience allow emotions to take shape and surface. In these cases, death is not immediate—otherwise waiting would be irrelevant and unnecessary. Yet, the nature of these cases causes us to pause and rethink the process of death through the eyes of significant others.

WAITING TO DIE

My Mother's Death

Jamil is a professor of sociology who is married, active in the community, and cares for his ailing mother, Grace. He loves his mother; she resides with him and wishes her a smooth and orderly transition. Such care is time consuming yet for the moment, Jamil realizes that "my time is not my own." His time clearly belongs to his mother—in the same way that a mother's time belongs to her newborn baby. Hence, Jamil might be characterized as a responsible son, desiring comfort for his mother at the close of her life. He is attentive to care, and at times, such devotion creates conflicts with his spouse, which further produces anger given his childhood relationship with his mother. Jamil writes, "When I was a child my mother did not spend much time raising me. My grandmother did that. Thus, I developed affection for my grandmother and my mother was not a critical person to me. Having to care for her now is doing for her what she never did for me. " Resentment is a real emotion expressed by Jamil; it is one of many emotions and stages experienced when losing loved ones. And while caring for a loved one may also prove problematic within one's own marriage, balancing becomes a relevant skill.

Jamil's mother, Grace, has lived with him since 1999 and was diagnosed with kidney failure in 2004. Given her worrisome personality, Jamil along with doctor decided against telling Grace; they believed "telling" would not serve any useful purpose. Grace is ninety-four and thus not a candidate for dialysis or a transplant; the initial prediction is that Grace may live through the end of the year. It was this diagnosis that commenced Jamil's waiting and such waiting has produced a series of emotions, ranging from anxiety to grief, anger, resentment, relief, comfort, blessing, and satisfaction. The emotional roller coaster has allowed Jamil to put care for his mother in perspective. He writes, "Overall, my feeling is one of satisfaction, knowing that my best efforts to provide for her life have been beneficial to her. Despite my ups and downs, I do feel a great sense of being blessed." While Grace is not in pain, Jamil realizes that there is little he can do for his mother, except "make her comfortable." And he has done so by cooking, reading, storytelling and showing Grace off to university students. Additionally, while waiting, Jamil travels with his mother, takes her to university basketball games and book signings. Their activity is an important distraction for both.

The doctor indicated "It is most likely that she will pass in her sleep, and that produces anxiety since each morning I look in her room to see if she is still breathing." Not knowing the day or time produces much concern, much worry, yet funeral arrangement must be made and relatives call for "Grace-updates," for example, "how is she doing and how are you and Priscilla (Jamil's wife) holding up." Making arrangements is part of the *doing* while waiting; it is the act of being prepared. Grace was a secretary who was very organized and kept meticulous notes. Such organization spilled over into her personal life in that she wrote her obituary, the order of service for her funeral, selected her casket and shroud. Providing updates increases communication among relatives and may create a stronger bond. It follows that experiencing the death of a loved one leads us to think and talk about life and death more frequently. Jamil contemplates, "Taking so much time to care for my mother while waiting out the remaining days of her life leaves me to think about my mortality. Is this taking a toll on my life, and possibly reducing my years?" According to Secunda (2000), the death of significant others definitely affects one's life and relationships; and yet it is clear that individuals (significant others) gain more perspective; persons are humbled and more grounded (see Kubler-Ross, 1975). Jamil then reflects on "waiting to die," and writes "It is a morbid thought sometime to consider that I am waiting for someone to die." Many thoughts enter ones' mind at any given time, however most times, our thoughts are governed by circumstance. Such a thought seems sensible given his circumstance of caring for a terminal mother, and yet the value of sharing and confiding makes the waiting process more bearable.

Jamil mentioned that he and his wife were caring for ailing parents simultaneously. His wife spent several months in North Carolina caring for her mother and Jamil cared for his mother at his California home. Significant others quickly realize that "my time is not my own"; it belongs to someone else. One of the most significant values is choice, one's ability to make choices. Yet, when time is not yours, choices are limited, and this may lead to frustration. Jamil writes, "It was not the dying that was tough for us, it was taking care of mothers while they were living." In short, *doing* for mothers what they cannot *do* for themselves, like taking them to the hospital, organizing their health care, their physical care, their business affairs, making sure mothers are feed, and maintaining their property. So, while death is unfortunate, there is a certain relief experienced at the point of death, the realization that "I've lost my mother but I've got my life back." In part, *getting your life back* means no longer caring for your mother, for example, the physical energy is unnecessary and the emotional energy shifts, while memories remain. Further, *getting your life back* means no longer waiting for loved ones to die.

My Husband's Death

Christine is a professor of sociology who enjoys research, cultural diversity, and encouraging students. She is a strong advocate for marginalized faculty who encounter injustice from university officials. Further, Christine is a prolific investigator, constructing and producing lengthy and revealing interviews. Readers learn as much about her methods (how to probe within interviews) as they do about her subjects. Like most researchers who immerse themselves in their work, Christine is driven by scholarship, interesting topics and deadlines. Generally, individuals develop routines for work and play; such routines allow our lives. "normality," that is, predictability. But what happens when the "normal" becomes "abnormal"? Suddenly, this was the case with Christine, when she learned of her husband's illness. Plans were put on hold, life became lop-sided, and a type of anomie (normlessness) emerged. Unlike Grace, Christine's husband, Hank, was fully aware of his condition. He knew the diagnosis was problematic. Hank was diagnosed with cancer, and the uncertainty of life—along with strange thoughts began to evolve. So, when does *the wait* begin? It is probable that "*the wait*" begins when one is diagnosed. Christine acknowledges that *her wait* began "with my husband's illness." But understanding one's *wait*, that is the beginning of *the wait*, is far more complex. For instance, what are you waiting for? One's medical condition could change? If conditions change, then the waiting for death stops. Initially, one is on the bubble. Is one waiting for life or death? Healing or infirmity? Christine recognizes that there are several layers of waiting, and one layer *may* gradually lead to the next. She writes:

> I recall "waiting" for the effects of chemo to subside so that my husband could have some joy in the present. I remember "waiting" for result of tests, for the blood count to climb so that he could have chemo again, etc. Thus, I had to "wait" to find out what kind of "meta-waiting" I would engage—would I be waiting for him to heal or waiting for him to die? I found it frustrating not to know what kind of "waiting" I needed to be doing.

Waiting then does not simply begin, it is a process involving various *wait-stages* and such stages are not necessarily linear. In part, the beginning of one's *wait-stage* is reflected in one's realization of the *future*; for Christine, "the waiting begins when the *future disappears*." The realization that Christine and Hank no longer have a future together; will not celebrate anniversaries; will not rear their child; will not witness their child's high school graduation or wedding. The realization that Christine and Hank will not grow old together. It follows that the point of wait-origin varies from person to person and situation to situation, yet it is probable to say that one's initial wait stage begins when the *future disappears*. The other wait-stages emerge shortly after the first, for example, *doing* and *coping*, and it is possible that these stages overlap. The *doing wait stage* focuses on doing for others, doing for self and taking care of funeral business. The *coping* process concentrates on managing one's self, for example, getting through the death of a loved one.

Life and routine are interrupted by a serious illness and eventual death. There is an unevenness to life, an unpredictability of sorts. What do you do? How do you hold yourself together? Part of the *doing* involves paying closer attention to a child's well-being; planning trips for her and making sure that she is mentally secure. Informing school teachers, coaches, and other significant persons in her life. It was important that Sandra's, Christine's daughter, emotions were properly channeled given Christine's childhood experience. She shares, "I lost my father when I was 10. My daughter and I lost our fathers to cancer in February of our fifth grade year in elementary school. As a child, I worried my father had become *nothing*, had ceased to be, and that created a lot more grief for me. I didn't want my daughter to endure the same pain." So, Christine commenced the counsel of spiritual leaders and therapists. The idea was for her daughter to "develop a confidence that her father was okay and did not cease to exist on all levels."

Additionally, the *doing* involves making funeral arrangements, informing others, keeping it together at work, for Hank, and comforting the loved one. The *coping*, however, is the focus of one's self. That is, part of Christine's coping strategy was to release her feelings by grieving. She also engaged in lots of thinking. Christine thought about what the future would hold—like daughter, dating and remarrying—for being alone would prove difficult, scary. She thought about the experience of being a widow and whether grief would immobilize her. Is there a set time to grief? How quickly would she recover, build a new life, and get back to "normal"? Getting back to *normal* is rough when life is in transition, when waiting means having little control over your life and the situation. Christine acknowledges such "frustration" but recognized the significance of the wait process. Moreover, getting back to *the everyday* means weeping, depression, and communication. The *doing* and *coping* includes attempts to sort through the aforementioned situations. In order to return to normalcy, the *doing* and *coping* are important features, for without them, one's life remains in limbo, a continued state of anomie. While doing/coping is positive and negative, it is an important part of healing and hence returning to "normal."

Waiting for a loved one to die is not a daily experience and often requires on-the-job training. "I think one learns to live a bit more for *today* when facing those challenges." For Christine, the loved one will not die today but soon. This means comforting Hank through his pain and rearranging one's schedule to have more family time or Hank time. So often we postpone dinner, taking for granted that there is "tomorrow." But when "tomorrow" is uncertain, it means taking Hank to cheer the Dodgers or buying his favorite ice cream, *today*! There are fewer arguments about toilet seats and toothpaste caps; they are no longer important. Here is where life is lived to its fullest, and one begins to define for him/herself what is trivial and what is not. The introspection provides an appreciation for life, *for today* and a reinterpretation of what is *really* important. *Death challenges significant others in ways that normalcy cannot.* Such challenges are unexpected and unpredictable, and yet we learn more about ourselves, that is our strengths, our weaknesses, and how to cope with and manage the passing of a loved one.

My Son's Death

One of the most difficult situations is losing a child, a son to liver failure. Benito (Benny) Agrelo was a child who underwent two liver transplants, one at age eight and the other at age fourteen. One undergoes transplants to lengthen life and even normalize life; yet, one cannot have a transplant surgery unless there is a donor, a liver from someone else. Like waiting to die, Benny awaited a liver, and when it came available, Amanda Agrelo, Benny's mother, was ecstatic. She realized that Benny had another chance at life, a chance to outlive her. For no mother wants her child to suffer, and when children experience pain, mothers equally feel pain and hurt. Amanda then did what was necessary to comfort and honor Benny.

In order to prevent rejection of an alien organ, certain antirejection drugs are necessary, like cyclosporine and at the time (1994), an experimental treatment called FK506. In Benny's case, when cyclosporine no longer worked, Dr. Andreas G. Tzakis performed another surgery, and then prescribed several medications including FK506. Soon Benny complained of the pain though his mother encouraged him to endure. The painful side effects included fierce headaches, back pain, leg pain, and irritability. Benny's brother, Frank told the Sun Sentinel that, "He cried all the time and was very agitated" (Lassiter and Walsh, 1994). The medication kept him from playing outside with his friends, reading, and at times, immobilizing Benny. Agonizing each dosage, Benny stopped taking his medicine. Though he told no one and concealed his behavior, there was less pain and irritability, as he did not swallow medication. Amanda assumed Benny was getting better, but a tip from Dr. Tzakis alerted Amanda that Benny was not taking medicine, leading Amanda to pay closer attention as to whether Benny was swallowing his medicine. Discovering that medicine was being flushed, Amanda objected to Benny's behavior and insisted that he take his medicine. She realized that death was a real consequence. Arguments between Amanda and Benny ensued, yet Benny intelligently refused. Feeling the pain of her son, Amanda attempted to negotiate another (milder) medicine, but no other medicine was on the market and doctors insisted that Amanda force Benny to swallow his medication. Amanda found the doctor's orders objectionable and thus declined to force Benny into swallowing his medication.

Soon the Florida Department of Health and Rehabilitative Services (HRS) intervened, alleging medical neglect. One evening, HRS arrived at Benny's home with five police cars and two ambulances, forcibly taking Benny to Jackson Memorial Hospital. According to Mrs. Agrelo, "he kicked and screamed and yelled," though he was confined for three days. If Mrs. Agrelo was not going force Benny to take medication, no one else should force him either. So, while Amanda did not want Benny to die, she did not want to see him in pain. She struggled with her own dilemma but was impressed by her sons' maturity and logic. For instance, he clearly expressed the side effects to his mother and other sibling, confessing, "I'm tired of living in pain. I rather stay at home and live as close as I can to a natural life." Moreover, Benny recognized the magnitude of his decision and was at peace with it, stating, "I know the consequences, I know the problems. Taking the medication could make me better, but not for long."

The conflict between HRS and the Agrelo family called for legal intervention. Judge Arthur Birken of Broward County Circuit Court met with Benny and his doctors in the hospital. After a long visit with Benny that included four hours of testimony from doctors who treated him (see *L.A. Times*, 1994), Judge Birken ruled that Benny could not be forced to take the antirejection medications and released to his family. According to Mrs. Agrelo, Benny's release was conditioned on his getting psychological counseling (see *The New York Times*, June 1994). While the Health Department apologized for their actions, the Agrelo family applauded the decision. Amanda says, "Benny was granted exactly what he deserves. He will get to live his life the way he wants. There will be no forcing of drugs for him" (see *L.A. Times*, June 12, 1994). Benny agrees that "the Judge made the right decision; I should have the right to make my own decisions. I'm tired of living in pain" (*L.A. Times*, June 12, 1994).

One can only imagine the emotional ride of Amanda Agrelo; she has waited for two liver donors and experienced two transplant surgeries; she has witnessed the joy and pain of her son; she was disappointed by medicine that did not work; doctors who were only interested in research, an invasion by HRS; the public who did not understand her situation; the media who only wanted a story and a judge, who seemed to do the right thing. Such an ordeal is exhausting, and tiring to say the least. It can take away your will to fight but also broadens one's perspective. According to the *New York Times* (1994), Amanda "had learned to respect the wishes of a son she called mature and bright." In short, she came to accept Benny's decision to die, and hence *the wait*. Apparently, her faith helped her come to grips with accepting Benny's resolution, and thus answering reporters, "This means it's up to God only." It's up to God when Benny will die, though in the meantime, she kept a bedside vigil, so she could be aware of his condition and respond to various requests. Her faith seemed to guide and comfort the family, and as a way to bring closure, Ava Senra Agrelo told the media, "A few days ago, my mom told him that he was going to see Jesus before she did, and that when he sees Him to give Him a big hug for her" (*L.A. Times*, August 22, 1994). A hug, as opposed to a handshake, often reflects warmth, sensing that one is missed and/or excitement upon reacquainting. Still Amanda is at peace with Benny, for she feels he is going to a better *place*, experience no pain and that Jesus will care for him. According to the *L.A.*

Times (August 22, 1994), Benny had fallen into a coma two days before his death, only to wake and say goodbye to his mother. "Mami, hug," Benny said just before he died, opening his eyes and raising his arms to his mother. The two embraced, Benny smiled and took his last breath, said Ava Senra Agrelo.

LAYERS OF WAITING

Waiting for a loved one to die is a process that includes layers or stages of waiting. Medical results may signal an initial layer but subsequent tests may inform the waiting process. Subsequent tests may provide new results; research could produce additional drugs. In both instances, what one is waiting for could change. Each visit to the doctor, each medical test result and new drug is a hope for change. But a time comes when positive change will not occur and the "real" wait for death is recognized. This then gets at another layer to one's wait. Amanda realizes that death is imminent and Benny's earthly future is no more. She will not see him graduate, marry, or have children.

Waiting for death is complex; one is not only waiting for death but one could be waiting for *relief.* Jamil recalls that "there was a sense of 'relief' after having devoted so many years to the care of my mother." Caring for a loved one, being at their beck and call, having no life, experiencing *their* emotions, which are tied to *your* emotions may initiate a longing for change, for relief, an end to the current situation. The relief layer is wrapped with exhaustion and a desire to get back to *the everyday*. Such a stage cannot be rushed, for no one knows the time or date of death, which further influences the difficulty, uncertainty, and complexity of waiting.

When death finally occurs, has the waiting ceased? On one level—yes. On another level, an additional layer is added. That is, how does one get beyond grief and depression? Waiting for death is physical. Waiting for grief and depression to subside is mental. All may not experience these complex layers and there is no defined time frame as to when depression and/or grief subsides. *But it is clear that waiting for death is far more complex than simply waiting for a loved-one to die.* There are numerous *before-and-after* emotions—and *timeframe* uncertainties (of death, grief and depression) have consequences for our handling death.

FAITH

Durkheim (1965, original 1915) argues that religion serves several critical functions for members of society. In the face of catastrophe, religion provides meaning and purpose. It helps us understand that there is a reason for earthquakes or death, events we cannot control. Ava Senra Agrelo, Benny's sister, explains, "I think everything was meant to happen exactly the way it happened. I was raised to believe that everything happens for a *reason*. I know it through so many different things that have happened through the past few months, through things that Benny said and did" (see *L.A. Times*, August 22, 1994). Religion offers meaning to the unexplainable, yet providing a certain level of comfort and reassurance. In part, one's faith tradition is the aid that gets them through difficult experiences. Benny's mother, Amanda, frequently invoked God and Jesus as a source of comfort, and thus leaving it to a higher power who knows best; she was resigned to let God take over, for example, "this means it's up to God only." The same is true with Christine, who maintains, "My faith is very relevant to me." She confided in spiritual counselor George Marley, who eased her pain, reassured her that Hank had something to look forward to and helped her daughter develop confidence that (Hank) her father was okay. Jamil often used the term "blessed" to describe his efforts to care for his mother. He writes, "My feeling is one of satisfaction knowing that my best efforts to provide for her life have been beneficial to her. Despite my ups and downs, I do feel a great sense of being *blessed*. I often say to myself that I hope I'm getting *credit* for this effort I'm putting in." *Credit* from whom? And *credit* for what? Does he care for his mother out of obligation or love? Seemingly, Jamil is looking to God for *credit*, and since the Christian church recognizes God as sovereign, it is likely that Jamil hopes God sees his deeds. Yet, the type of *credit* is unclear. What type of credit is due Jamil for caring for his ailing mother? Financial credit? Health credit? Extra credit? Heavenly credit? Or All of the Above? His acknowledgment of being "blessed," looking for "credit," and "belonging to a church" suggests that he too depends on a higher power. Fortunately, at the end of the day, Jamil would rather "light a candle" than complain about his situation.

While waiting for a loved one to die is a social fact, to what extent does religion advocate and urge waiting? Generally, religion is a social institution that places emphasis on waiting. Unlike business institutions, religious institutions recognize the value of patience although delay may prove detrimental in business. Business is interested in efficiency and rapid service, and given market competition—there is fear that customers will shop elsewhere. Marketing agencies assist business in advertising by crafting various slogans, like, "can't wait one minute more," "don't wait, these rates won't last long," "what are you waiting for," and "why wait in line for textbooks." The idea is to avoid waiting and obtain your desired product *now*. As mentioned early, technology has sped up the waiting process in that gratification is less delayed. Nowadays, socialization reflects a type of haste, quickness, and impatience. But are there consequences? Have we become a more impatient society? An anxious society given our inability to wait?

Religion then may be that social institution which provides balance and a type of patience to reevaluate life and circumstance. Whether waiting to exhale or waiting to die, religion allows and requires believers to patiently wait. Biblically then, waiting is contextual—in the same way that waiting occurs in everyday life; in short, biblical waiting is determined by the situation. For instance, Psalm 37 encourages believers to remain righteous even though "evil men" and "the wicked" appear successful. Their success is limited, and they will eventually perish. But those that *wait* and those who are righteous will be exalted to inherit the land. Additionally, James 5 calls on believers to be patient and wait, like the farmer, who *waits* for the land to yield valuable crops. And finally, Job represents a most righteous and patient servant of God. While being ridiculed by "friends" and advised to curse God and die, Job remained strong in his faith. Job patiently *waited* and received his *change* and thus reward. Such instances get at the contextual framework of waiting and that biblically waiting is *viewed* as active. At the conclusion of one's wait, a promise fulfilled or a reward is likely. Is this what Jamil means by credit?

SUMMARY

In part, this chapter has focused on the emotions of individuals who lose loved ones; how they manage their emotions as they wait for loved ones to die. Such a situation produces a range of emotions, yet individuals are required to remain composed. Clearly, emotions have a role in the organization of action; it has an important role in one's behavior. Whether the loved one is comforted, nursed, or funeral arrangements made, certain emotions are designed to gear us into action (or nonaction). What shall be done and how shall we do it? The analysis includes three significant cases, for example, the professor who waits for his mother to die; a professor who waits for her husband to die; and a mother who waits for her son to die.

Jamil raises certain issues about resentment in that he was caring for his mother in ways that she never cared for him; additionally, resentment was expressed by recognizing that "my life is not my own." That is caring for a dying mother reduces one's social options and caring for mother becomes a full-time commitment. Indeed, caring for mother is like caring for one's infant child. Still, in the end, being there for his mother was the right thing to do, and Jamil communicates a certain satisfaction "knowing that my best efforts to provide for her life have been beneficial."

Christine guides us through a deeper and yet another analysis of *waiting to die*. She forces us to address "wait-origins" and "wait-stages," recognizing that waiting is not a linear process. The question is raised: when does *the waiting* begin? The answer reflects her situation and whether one is waiting for Hank to heal or depart this life. This gets at the complexity of waiting and the emotions tied to loved ones. Christine further guides the emergence of our wait-stages, for example, *future disappearance, doing,* and *coping.* For Christine, the waiting begins when the future disappears; doing is wrapped up in caring for others, doing for others and doing for self. Coping becomes the final wait-stage, involving grief, thinking, depression, communication, and relief (not necessarily in that order).

Amanda Agrelo is our final case study, as she permits society to witness her son's death. Benny is a young man who underwent two liver transplants; the joy of having a donor represents an emotional high that extends the life of her son, Benny. But while the transplant is successful, the antirejection drugs may prove problematic. In Benny's case, such drugs caused excruciating pain that prevented him from normal adolescent activity. Thus, he decided to forgo his medicine and physically felt better as a consequence. Doctors were disturbed and the state intervened, only to have the judge rule that Benny could not be forced to take the antirejection medication and thus released to his family. Amanda, Benny's mother, came to accept and support Benny's decision; keeping a bedside vigil so she was aware of his condition and respond to various requests. Benny's situation represents a type of dignity in dying and the gradual support of his family reflects an understanding of Benny's experience, and a patience that emerges as Benny and others come to grips with his calling. For Benny's family, understanding and sensitivity to his experience lead to patience that would eventually shield, support, and protect Benny from critics.

Jamil, Christine, and Amanda reveal the emotional complexities of waiting for a loved one to die. Here, one discovers that there are layers of waiting and each layer guides and/or informs how significant others wait. One must first discover what he or she is waiting for, that is, life or death. During the process, there is a certain amount of sadness, fatigue, anomie, and even frustration. A relief layer is often experienced at the moment of death, and yet another layer is probable given one's relationship with deceased loved one. That is, grief and depression often emerge and there is no time frame as to when such symptoms subside.

Each individual expressed a certain faith in God; a belief that assisted them in getting through the death of their loved one. Presumably, death may not only cause one to pause, but critically reevaluate one's life and society. The Christian faith seemingly emphasizes patience and long suffering, while at the same time it nourishes and supports significant others while waiting. Death is imminent and "out of my hands" so "this means it's up to God only." In short, one is giving the situation to God, and one takes comfort in

God's choices. The scripture is the foundation, song reinforces scripture, and believer activity is a reflection of scripture and song; one is demonstrating his or her faith.

Waiting to die takes on a dramatic shift when examining a horrific case in New York. According to *The Final Call* (Muhammad, 2008:4), a Brooklyn woman, Esmin Green, died on the waiting room floor of Kings County Hospital Center. She waited nearly twenty-four hours as surveillance video showed her leaning in her seat, falling to the floor, and unable to respond when tapped. Muhammad (2008:4) reports that hospital staff seemingly ignored her, and their written documentation was inconsistent with video surveillance footage. A study conducted by the Cambridge Health Alliance/ Harvard Medical School (2007) indicated that African Americans and Hispanics endure longer emergency room waits than other groups. Resources are essential in delivering equitable health care, and the lack of resources and empathy for patients could in fact lead to death.

It follows that waiting to die varies by situation, for example, from being trapped in a mine, to sinking submarines, to airplane crashes, to car accidents, to cancer diagnosis, to inadequate hospital services (see Schwartz, 1975; Andersen et al., 1971). Death is further complicated by death row inmates, police brutality, and lynching. These deaths are different from cancer. Cancer is a physical disease; racism is a social disease. Deaths resulting from death row, police brutality, and lynching are imposed; they are done for social control; to set an example. Still the emotion remains, but a different type of emotion. A type of anger and rage that questions whether whites really care for African Americans, whether police officers are properly trained, or will this happen to my son. It is a wait that is chilling. Being suppressed by white policemen (knee on the neck, shooting unarmed Black men, lynching, etc.) shortens the wait, and *layers of emotions* are not experienced before death but after. Cancer patients may be given X-amount of days to live and the idea is to make their remaining life comfortable. Such was not the case with George Floyd and other African Americans. Their deaths were not anticipated, not planned. So, the emotional rollercoaster of death is filled with anxiety and uncertainty. Death is mysterious in that (generally) no one knows the time or place. (Sort of like God. No one knows when God/Jesus will return. Seemingly, God returns to all of us individually, for example, when death is experienced.) And while others try to play god, death as an outcome is solely decided by God! Additional research is urged on these untapped and fruitful research topics. Yet, how one waits to die is situational, recognizing that context has consequences for our understanding of death and various emotions expressed.

Conclusion

Toward a Theory of Waiting

WAITING GAME AND WAIT-AND-SEE

The *waiting game* is a process by which one contemplates and critically thinks through before making decisions. Whether lengthy or short, one waits to acquire relevant information; a type of chess game waiting. The waiting game may further result in stall-tactics, as a strategy for advantage in decision-making. Decisions might involve events, situations, issues, and/or individuals. Card and board games serve as strong examples; one's move is frequently dependent on the other. Strategies are consistently evolving. Another example is dating. Women (or men) who "play hard to get" find themselves in advantageous positions. They keep interested parties at bay, while such individuals (interested parties) wonder and wait. (Is she/he interested? Will she/he call? Will she/he text? Was I too forward?) It follows that persons with the least interest in the relationship has the most power (see Dale Wright, 1999). In part, playing-hard-to-get functions to stratify relationships; and the other is likely to wait on a return call, email, or text. Not receiving communication in a timely manner may lead the other to text several times before a single response is rendered.

The waiting game is different from a *wait-and-see situation*. That is, a *wait-and-see situation* focuses on results before decisions are made; and the outcome may include more than one option. Deciding how to treat a disease is an important example; men diagnosed with prostate cancer may elect to have surgery. Yet, "a study in the Journal of the American Medical Association showed that men with very low Gleason-scores can safely skip treatment for several years" (see Newsweek, May 23, 2005, p. 79). In part, a *wait-and-see situation* involves thinking through all possible outcomes, and any additional information is crucial to making decisions. While prostate cancer is not a game, it really requires that one make an informed medical decision, a "waiting decision." Barring *early-decision,* another example is selecting a college. While students apply to several universities, their final choice depends on many factors. Some of which include financial resources, college location, academic interests, institutional status, etc. Usually, a decision is not made until relevant information is received. It is normal that students and parents *wait and see* before investing in college. *Wait and see* allows one to weigh all options, critically think through one's choices, then decide.

The phrase "waiting game" is really a metaphor that illustrates a form of decision-making. Negotiators who are skilled at waiting games recognize that a major feature of such games is bluffs (see Kaufmann et al., 2017). In this sense, the game involves misleading others to close a deal or obtain the best deal. Here then, some approach the negotiation table with more power and knowledge than others, having abilities to influence outcomes. Others make decisions, then place the ball in your court, for example, "I've made my decision, now what are you going to do?" On one level or another many are drawn into waiting games, recognizing that each move or each game encounter has consequences for the next.

The major difference among *waiting games* and *wait-and-see situations* is that *waiting games* involve bluffs and the real possibility of deceiving others. In contrast, *wait-and-see situations* rely on sound data, and here, misleading others is unacceptable and unethical. The *waiting game* may in fact be a game that one plays with the other; it is not likely to have the same consequences as *wait-and-see attitudes*, in that *wait-and-see situations* should not be viewed as games but serious on all levels. *Waiting games* may transition into more important events, but *wait-and-see situations* maintain their seriousness and significance.

THEORY OF WAITING

The waiting game may involve anticipation, strong clues, patience, hunches, luck, and/or valid information. Yet, in moving toward a *theory of waiting*, my concern is explanation, for example, a theory of waiting gets how we explain waiting, and how we make sense of waiting. Much of our waiting centers around wait-management, for example, how we manage and achieve our waiting. Wait-management includes physical waiting, structural waiting, and mental justification as why we wait. Physical waiting is the physical act of waiting, whether waiting in line or waiting for a phone call. Structural waiting gets at the props that pattern our wait-lines, and mental-wait-justification gets at reasons why we wait. Part of wait-management is *doing*. Generally, persons manage waiting by *doing* something, for example, knitting, talking on the phone, watching others, reading, etc. The *doing* is more or less a coping strategy to get through waiting.

Anticipation becomes a key feature in explaining how individuals wait. That is, *the anticipation of waiting may lead to modification in behavior.* For example, while driving one notices a bus or semi-truck, which is approximately two car spaces ahead. Anticipating that the bus will stop for pickup, some drivers are likely to change lanes to avoid delays. Likewise, when games are decided, leaving major sporting events early is done to avoid traffic. The same is true for Black Friday shoppers. Again, predicting long lines for choice products and door buster deals, shoppers arrive early, often several hours early, to stake out a waiting place that ensures product availability and purchase. Implied in *wait-anticipation* is preparation. While waiting in line for iPhones, one comes prepared by bringing food, reading materials, games, tents, chairs, blankets, etc. Moreover, implied in *wait-anticipation* and thus one's behavior is an important cultural norm of "first come, first serve." Those arriving early believe that they should be served first. And therefore, a certain strategy develops when one anticipates waiting; a strategy to avoid additional waits after stores open. But more generally, strategies reflect anticipation and specific wait-environments, which then has consequences for wait-management.

Other delays have been institutionalized in that airlines recommend early arrivals when traveling, and thus one learns to anticipate long delays in airports. Spacing is also an important consideration. Our behavior reflects an institution that requires waiting; there is little debate about the need to wait given safety is the ultimate goal. In such situations, travelers are willing or forced to wait and undergo several inconveniences. Institutionalized delays, as with deliveries, court proceedings, and airline travel, often influence our wait-patterns by bringing something to *do* and the anticipation of a long wait. Mentally, one prepares for an extended wait. And so, while the anticipation of waiting tends to modify our behavior, it also has consequences for one's mental health. In short, whether institutionalized or not, the anticipation of waiting modifies our behavior.

Conversely, *unexpected waits may lead to anxiety, frustrations, and feelings of stagnation.* A sentiment of "time wasted" could emerge given one's unforeseen delay. This condition might also modify an individual's behavior but probably in more negative ways, like cutting in line or confronting the source of delay, especially when one is hurried. Ultimately, those involved in unexpected waits desire relief, which could lead to abandoning the line or moving to another line. Others handle unexpected waits differently, like adjusting to the problem, maintaining one's place in line and/or simply waiting-it-out. It follows that wait-strategies are linked to both unexpected waits and anticipated waits, yet the former is more spontaneous and taxing than the latter.

Extended-group waiting refers to individuals who wait prolonged periods of time for specific products or events. For example, those who wait for the release of iPhones, Harry Potter books, Nintendo Switch, and X-boxes typically line up to form a group of "iPhone waiters." Those who wait for events like the Rose Parade, Macy's Thanksgiving Day Parade, Jazz Festival entrance, Coachella Valley Music and Arts Festival, Million Man March or buying tickets to the final Michael Jackson concert/documentary represent groups who make conscious plans to wait. These groups recognize that a lengthy wait is probable, and so the *anticipation of waiting* clearly affects their behavior. Again, wait-management becomes a key feature. In these situations, and others, what is often overlooked is the *development of community*. A type of community develops; and thus, *the longer one waits in extended-group environments, the more likely community emerges, or the development of a short-lived community is more probable.*

For example, each such wait-community is brought together by a common interest, for example, Coachella, Black Friday, iPhone, Comic Con, etc. Among other things, conversations are likely to emerge about the object of desire. Extended-group waiting allows the "strange to become familiar" in that more attention is paid to those around us; faces and verbal patterns become recognizable. Objects like bags, chairs, blankets, computers, tents, and so forth attach themselves to specific owners, and in time, looking out for the other evolves naturally. While waiting to purchase an iPhone, one respondent mentioned that, "I've been talking to this guy all night." I asked whether they knew one another by name, and John called each person in his immediate circle by name. Fred added that, "When I need a restroom break or to go buy food, these guys will watch my stuff for me. We'll watch each other's stuff."

Communities then develop a life of their own. It is true that wait-communities are influenced by larger and more stable communities in that rules of conduct often reflect norms of the larger society. It follows then that cutting in line by outsiders or other infractions is likely sanctioned, but pushing or challenging boundaries gets at group consensus or group variance. For instance, purchasing one's wait-place is allowed if there is no cost to others. Infractions then are often handled informally, recognizing that group members must coexist until wait-event has ended. The end represents a conclusion to a temporary community, a community that was brought together by similar interests.

The anticipation of waiting and the development of wait-communities require additional probing and thus additional questions. Three questions logically emerge from the above theoretical analysis: Why are people *willing* to wait? Under what conditions is waiting more tolerable? And, under what conditions is waiting less tolerable? Given that most waiting is imposed, naturally or institutionally, the first question implies a choice in waiting. Waiting when it is not required, for example, an extracurricular choice to participate in a self-gratifying event. For example, waiting hours to watch celebrities walk the red carpet is a choice; waiting in line to ride your favorite rollercoaster is a choice; and waiting in line or online to purchase playoff tickets is clearly a choice. One respondent reasoned, "Everyone has something they are willing to wait for." He had spent several hours in an iPhone line and eventually purchased one of the first of such phones. While the iPhone may not interest others and inspire them to wait in long, time-consuming lines, there is however *something* that will. It may be concert tickets, opening night of star trek or a charismatic evangelist. And that is the point: *We are all willing to wait for something*, something that holds intrinsic value to oneself; something that one has determined is worth the trouble of waiting (which may be no trouble at all). Therein lies the choice to wait and all that is accompanied with such delays. For those choosing to wait, there is a perceived benefit, that is, a social, material, mental, moral, political, or economic gain.

The first question is a natural lead-in to the second, which considers choice and non-choice waiting. The question is raised, under what conditions is waiting more tolerable? One's willingness to wait suggests that they not only anticipate delays but holdups are built into their psyches as well, providing higher levels of tolerance, that is, more patience during unforeseen circumstances. For instance, there was a horrible punch spill at opening day of the annual Knit Gallery Gumball sale that attracts many knit enthusiasts. Having waited nearly two hours, customers were further delayed another fifteen minutes—due to punch spill and cleanup; and according to one shopper, "We all took it in stride." Regarding consensus, many shoppers believed that it was best to wait rather than track punch throughout the gallery. While Knit Gallery personnel were apologetic, customers logically realized that refusing to comply and thus track punch throughout store would make shopping worst for all involved; and therefore, a few extra wait-minutes was bearable. It follows that witnessing the wait-explanation, spilled punch, has consequences for wait tolerance. In short, *extended wait groups* often develop consensus and are more willing to work around believable/observable wait explanations.

In contrast, waiting in imposed environments is somewhat different in that it is a necessary means to an end, that is, one must buy stamps and mail bills, yet postal service offers options to email bills, buy stamps online or in grocery stores. It follows that both imposed and volunteer waiting environments offer a type of "choice." Imposed wait environments offer alternatives and volunteer wait environments recognize that one's willingness to wait is a choice. Waiting at DMV, the auto shop or airport invites a hold new meaning to tolerance. For one, waiting at DMV seems more hectic than waiting for the latest Nintendo Switch. Regarding imposed wait environments, our tolerance to waiting is linked to explanations given by authorities. Explanations concerning security and airport safety are rarely disputed, and physical evidence is seldom requested or required. Explanations that are consistent with observation are also more tolerable, for one can see that the bank is crowded with lots of people waiting. In short and with regard to imposed wait environments, wait-tolerance is tied to explanations that involve security, safety, and observable facts.

Generic explanations then speak to our final question: Under what conditions is waiting less tolerable? Generic explanations might generate concern and therefore invite challenge and speculation. Generic explanations are excuses used by varying establishments for a host of troubles; the establishment is not willing to divulge problems, so common and familiar excuses are used. Excuses like "understaffed," "technical problems," "software malfunctions," and "the doctor is with a patient" rarely provide satisfactory clarification and yet they are routinely used to stall customers. One is left to his or her imagination to determine the meaning of "understaffed" or "technical problems." Such excuses are challenged because of their vagueness, not to mention the additional time one must wait. They function as cover-ups for other, more embarrassing predicaments, like mistakes in service, for example, giving the wrong order to chefs. Detecting such excuses and even lies, customers are likely to leave and/or contest stated reasons, leaving the company open for criticism and negative reviews.

Additionally, waiting is less tolerable when mental health is affected and timing is inconvenient. One respondent clearly confessed that, "In everything I do, I try to figure out how I can avoid waiting. Because I can't wait, it drives me crazy!" Another respondent who walked into Sears Auto Department viewed the line and declared, "I'm not waiting in that line!" The long line, along with the perceived amount of wait-time discouraged her, possibly affecting other commitments. Consequently, she returned the following day where the line was manageable. In these two instances where mental health is affected and timing is inconvenient, persons are likely to search for alternatives, options that fit their personalities and schedules. Taken together, waiting is less tolerable when perceived sincerity of explanation and length of wait are questioned by clients. While one's schedule may prevent them from waiting, a perceived lie could lead one to walk out and never return.

In part, waiting is a sociopsychological situation that we all experience. It is unavoidable in any society or community—waiting is universal. Within our culture, we are socialized to wait; one's ability to wait implies a certain civility and consideration, a certain need for order and organization. It suggests that our "wait socialization" has gone deep, for example, internalized. Our "wait socialization" has become so internalized and therefore routinized that wait-manipulation is possible. Boarding planes is a solid example.

Individuals needing assistance along with parents and small children board airplanes first. This is followed by first class, then zones one, two, three, and four. Given order and patience in which boarding occurs, it is probable that most adhere to boarding procedures. Not all. One respondent, Thurston, mis-used the wait-cooperation premise. Thurston shared that he regularly skips a zone. For instance, "If I have zone four, I'll go in with zone three, or if I have zone three, I'll go in with zone two. No one seems to care or they (attendants) are not paying attention. I get in line and hand them my boarding pass—like I'm supposed to be with that group."

Thurston's assumption appears probable in that—it is the perception that we are following wait rules when we are not. Put simply, Thurston did not wait his turn. *Cooperative deviance* is mixed with *cooperative norms* and no one knows the difference. No one knows Thurston's zone number, except Thurston and the attendant; passengers however, do not—and yet they assume he is doing the right thing. While attendants may confront zone violators, Thurston claims that he's never been "stopped." Is it possible that attendants don't care, they are too busy, they are not paying attention, they simply desire a smooth transition, that privilege clouded their ability to act, or that Thurston is lying? Whatever the reason, wait encounters are con-stant and ever evolving. In the words of Peter Berger, "The fascination of sociology lies in the fact that its perspective makes us see in a new light the very world in which we have lived all our lives." The sociology of waiting captures that excitement, while *cooperative deviance* unveils another layer of waiting.

Theoretically, while *wait props* are designed to organize waiting and rou-tinize the process, *failure to follow signs (or written instructions) and verbal directions could result in longer waits, for the client and those in his wait space.* The extended wait is directed at those who do not follow instructions.[1] That is, if the clerk asked those in line to present their Kaiser medical card, and when X-person arrives at the clerk's counter and cannot produce a Kaiser medical card, the clerk is likely to ask X-person to "step to the side." Wait on the outskirts of the line until he finds card, or wait until the clerk has time to service X-person. Why should X-person "step to the side"? On the one hand, X-person cannot produce his Kaiser card; on the other, there are several persons awaiting service who can produce Kaiser cards. Seemingly, the clerk does not want others affected by X-person's inability to follow instructions. Why should other customers wait? The clerk then must keep the line moving and maintain the appointment schedules. It is a systemic issue; a situation that keeps pace with hospital operations. The longer wait is often a consequence of failure to follow instructions, not to mention the possible impatience of those waiting. Put simply, it behooves individuals who are waiting in *any* line to follow verbal and written instructions. Conversely, were the clerk to extend consideration, and wait for X-person to find his Kaiser card, the wait affects all involved, adding another layer to the wait situation.

Students are unlikely to cut line in the presence of teachers; motorists are less tempted to cross red lights during police presence; concert-goers are less likely to cut line when security is present; and bike riders are less likely to cross red lights while police are nearby. Essentially, *persons are more likely to observe wait-rules in the presence of authority figures.* In such cases, it is likely that officials will enforce wait rules. Openly defying officials and wait rules are dangerous; mild or severe sanctions may result (see Price, 2005). An official response and/or sanction is probable and likely expected by those watching. Clearly, few will object to the official's actions. The issue is wait rules and authority figures; and though Sheila is in a hurry, she is less likely to speed when police are approaching.

Wait theory guides our understanding of waiting, for example, how people wait, why they wait, and where they wait. Waiting is a situation that all experience; it is one of life's realities; it may be fun, boring, or stressful. Waiting is optional and/or necessary. "Everyone has something they are willing to wait for" reflects optional waiting. "Do I have to wait?" reflects necessary waiting; for instance, waiting for babies to come to term is required, and waiting for an iPhone represents choice. Waiting is better understood culturally and regionally. Some societies and regions are laid back; other regions, like New York, can't seem to slow down. Different environments and situations help us understand and manage waiting.

Consider the corona pandemic; there is more waiting. For instance, waiting to take a corona virus test, waiting for test results, waiting for the curve to flatten, waiting to reopen, waiting to enter stores, waiting in post offices, waiting at the DMV, waiting online, waiting in line, waiting to enter aircrafts, and waiting for a vaccine. Waiting is built into our errands and compounded by maintaining safe distance and masks to prevent the spread of COVID-19. We are more cautious and cognizant of our neighbors and those around us; those whom we share the same wait-line, the same wait-space, or those who we pass in stores, in hallways, in elevators, on streets, and those who refuse masking. Here, community is less likely. During this crisis, *we know why we wait.* Our wait is implied and explained by several media outlets, medical professionals, politicians, parents, teachers, store and restaurant managers. We wait, space, and mask to prevent the spread of COVID-19, while social distance and masks assist us in managing corona-waits. *Individuals then are more tolerant of waiting during crises than ordinary times.* If we don't follow corona-protocol, what are the possible outcomes?

Finally, *wait theory* accounts for different types of waiting. There are some waits that require little or no explanation; other waits require more detail. Whether it pertains to business, education, recreation, shopping, or health, understanding why we wait helps us comply and *manage* our waiting. A *theory of waiting* is designed to do just that, explain waiting. Our culture has consequences for our wait-behavior, yet, at the heart of waiting is *consideration*, not fairness. Just because you are in line before me, does not mean that you should receive service first. Seniors and pregnant women who cannot hold their urine deserve consideration, not fairness, particularly when restroom lines are long. All things being equal, fairness should apply, but do we know everyone's personal circumstance? No. Thus, in time and space, waiting an extra five-minute seems harmless; and culturally, most citizens will follow rules. How do we know? Wait lines are not chaotic, they are quite functional; and overt wait-violations are often meant by resistance.

NOTE

1. Note the case of Farrad, the Kaiser member who could not produce his Kaiser card. This case is recorded in the chapter, "Structure of Waiting." Given his inability to locate his Kaiser card, he was asked to "step to the side," resulting in a longer wait.

Glossary

CALCULATED DISTRACTIONS: planned manipulations by industry.

CASUAL THINKING: recollections about events or persons, along with impromptu thoughts about loved-ones and other situations.

CHOICE WAITING: consciously making a decision to wait.

COMMUNICATION DISINTEREST: having no interest in conversing with strangers and other persons.

COMMUNICATION INTEREST: showing interest in talking with strangers and other persons.

CULTURE OF EXPLANATION: a society that anticipates and expects a reason for someone's actions and behaviors, like lateness, cheating, incorrect restaurant orders, etc.

CULTURE OF WAITING: Environments where waiting is expected and normalized.

ENCLOSED WAIT SECTION: a prescribed wait area or region.

EXPLANATIONS STRATEGIES: approaches used to deliver wait explanations.

EXTENDED WAITING: lengthy waits that are unusual, often unanticipated, and infrequent.

EXTENDED-GROUP WAITING: refers to groups who wait prolonged periods of time for specific products or events.

IMPERSONALITY OF WAITING: waiting in a similar space but social distance, utilitarian communication (if any), and lack of eye contact are evident. Individuals are uncomfortable and guarded.

INANIMATE WAIT EXPLANATIONS: explanations provided by sources other than humans, e.g., signs, video recordings, etc.

INSTITUTIONAL WAIT-MANAGEMENT: organizing and monitoring those who wait.

INTERMITTENT CONVERSATIONS: conversations that are irregular and interrupted by other situations, yet conversations resume later.

NATURAL DISTRACTIONS: spontaneous and unpredictable interruptions, grabbing our attention in ways that spark emotion and thought.

OBJECT OF WAIT: waiting for a specific item, individual, or event.

OPEN WAIT AREA: waiting in a public space; generally, individuals wait outside and visible to the public.

ORDINARY WAITING: the routine process of waiting.

SELF-IMPOSED WAITS: intentional waits with prescribed goals; a type of deferred gratification.

STAND WAITS: standing while waiting.

STRUCTURAL ANOMIE: Difficulty understanding where to wait, how to wait, and/or where line starts. Rails, ropes, signs, etc., are absent.

TACTICAL THINKING: thoughts and planning about how to accomplish a task, develop a design, or defeat a rival.

UTILITARIAN CONVERSATION/COMMUNICATION: a type of talk that is short, practical, and informative.

VIRTUAL LINE: a waiting line that is accessed and stored by a computer network.

WAIT-AUDIENCE: an assembly of onlookers who are waiting and viewing an encounter or event.

WAIT-BEHAVIOR: how one conducts him or herself while waiting.

WAIT-DECISION: options in waiting.

WAIT-DISTRACTIONS: diverting one's attention away from waiting.

WAIT-ENVIRONMENT: the place or surrounding where one waits.

WAIT-EXPLANATIONS: reasons for waiting.

WAIT MANAGEMENT: strategies developed by individuals that assist them in coping with and adjusting to delays.

WAIT NORMS: adhering to the cultural folkways and rules of waiting.

WAIT-ORIGINS: the beginning of one's wait.

WAIT-PATTERNS: wait designs that an industry or culture constructs, e.g., waiting in line, waiting on the phone, waiting online, waiting in car lines, waiting in line six feet apart, etc.

WAIT-ROOM: enclosed settings that are best exemplified in hospitals; these rooms are somewhat confine.

WAIT-SHIFT: rotating periods of time delegated for waiting.

WAIT-SOCIALIZATION: the process of learning how to wait.

WAIT-STAGES: phases of waiting that lead to specific outsomes. Wait stages are not necessarily linear.

WAIT-STRUCTURES: areas of wait and places where waiting occurs, like banks, amusement parks, freeways, post offices, mazes, etc.

WAIT-TIME: the amount of time waiting and/or the length of time that is anticipated.

WAIT-TYPES: different situations of wait, e.g., waiting on decisions, waiting for an appointment, waiting for results, waiting for Christmas, etc.

WAIT-UTILIZATION: what we *do* while waiting, e.g., knitting, reading, computing, etc.

WAITING CONSISTENCY: regular patterns of wait behavior; waiting consistency may occur hourly, daily, weekly, and even monthly. Here, individuals develop routine and regular wait-patterns.

WAITING IN VAIN: waiting for something that does not materialize.

WAITING PLACE: a certain seat or area where persons spend time waiting.

WAITING PROPS: consist of rails, ropes, ropes connected to poles, floor markings (such as arrows & lane lines), floor signs, symbols, and signs directing people how, where, and what to expect while waiting.

WORTH THE WAIT: a wait situation that is valued, and worth one's time and investment.

References

Allred, K.G. 1999. "Anger and Retaliation: Towards an Understanding of Impassioned Conflict in Organizations." in R.J. Bies, R.J. Lewicki and B.H. Shepard (eds.), *Research on Negotiation in Organizations.* Greenwich: JAI Press.

Anderson, David, Dennis Sweeney, Thomas Williams & Kipp Martin. 2008. *An Introduction to Management Science: Quantitative Approaches to Decision Making,* 12th edition. Mason: Thomson.

Anderson, Elijah. 1999. *Code of the Street.* New York: W.W. Norton & Company.

Anderson, Elijah. 2011. *Cosmopolitan Canopy: Race and Civility in Everyday Life.* New York: W.W. Norton and Company.

Aneshensel, Carol S. 2005. "Research in Mental Health: Social Etiology Versus Social Consequences." *Journal of Health and Social Behavior,* 46:221–228.

Armstrong, Sarah. 2018. The Cell and the Corridor: Imprisonment as Waiting, and Waiting as Mobile. *Time and Society,* 27(2):133–154. doi:10.1177/0961463X15587835

Aronson, Elliot. 1999. *The Social Animal,* 8th edition. New York: Worth Publishers.

Aronson, Elliot. 2004. *The Social Animal,* 9th edition. New York: Worth Publishers.

Aultman, Julie M. & Delese Wear. 2006. "Medicine and Place." *Perspectives in Biology and Medicine,* 49:84–98.

Auyero, Javier. 2011. "Patients of the State: An Ethnographic Account of Poor People's Waiting." *Latin American Research Review,* 46:5–29.

Baldwin, Ann Linda. 2012. How do Plants in Hospital Waiting Rooms Reduce Patient Stress? *Journal of Alternative & Complementary Medicine,* 18(4):309–310. doi:10.1089/acm.2012.0116

Baptista, Alistair & Rajamanickam, Nithya. 2007. "Harry Potter Magic Cast Spells on Fans." July 22, 2007, *Daily News.* gulf-daily-news.com.

Barker, Tom & David Carter. 1990. "'Fluffing Up the Evidence and Covering Your Ass': Some Conceptual Notes on Police Lying." *Deviant Behavior,* 11(1):61–73. Washington, DC: Taylor & Francis, Inc.

Benewick, Robert & Robert Holton. 1987. "The Peaceful Crowd: Crowd Solidarity and the Pope's Visit to Britain." in George Gaskell and Robert Benewick (eds.), *The Crowd in Contemporary Britain.* London: Sage Publications.

Bennett, Lerone, Jr. 1993. *Before the Mayflower,* 6th edition. New York: Penguin Books.

Berger, Peter. 2007. "Invitation to Sociology." in James Henslin (ed.), *Down to Earth Sociology*, 14th edition. New York: Free Press.

Blassingame, John W. 1979. *The Slave Community.* New York: Oxford University Press.

Bonilla-Silva, Eduardo. 2006. *Racism Without Racists: Color-Blind Racism and the Persistence of Racial Inequality in the United States,* 2nd edition. New York: Rowman & Littlefield Publishers.

Bottero, Wendy. 2005. *Stratification: Social Division and Inequality.* London & New York: Routledge.

Brady, Michael K. & J. Joseph Cronin, Jr. 2001. "Customer Orientation: Effects on Customer Service Perceptions and Outcome Behaviors." *Journal of Service Research*, 3:241–251.

Branch, Taylor. 1988. *Parting the Waters: America in the King Years 1954-63.* New York: Simon and Schuster.

Brooks, Daniel. 2018, June 14. *The Russian Zen of Standing in Line.* Retrieved from http://www.russiaknowledge.com/2018/06/14/the-russian-zen-of-standing-in-line/

Busch, Fred. 2006. "Talking with Strangers." *Psychoanalytic Review*, 93(3):463–475.

Cone, James H. 1992. *Martin & Malcolm & America: A Dream or a Nightmare.* New York: Orbis Books.

Cooley, Charles Horton. 1964/1902. *Human Nature and Social Order.* New York: Scribner.

Davidow, William H. & Uttal, Bro. 1990. *Total Customer Service: The Ultimate Weapon.* New York: Harper Perennial.

Delta the Worst Airline. 2009. *Delta Airlines Complaint: Delta is the Worst Airlines Ever 7 Hours on Tar Mat.* Retrieved April 16, 2010, from http://www.my3cents .com/showReview.cgi?id=46567

Deshpande, Rohit & Frederick E. Webster. 1989. "Organizational Culture and Marketing: Defining the Research Agenda." *Journal of Marketing,* 53:3–15.

Duneier, Mitchell. 1992. *Slim's Table.* Chicago/London: University of Chicago Press.

Dunnett, A. Jane. "The Role of Organizational Culture in Customer Service." *The Business Review, Cambridge,* 7:38–44.

Dunning, Eric, Patrick Murphy & J. Williams. 1986. "Spectator Violence at Football Matches." *British Journal of Sociology,* 37:221–244.

Dunning, Eric, Patrick Murphy & J. Williams. 1987. *The Roots of Football Hooliganism.* London: Routledge and Kegan Paul.

Durkheim, Emile. 1965, orig. 1915. *The Elementary Forms of Religious Life.* New York: The Free Press.

Dyson, Michael Eric. 2006. *Come Hell or High Water: Hurricane Katrina and the Color of Disaster.* New York: Basic Civitas.

Ellison, Ralph. 1972. *Invisible Man.* New York: Vintage.

Emerson, Robert M. 1981. "On Last Resorts." *American Journal of Sociology,* 87:1–22.

Emerson, Robert M. 1974. "Role Determinants in Juvenile Court." In Daniel Glaser (ed.), *Handbook of Criminology*. New York: Rand McNally College Publishing Company.

Farman, Jason. 2018. *Delayed Response: The Art of Waiting from the Ancient to the Instant*. New Haven: Yale University Press.

Flaherty, Michael. 1999. *The Watched Pot: How We Experience Time*. New York: New York University Press.

Freud, Sigmund. 1955. "Group Psychology and the Analysis of the Ego." In J. Strachey et al. (eds.), *The Standard Edition of the Complete Psychological Works of Sigmund Freud*, Vol. 18. London: The Hogarth Press.

Garfinkel, Harold. 1967. *Studies in Ethnomethodology*. New Jersey: Prentice Hall.

Gieryn, Thomas F. 2000. "A Space for Place in Sociology." *Annual Review of Sociology*, 26:463–496.

Goffman, Erving. 1959. *The Presentation of Self in Everyday Life*. Garden City: Anchor Books.

Goffman, Erving. 1961. *Encounters*. Indianapolis: Bobbs-Merrill.

Goffman, Erving. 1963. *Behavior in Public Places: Notes on the Social Organization of Gatherings*. New York: Free Press.

Gong, Caroline. 2005. "I Can't Live Without My Darling iPod." *Newsweek,* May 16, 2005, p. 14.

Gonnerman, Jennifer. 2004. *Life on the Outside: The Odyssey of Elaine Bartlett*. New York: Picador.

Grint, Keith & Steven Woolgar. 1997. *The Machine at Work: Technology, Work and Organization*. Cambridge, UK: Polity.

Gronfeldt, Svafa & Judith Strother. 2006. *Service Leadership: The Quest for Competitive Advantage*. Sage Publications: Thousand Oaks.

Grushin, Olga. 2010. *The Line*. New York: Marian Wood/Putnam's Sons.

Haley, Alex. 1965. *The Autobiography of Malcolm X*. Grove Press: New York.

Hall, Edward T. & Mildred R. Hall. 2005. "The Sounds of Silences." In James M. Henslin (ed.), *Down to Earth Sociology,* 13th edition. New York: Free Press, pp. 99–107.

Harvey, O.J. 1962. "Personality Factors in Resolution of Conceptual Incongruities." *Sociometry,* 25(4):336–352.

Haslett, Adam. 2002. "The Good Doctor." In *You Are Not A Stranger Here*. New York: Random House.

Hoffman, Elizabeth A. 2006. "The Importance of Place: Using Local-Focus Videos to Spark the Sociological Imagination." *Teaching Sociology,* 34:164–172.

House, James S. 1981. "Social Structure and Personality." In Morris Rosenberg and Ralph Turner (eds.), *Social Psychology: Sociological Perspectives*. New York: Basic Books.

Hudson, Ray. 2001. *Producing Place*. New York: Guild Press.

Jackson, James Thomas. 1993. *Waiting in Line at the Drugstore and Other Writings of James Thomas Jackson*. Houston: University of North Texas Press.

Kagan, Jerome. 2007. *What is Emotion?* New Haven: Yale University Press.

Kaufman, Lutz, Joerg Rottenburger, Craig R. Carter & Christian Schlereth. 2017. "Bluffs, Lies and Consequences: A Reconceptualization of Bluffing in Buyer-Supplier Negotiations." *Journal of Supply Chain Management*, 52(2):21–33.

Kent, Richard. 2007. "Secrets and Lies." *Nursing Standard,* 21(46):24–25.

King, Martin Luther, Jr.1963. *Why We Can't Wait.* New York: Mentor Books.

King, Martin Luther, Jr. 1958. *Stride Towards Freedom: The Montgomery Story.* San Francisco: Harper & Row Publishers.

Kubler-Ross, Elisabeth. 1975. *Death, The Final Stages of Growth.* New Jersey: Prentice-Hall.

Kuhn, Manford H. 1964. "Major Trends in Symbolic Interaction Theory in the Past Twenty-Five Years." *Sociological Quarterly,* 5:61–84.

Lai, Gina & Rance P. Lee. 2006. "Market Reforms and Psychological Distress in Urban Beijing." *International Sociology: London,* 21(4):551.

Lassiter, Tom & Barbara Walsh. 1994, June 15. "Survivors: Benito, Reconsider Transplant Recipients Empathize with 15-Year-Old's Pain." *Sun Sentinel.* Fort Lauderdale, p. 1.B.

Lawless, Jill. 2007. "Fans Lining-up for Harry Potter Book." *USA Today.* July 21, 2007.

Levine, Robert. 1997. *The Geography of Time.* New York: Basic Books.

Liljander, V. & Strandvik, T. 1995. "The Nature of Customer Relationships in Services." in T.A. Swartz, D.E. Bowen, and S.W. Brown (eds.), *Advances in Service Marketing and Management,* Vol. 4. London: JAI Press.

Liljander, V. & Strandvik, T. 1997. "Emotions in Service Satisfaction." *International Journal of Service Industry Management,* 8(2):148–169.

Lipsky, Michael. 1980. *Street-Level Bureaucracy: Dilemmas of the Individual in Public Services.* New York: Russell Sage Foundation.

Litwack, Leon. 1998. *Trouble in Mind: Black Southerners in the Age of Jim Crow.* New York: Knopf.

Lofland, John. 1981. "Collective Behavior: The Elementary Forms." In Morris Rosenberg & Ralph Turner (eds.), *Social Psychology: Sociological Perspectives.* New York: Basic Books.

Los Angeles Times, Los Angeles, California: 1994, August 22, p. 11. "Boy Who Refused Liver Transplant Drugs Dies Medicine: Florida 15-Year-Old Draws Last Breath in His Mother's Arms Two Months After Court Let Him Stop Taking Anti-Rejection Medication." ProQuest. URL: http://ezp.pasadena.edu/login?url=http:// proquest.umi.com/pq dweb?did=59578784$sid=4&Fmt=3&clientld=7617&RQT =309&VName=PQ D

Los Angeles Times, Los Angeles, California, 1994, August 12. "Teenage Patient Gets OK to Stop Transplant Drug." URL: http://articles.latimes.com/1994-06-12/news/ mn-3436_1_transplant-patient

Lyon, Margot L. 1996. "C. Wright Mills Meets Prozac: The Relevance of 'Social Emotions' to the Sociology of Health and Illness." In Veronica James and Jonathan Gabe (eds.), *Health and the Sociology of Emotions.* Cambridge: Blackwell Publishers.

Maines, D.R. 1977. "Social Organization in Symbolic Interactionism." In A. Inkeles, J. Coleman and N. Smelser (eds.), *Annual Review of Sociology,* vol. 3. California: Annual Reviews, Inc., pp. 235–259.

Maister, David. 1985. "The Psychology of Waiting Lines." In J. A. Czepiel, M. R. Solomon and C. F. Surprenant (eds.), *The Service Encounter: Managing Employee/*

Customer Interaction in Service Businesses. Lexington, MA: D.C. Heath and Company, Lexington Books.

Mandler, George. 1975. *Mind and Emotion.* New York: Wiley.

Mann, Leon. 1969. "Queue Culture: The Waiting in Line as a Social System." *American Journal of Sociology,* 75:340–354.

Mann, Leon & K.F. Taylor. 1969. "Queue Counting: The Effect of Motives upon Estimates of Numbers in Waiting Lines." *Journal of Personality and Social Psychology,* 12:95–103.

Martelli, Don. 2009. *New Federal Transportation Rule Limits Airline Tarmac Delays.* Retrieved April 16, 2010, from http/technorati.com/lifestyle/travel/article/new-federal-transportation-rule-limits-airline/

Marx, Karl & Frederick Engels. [1848] 1988. *The Communist Manifesto.* New York: Norton.

McCarthy, J.D. & M.N. Zald. 1977. "Resource Mobilization and Social Movements: A Partial Theory." *American Journal of Sociology,* 82:1212–1239.

Mead, George Herbert. 1934. *Mind, Self and Society.* Chicago: University of Chicago Press.

Miao, Hong & Mia Wang Bassham. 2007. "Embracing Customer Service in Libraries." *Library Management,* 28:53–61.

Milgram, Stanley. 1963. "Behavioral Study of Obedience." *Journal of Abnormal and Social Psychology,* 67:371–378.

Mills, C. Wright. 1959. *The Sociological Imagination.* New York: Oxford University Press.

Morris, Aldon D. 1984. *The Origins of the Civil Rights Movement: Black Communities Organizing for Change.* New York: Free Press.

Muhammad, Ashahed M. 2008, July 15. "Dying for Care: Video Captures Emergency Room Death." *The Final Call,* p. 4.

Nabokov, Peter. 2006. *Where the Lightning Strikes: The Lives of American Indian Sacred Places.* New York: Viking-Penguin Group.

Newsweek. "Playing the Waiting Game." Vol. CXLV, No. 21, May 23, 2005, p. 79.

New York Times, nytimes.com. 1994, June 13. "Behind a Boy's Decision to Forgo Treatment." URL: http://www.nytimes.com/1994/06/13/us/behind-a-boy-s-decision-to-forgo-treatment.html?pagewanted=print

Norman, Donald. 2009. "Waiting: A Necessary Part of Life." http://jnd.ord/dn.mss/waiting_a_necessary_part_of_life.html

Parsons, Talcott. 1937. *The Structure of Social Action.* New York: McGraw-Hill.

Pearlin, Leonard I. 1989. "The Sociological Study of Stress." *Journal of Health and Social Behavior* 30:241–256.

Popke, Sean. 2007. "Activation Nightmare." *USA Today.* July 6.

Powsner, Seth & Richard Spitzer. 2003. "Sex, Lies and Medical Compliance." *The Lancet,* 361:2003–2004. www.thelancet.com

Price, Paul-Jahi Christopher. 2005. *Social Control at Opportunity Boys' Home: How Staff Manage Juvenile Inmates.* New York: University Press of America.

Raines, Howell. 1977. *My Soul is Rested: Movement Days in the Deep South Remembered.* New York: G. P. Putnam's Sons.

Relph, E. 1976. *The Placelessness of Place.* London: Pion.

Ritzer, George. 1993. *The McDonaldization of Society.* Thousand Oaks: Pine Forge Press.

Robson, Douglas. 2007. "Williams: Rain Brings 'Clarity.'" *USA Today,* July 6, 2007, p. 11c.

Rogelberg, Steven G., Janet L. Barnes-Farrell & Victoria Creamer. 1999. "Customer Service Behavior: The Interaction of Service Predisposition and Job Characteristics." *Journal of Business and Psychology,* 13:421–435.

Rosenberg, Morris & Ralph Turner, eds. 1981. "Social Structure and Personality." in *Social Psychology: Sociological Perspectives.* New York: Basic Books.

Schneekloth, L.H. & R. G. Shibley. 1995. *Placemaking: The Art and Practice of Building Communities.* New York: John Wiley and Sons.

Schwartz, Barry. 1974. "Waiting, Exchange and Power: The Distribution of Time in Social Systems." *American Journal of Sociology,* 79:841–870.

Schwartz, Barry. 1975. *Queuing and Waiting: Studies in the Social Organization of Access and Delay.* Chicago: University of Chicago Press.

Schwartz, Sharon. 2002. "Outcomes for the Sociology of Mental Health: Are We Meeting Our Goals?" *Journal of Health and Social Behavior,* 43:223–235.

Schweitzer, Maurice E. & Donald E. Gibson. 2008. "Fairness, Feeling and Ethical Decision-Making: Consequences of Violating Community Standards of Fairness." *Journal of Business Ethics,* 77:287–301.

Secunda, Victoria. 2000. *Losing Your Parents, Finding Yourself: The Defining Turning Point of Adult Life.* New York: Hyperion.

Shostack, L.G. 1985. "Planning the Service Encounter." in J.A. Czepiel, M.R. Solomon and C.F. Surprenant (eds), *The Service Encounter.* Lexington: Lexington Books.

Skipp, Catharine & Arian Campo-Flores. 2009. "A Bridge Too Far." In *Newsweek,* Vol. CLIV, No. 5, August 3, 2009, pp. 46–51.

Smith, F. Carter. (1990, November 3). "Woman is Acquitted in Trial for Using the Men's Room." *Special to The New York Times.* https://www.nytimes.com/1990/11/03/us/woman-is-acquitted-in-trial-for-using-the-men-s-room.html

Solis, Nathan. 2007. "The Wait, The Money. Was It Worth It?" *Weekly Courier,* 95(3):2.

Stegner, W.E. 1992. *Where the Bluebird Sings to the Lemonade Springs: Living and Writing in the West.* New York: Random House.

Stevenson, Harold, Rachel Keen & Robert Knights. 1963. "Parents and Strangers as Reinforcing Agents for Children's Performance." *Journal of Abnormal and Social Psychology,* 67(2):183–186.

Stokowski, Patricia A. 2002. "Language of Place and Discourse of Power: Constructing New Senses of Place." *Journal of Leisure Research,* 34:368–382.

Suzman, R.M. 1977. "The Modernization of Personality." In G.J. DiRenzo (ed.), *We, the People: American Character and Social Change.* Connecticut: Greenwood Press, pp. 40–77.

Timm, Paul R. 2008. *Customer Service: Career Success Through Customer Loyalty,* 4th edition. New Jersey: Pearson-Prentice Hall.

Tracy, Jessica, Richard Robins & June Price Tangney. 2007. *The Self-Conscious Emotions: Theory and Research. Ed.* New York: Guildford Press.

Turley, Jonathan. 2005. "Shame on You." (Sunday, September 18, 2005) *Washington Post.* http://www.washingtonpost.com/wp-dyn/content/article/2005/09/17/AR2005091700064_pf.html

Turner, Jonathan T. 1978. *The Structure of Sociological Theory.* Homewood: The Dorsey Press.

Turner, Ralph H. & Lewis M. Killian. 1987. *Collective Behavior,* 3rd edition. New Jersey: Prentice-Hall.

USA Today. (2007). *LAPD in May Day Melee off the Street.* Retrieved March 31, 2011, from http://www.usatoday.com/news/nation/2007-05-06-immigration-rally_N.htm#

Walton, David. 1975. *Waiting in Line.* Ann Arbor: Ardis.

Weller, Chris (2016, January 7). *The Japanese People are Insanely Good at Standing in Line.* Retrieved from https://www.businessinsider.com/why-japanese-people-stand-in-line-so-well-2016-1

Williams, Juan. 1987. *Eyes on The Prize: America's Civil Rights Years 1954-1965.* New York: Penguin Books.

Wong, Amy, 2004. "The Role of Emotional Satisfaction in Service Encounters." *Managing Service Quality,* 14(5):365–376.

Wright, Dale E. 1999. *Personal Relationships: An Interdisciplinary Approach.* California: Mayfield Publishing Company.

Zeithaml, V.A. & Bitner, M.J. 2003. *Service Marketing: Integrating Customer Focus Across the Firm.* New York: McGraw-Hill Higher Education.

Zola, I.K. 1997. "Medicine as an Institution of Social Control." In Peter Conrad (ed.), *The Sociology of Health and Illness: Critical Perspectives,* 5th edition. New York: St. Martin's Press.

Zuberi, Tukufu, 2001. *Thicker Than Blood: How Racial Statistics Lie.* Minneapolis: University of Minnesota Press.

Index

About the Author

Paul Christopher Price is the author of *Social Control at Opportunity Boys Home: How Staff Control Juvenile Inmates*. It is an ethnographic project about group home detainees, and referenced by many scholars. In fact, Price was invited, and attended the Urban Ethnography Project at Yale University, where ethnographers present and critically discuss their research. Teaching sociology for more than thirty years, Price has interacted with students from all walks of life. African American male students captured his attention, and recently became the co-chair of the Young African American Male Conference at Pasadena City College. His research interests include waiting, student excuses, social control, self-esteem, race, and social theory.

* 9 7 8 1 7 9 3 6 4 0 7 1 0 *